Contents

Acknowledgements

We gratefully acknowledge permission to use copyright material, the sources of which are as follows:

From W. Christaller, *Central Places in Southern Germany*, © 1966, Prentice–Hall Inc., Figs. 1.12, 1.14, 1.15; from A. Lösch, *The Economics of Location*, Yale University Press, Fig. 1.16; from W. Isard, *Location and Space Economy*, M.I.T. Press, Fig. 1.18; from *Central Lancashire: Study for a City 1967*, H.M.S.O., Fig. 1.20; from B.J.L. Berry and W.L. Garrison, *Economic Geography*, Vol. 34 (1958), Fig. 1.22; from *Papers and Proceedings, Regional Science Association*, Vol. 9 (1962), Fig. 1.23; from R.M. Prothero, *Economic Geography*, Vol. 33 (1957), Fig. 2.11; from O. Jonasson, *Economic Geography*, Vol. 1 (1925), Fig. 2.12; from S. van Valkenburg and C.C. Held, *Europe*, John Wiley & Sons Inc., Fig. 2.13; from C.D. Harris, *Annals* of the Association of American Geographers, Vol. 44 (1954), Figs. 3.11, 3.12; from R. Vining, *Economic Development and Cultural Change*, Vol. 3 (1954/5), University of Chicago Press, Fig. 4.4; from B.T. Robson, *Urban Growth*, Methuen & Co. Ltd., Figs. 4.5, 4.6; from B.J.L. Berry and F.E. Horton, *Geographic Perspectives on Urban Systems* (based on B.J.L. Berry, *Economic Development and Cultural Change*, July 1961), Prentice–Hall Inc., Figs. 4.7, 4.8, 4.9; from G. Bell, *Ekistics*, Vol. 13 (1962), Fig. 4.10; from E.W. Burgess and R.E. Park, *The City*, University of Chicago Press, Fig. 5.1; from H. Hoyt, *The Structure and Growth of Residential Neighbourhoods in American Cities*, Federal Housing Administration, Figs. 5.2, 5.3; from R.J. Johnston, *Urban Residential Patterns*, G. Bell & Sons Ltd., and B.T. Robson, Fig. 5.4; from P.J. Smith, *Economic Geography*, Vol. 38 (1962), Fig. 5.5; from P.H. Mann, *Approaches to Urban Sociology*, Humanities Press, Routledge & Kegan Paul Ltd., Fig. 5.6; from C.D. Harris and E.L. Ullman, *Annals* of the American Academy of Political and Social Science, Vol. 245 (1945), Fig. 5.7; from *Commerical Structure and Commercial Blight*, Chicago Research Paper No. 85, University of Chicago, Fig. 5.13; from B.J.L. Berry and F.E. Horton, *Geographic Perspectives on Urban Systems* (based on P.H. Rees's Master's Thesis), Prentice–Hall Inc., Fig. 5.14; from A. Hay, *Transport for the Space Economy*, Macmillan London and Basingstoke, Fig. 6.15; from E.J. Taaffe, R.L. Morrill, and P.R. Gould, *Geographical Review*, Vol. 53 (1963), Fig. 6.16, from E.M. Hoover, *The Location of Economic Activity*, McGraw–Hill Book Company, Fig. 7.7; from T. Hägerstrand, *Innovation Diffusion as a Spatial Process*, University of Chicago Press, Figs. 9.1, 9.4, 9.6, 9.7; from R.L. Morrill, *Geographical Review* Vol. 55 (1965), Fig. 9.8; from N.M. Hansen, *Growth Centres in Regional Economic Development* (B.J.L. Berry's article), Free Press, Figs. 9.9, 9.10, 9.11; from H. Perloff, *The Quality of the Urban Environment* (A.J. Krim's thesis), Resources for the Future, Fig. 9.12; from W. Petersen, *Population*, Macmillan Inc., Figs. 10.1, 10.7; D. Meadows, *et al, The Limits to Growth*, a Potomac Associates book published by Universe Books, New York, 1972, Fig. 10.4; from M.J. Moseley, *Growth Centres in Spatial Planning*, Pergamon Press Ltd., Fig. 12.3, from J. Friedmann, *Regional Development Policy: A Case Study of Venezuela*, M.I.T. Press, Figs. 12.4, 12.5, 12.7.

Appreciation is due to the following examining boards and universities for permission to use the examination questions which appear at the end of each chapter: Joint Matriculation Board; Oxford and Cambridge Schools Examination Board; University of Cambridge Local Examinations Syndicate; University of Cambridge; University of London; University of Manchester; University of Southampton.

Maps and diagrams drawn by Joyce Batey and Clive Thomas, Department of Geography, University of Manchester.

Introduction

There have been great changes in geography in the last twenty years. They reflect research conducted in the nineteenth century as well as in more recent times. Many of the new ideas which were once taught in the final year of university are now being studied in the first year of university and increasingly in the sixth form as 'A' level syllabuses are modified. Some elements of these ideas are included even in new 'O' level and C.S.E. syllabuses and lower secondary school books like the *Oxford Geography Project* and *Location and Links.*

'A' level teachers and pupils and, to some extent, first-year university and college students find difficulty in fully understanding these new ideas. The primary sources of these ideas are scattered and, for schools, inaccessible. The secondary sources are sometimes incorrect, are often difficult, and rarely place the ideas in perspective. There seems to be a need to incorporate many of the new ideas into one book, where they can be clearly and correctly explained, and to take them directly from the original sources, where examples can be shown, problems and modifications demonstrated and where the new ideas can be seen in relation to existing ones. To this end a university lecturer and the head of a school geography department have combined as co-authors of this book.

The book as part of the *Science in Geography* series

The previous books in this series have studied the scientific approach to geography and the collection, analysis, and presentation of data. This book examines the ideas and principles which have been established largely from this scientific approach. The approach has numerous aspects which are reviewed by Brian FitzGerald (S.I.G.1). For the purposes of this book, some discussion of the major aspects is useful.

Traditionally, geographers have examined the differences between places and regions, rather than their similarities. They have not attempted to establish **generalizations** based on existing similarities. The modern geographer has become concerned with **similarities** as well as **differences** at many scales of study. Like the scientist, he has attempted to discover some **order** in the apparent chaos. Unlike the scientist, he cannot, at least in human geography, use a laboratory and hold some factors constant while studying the relationship between others. If he uses a region as a 'laboratory', there are too many operating factors, few of which can be held constant. One approach has been to build simplified **models**. It has often been largely **deductive**, in that simplifying assumptions are made about the environment and people from which basic principles are derived. The end result of the models is a set of predicted spatial patterns. These reflect the simplifying assumptions of the model rather than conform to actual patterns, but as these assumptions are relaxed, the spatial outcome tends toward the pattern observed in reality. The importance of this approach is the discovery of the basic principles, the generalizations, which provide the order that underlies what appears to be the chaotic pattern of economic and social activity. This deductive approach is particularly followed in Chapters 1, 2, 3, and 9.

Similarities have also been sought directly by examining reality. If a phenomenon is commonly observed, it is called an **empirical regularity**. One such is the rank-size rule discussed in Chapter 4. Other observations of reality have yielded descriptive models, like those in Chapters 5, 11, and 12. Sometimes these are based on case studies, but they may be applied to many other situations. When theories are constructed from an analysis of a number of specific cases, the approach is called **inductive**.

Other models are derived from analogies with parts of science. The simple gravity model in Chapter 8 is a good example, for it is based on Newton's physical laws and is applied to the movement of people, goods, and ideas. The diffusion models of Chapter 9 are based partly on an analogy with the behaviour of gases. The behaviour of a mass of gas particles can be predicted, whereas the behaviour of an individual particle cannot be. The diffusion models assume that the behaviour of a mass of people may be explained but not that of any one person. In Chapter 5 a biological analogy is employed as people are compared to plants instead of particles. The ideas of plant invasion and succession are applied to people living in a city.

Scientific study is characterized by experimentation. This approach can be applied in geography using simulation models as is seen in Chapters 6, 9, and 10. Here the researcher can modify the assumptions and rules of his model and experiment, by running the model, to see which ones produce a spatial distribution with the closest fit to reality. Insight into the workings of reality is gained then by experimenting with the model. Finally, a scientific approach emphasizes measurement. Simple mathematical measures are used, particularly in Chapters 4, 6, 8, and 10 to make descriptions precise and concise.

Although the series is based on science in geography, the use of a scientific approach should be seen as an addition to, not a replacement of, traditional approaches. Language can be precise and concise if used correctly. Observations by fieldwork and case studies are still very necessary. Similarly, a scientific approach should be used with caution, just as should any other approach. Analogies must not be extended too far. People are not particles or plants: they make decisions. However, it is too easy from ignorance to dismiss a scientific approach as inapplicable. For example, mathematics may be thought to lend an incorrect precision and predictability to human behaviour. In fact, a branch of it, probability theory, can usefully represent this unpredictability (Chapter 9). Any approach that provides insight and further understanding should be employed.

Using this book

This book is designed for the sixth-former, the college and first-year university student, the sixth-form teacher, and the trainee teacher. It may be read from cover to cover since there is a logical progression with links between chapters. On the other hand, each chapter may be read as a unit.

The book has three main sections. In Section 1, the theories make very simplified assumptions so that basic principles may be established. It contains chapters on settlement patterns, agricultural land use, industrial location, and urban land use and social patterns. In Section 2, more of these assumptions are relaxed in order to allow a dynamic aspect to be introduced. It contains chapters on transport routes and costs, movement, and diffusion. Finally, in Section 3, the complexities of reality are more closely approached as the growth and development of populations and economies are examined over time and space. By then all of the initial simplifying assumptions have been relaxed. In the final chapters, in particular, only a few of the many possible theories are examined. It is very important that the reader follow up the references in order to gain a more complete understanding of these complex topics.

Within this overall approach, it is still possible to read individual chapters on their own, so that the teacher and student can follow their own sequence of study. To help the reader a **standard format** has been adopted in each chapter, wherever possible.

Introduction and link provides the link with preceding chapters, puts the main ideas of the chapter in perspective with existing geographical thought, and introduces the main author(s) of the work to be discussed.

Main aim crystallizes the point of the chapter.

Principles states the basic principles established by the theory.

Author's example, where applicable, shows how the author related his ideas to, or obtained them from, the real world.

Present-day examples draws on published examples and our own work. The examples are often taken from Great Britain and North America, but there are also examples from as many other parts of the world as possible in order to achieve a more complete areal coverage.

Problems and applicability is a discussion of the problems and modifications of the basic principles and theories, their general applicability to reality, and, where appropriate, their relevance to planning and policy making.

Conclusion brings the chapter into perspective, points out the major contributions of the theories discussed in it, their place in geography, and the stimulus to further research that they might have created.

Finally, a brief *bibliography* is added for the teacher and the student, with some relevant *essay questions* taken from past 'A' level and university papers.

Bibliography

FitzGerald, B.P., *Science in Geography 1: Developments in Geographical Method* (Oxford University Press, 1974)

Rolfe, J., *et al., Oxford Geography Project*, Books 1–3 and Teacher's Guides (Oxford University Press, 1974 and 1975)

Walker, E.A., Walker, M.J., and Wilson, T., *Location and Links,* Books 1–5 (Blackwell, 1972 and 1973)

Useful general references

Abler, R., Adams, J.S., and Gould, P., *Spatial Organization* (Prentice-Hall, 1971)

Haggett, P., *Locational Analysis in Human Geography* (Arnold, 1965)

Hoover, E.M., *An Introduction to Regional Economics* (Knopf, 1971)

Lloyd, P.E., and Dicken, P., *Location in Space: A Theoretical Approach to Economic Geography* (Harper & Row, 1972)

Smith, R.H.T., Taaffe, E.J., and King, L.J., (eds.), *Readings in Economic Geography: The Location of Economic Activity* (Rand McNally, 1968)

Understanding Society: Readings in the Social Sciences (Macmillan for Open University Press, 1970)

Section 1

Location and land use

Chapter 1

Central place theory: Christaller's model

Introduction and link

One of the most important examples of the scientific approach to geography has occurred in the study of settlements. Walter Christaller, a German geographer, in his book on *Central Places in Southern Germany* derived a theory from a set of assumptions and principles that demonstrated that there was order in the patterns and functions of the settlements that he observed around him. The scientific approach may also be observed in his use of measurements of such concepts as centrality to test the theory in the real world.

The established approaches to settlement geography had been concerned with the physical site and situation of towns, their origins and functions, classifications based on these characteristics, and the delimitation of town or port hinterlands. Christaller's approach incorporated some of this tradition in that he classified settlements according to their functions and examined the relationship between settlements and their hinterlands. However, his work sought to explain the relative, rather than absolute, position of settlements, and he suggested that there was an overall organization to the system of settlements and hinterlands.

He wrote his book in 1933 but his work, with its emphasis on theory and order, did not become widely known till the 1950s. It was not translated into English until 1966. Christaller owed much to the ideas of von Thünen and Weber, two other Germans, whose work will be discussed in later chapters. His theoretical approach to settlement geography was similar to that of von Thünen to agricultural land use and to that of Weber to industrial location.

Main aim

The main aim of central place theory is to explain the spatial organization of settlements and hinterlands, in particular their relative location and size.

Assumptions and principles

Christaller based his theory on a set of assumptions that simplify reality. These were either explicitly or implicitly expressed.

1. There is an unbounded uniform plain on which there is equal ease of transport in all directions. Transport costs are proportional to distance and there is only one type of transport.

2. Population is evenly distributed over the plain.
3. Central places (settlements) are located on the plain to provide goods, services, and administrative functions to their hinterlands. Examples of these are hardware shops (goods), dry cleaners (services), and town planning departments (administrative).
4. Consumers visit the nearest central place that provides the function (good or service) which they demand. They minimize the distance to be travelled.
5. The suppliers of these functions act as economic men; that is, they attempt to maximize their profits by locating on the plain to obtain the largest possible market. Since people visit the nearest centre (4), suppliers will locate as far away from one another as possible so as to maximize their market areas.
6. They will do this only to the extent that no one on the plain is further from a function than he is prepared to travel to obtain it. Some central places offer many functions. These are called higher order centres. Others, providing fewer functions, are lower order centres.
7. It is assumed that these higher order centres supply certain functions (higher order functions) which are not offered by lower order centres. They also provide all the functions (lower order functions) that are provided in lower order centres.
8. All consumers have the same income and the same demand for goods and services.

There are two major principles underlying Christaller's theory: the range of a good and the threshold of a good. These will be illustrated in the simple case of one good and one supplier. The demand for a good will depend upon its price (Fig. 1.1). As price increases, demand decreases. Christaller assumed that all consumers have the same amount of money available to buy a particular good (assumption 8). So a consumer who has to travel to a central place to buy a good will have less money available than one living in the central place, because he has incurred transport costs. He will, therefore, be able to buy less. This **frictional effect** of distance, realized through transport costs (assumption 1), results in demand decreasing with distance from the central place (Fig. 1.2). People at C cannot afford to buy the good at all because transport costs take up all the money they have available for the good. The distance from the supplier at which the consumer becomes unwilling to travel to purchase the good is called the **range of the good** (the distance AC in Fig. 1.2).

Fig. 1.1. *Graph showing demand and price relationship*

Fig. 1.2 *Graph showing demand and distance relationship*

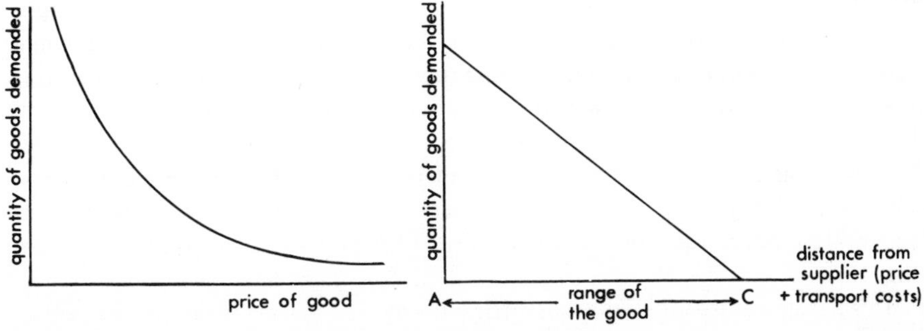

Fig. 1.3 *Map of minimum and maximum market areas*

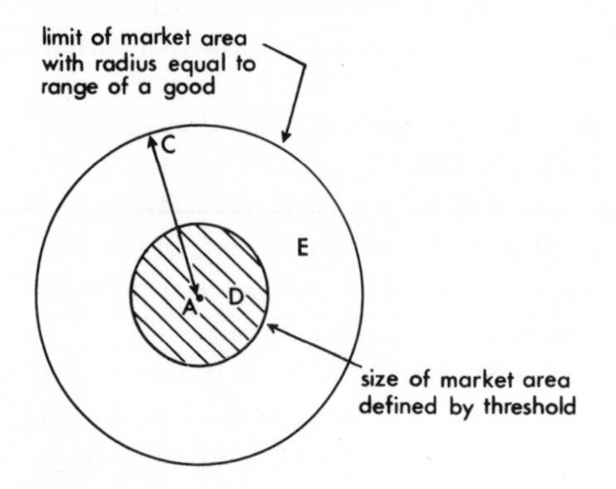

Fig. 1.4 *Evenly spaced triangular lattice pattern of suppliers (entrepreneurs)*

This is the radius of the maximum potential size of market area (Fig. 1.3). When the demands of all consumers in this area are added together, the total demand or maximum potential market size is derived.

For any particular good, there is also a minimum demand or size of market necessary for the profitable sale of the good. For example, a hairdresser must cut enough heads of hair in a week to pay for the shop rent, the upkeep of his equipment, and the wages of the boy who sweeps up. Below this number of customers he will run at a loss. This minimum demand or size of market is called the **threshold**. Since all consumers visit their nearest centre for a good, the threshold may be displayed on a map as the minimum size of market area necessary for production (Fig. 1.3). A supplier will attempt to obtain a much larger market than the threshold so as to maximize his profit. The range of the good defines the outer limit of the market area.

Usually the demand for a good will be sufficient for more than one supplier to establish himself on the plain. The maximum number of suppliers that can profitably sell the good is set by the threshold value. With a threshold of 100 units of demand a week and a total market on the plain of 10 000 potential units, a maximum of 100 entrepreneurs will be able to operate. However, they cannot locate just anywhere on the plain and still make a profit. They must be positioned as far away from their competitors as possible to ensure that their market area gives at least the threshold value. If all entrepreneurs act in this way, they will be evenly spaced over the plain in a triangular lattice pattern (Fig. 1.4). In this way each one is equidistant from his six nearest competitors. If anyone moves further away from a competitor, he only gets closer to one of the others. In the single case (Fig. 1.3) the maximum market area was circular, the radius being the range of the good. When competitors enter the plain, they will ensure that they serve some of the customers in area E (Figs. 1.3 and 1.5), while the original entrepreneur still serves those in D. In order to ensure that there are no unserved customers (Fig. 1.5), the circular market areas must overlap (Fig. 1.6). However, customers in these overlapping zones will visit their nearest centre (assumption 5) and so the final market areas will be hexagonal (Fig. 1.6).

This hexagonal pattern is the most efficient way that market areas may be packed

Fig. 1.5 *Non-overlapping market areas for seven suppliers*

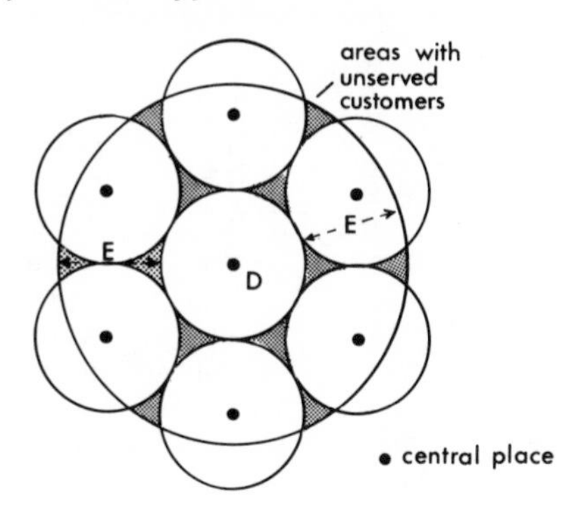

Fig. 1.6 *Overlapping market areas leading to hexagonal market areas*

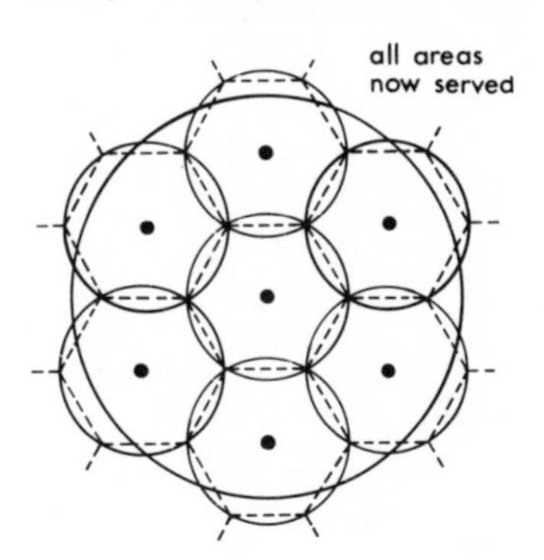

on to the plain so that every possible customer is served. The market areas are of minimum size for profitable operation. There are thus the maximum number of suppliers selling the good. Since these each locate in a central place there are the maximum number of central places selling the good. From the consumers' viewpoint, the sum of the distances that they all travel to obtain the good is minimized. With these properties this arrangement of central places and market areas is the most efficient for the marketing of goods. Christaller called it the **marketing principle**.

In order to construct the whole system, other goods must be considered. Each will have a different threshold and range. Suppliers selling different goods will locate together in **central places** for the convenience of customers. Goods of similar thresholds will be sold in the same central places. The lower the threshold, the greater the number of central places that will sell the good. Goods with low thresholds and small market areas are called **low order goods** (for example groceries, bread, and hardware items), while goods with high thresholds are termed **high order goods** (for example furs and expensive jewelry). The numerous centres that only sell low order goods are called **low order centres**. The few that offer high order goods are known as **high order centres.**

Fig. 1.7 *Orders of centres and associated market areas (*k = *3)*

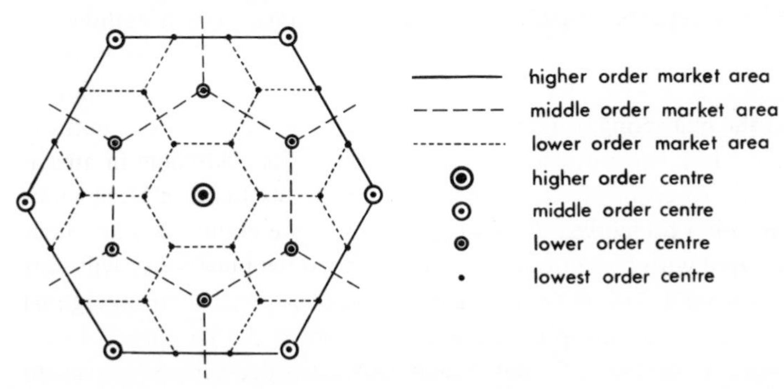

Fig. 1.8 k = *3 system, ideal description*

order	identification letter	number of places	number of complementary regions	range of region (km)	area of region (km²)	number of types of goods offered	typical population of places	typical population of region
lowest	*M*	486	729	4·0	44	40	1000	3500
	A	162	243	6·9	133	90	2000	11 000
	K	54	81	12·0	400	180	4000	35 000
middle	*B*	18	27	20·7	1200	330	10 000	100 000
	G	6	9	36·0	3600	600	30 000	350 000
	P	2	3	62·1	10 800	1000	100 000	1 000 000
highest	*L*	1	1	108·0	32 400	2000	500 000	3 500 000
	total	729						

Source: Christaller, W., *Central Places in Southern Germany* (Prentice-Hall, 1966), p.66

The lowest order centres will sell a set of goods {a, b, c, d} of the lowest order. Although of the same order, each good will have a slightly different threshold and thus minimum size of market area. The market area of a lowest order centre will be equal to the minimum market area of the good with the highest threshold of the set (say 'good d'). The other goods {a, b, c} with slightly lower thresholds are therefore sold to slightly larger markets than their thresholds. Since a good with a higher threshold than 'good d' cannot be sold profitably in the lowest order centre, it will be found only in higher order centres. Each order of centre thus sells a certain set of goods that have similar thresholds. Higher order centres also sell all the goods that lower order centres sell (assumption 7). The different orders of centres and their associated market areas are shown in Fig. 1.7.

Since successively higher order centres provide a larger set of goods and services, they employ more people. The population of central places is therefore assumed to be related to the number employed. It can be seen that the population of central places of a given order is similar and that there is a marked difference between the population of centres of one order and another (Fig. 1.8).

The different order centres are thus distinguished by the type and number of functions provided, market area, employment, and population.

The k=3 network: the marketing principle

Christaller's thinking has been illustrated by examining the construction of the model of the size and location of towns according to the marketing principle. He also considered two other principles, those of traffic and administration. The spatial arrangements associated with these principles are described for brevity by k–values. The k–value is explained below. It indicates the number of centres dominated by another centre, and the relationship between the number of market areas of each order. It can be seen from Fig. 1.7 that lowest (lower) order centres lie on the

Fig. 1.9 k = *3 network, explanation*

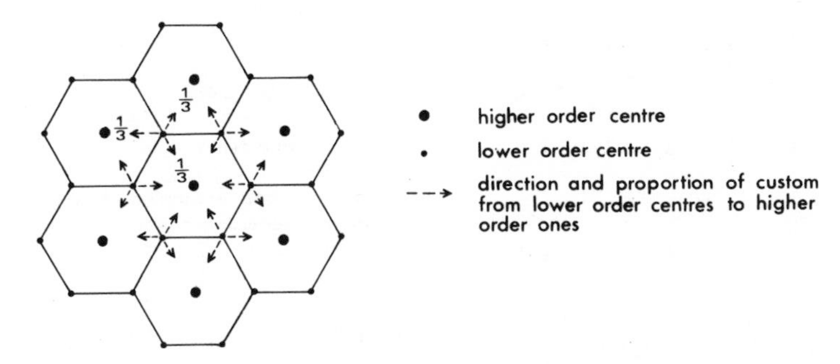

boundaries of the market areas of lower (middle) order centres. In the simplified case (Fig. 1.9) people in any lower order centre may choose between three higher order centres for higher order goods, since all three are equidistant. The custom of a lower order centre may then be considered to be split three equal ways between the three higher order centres. Each higher order centre then receives one-third of the custom of the six lower order centres which are located on the boundary of its market area (Fig. 1.9). It can thus be considered to serve a population equivalent to two lower order centres ($6 \times \frac{1}{3}$). It also serves its own population (1). In total it then serves three central places (2 + 1). For centres of each order, it may be observed that they serve or dominate three centres of the next lowest order, including themselves. This spatial arrangement, which is characteristic of the marketing principle described above, is known as a $k = 3$ network. The k–value also shows the relationship between the number of market areas of each order. There are always three times as many as there are of the order above. The relationship between numbers of central places of each order is more complex but still based on the k–value except for the highest order place.

	market areas	central places		
highest order	1	1	9 (1 + 2 + 6)	27 (9 + 18)
	3	2		
	9*	6		
	27	18		
lowest order	81	54		

*The nine market areas of this order contain nine central places which sell the associated order of goods. Six are considered centres of this order because they do not sell anything of any higher order. Three of the nine sell higher order goods too, one being the highest order central place and the other two being the next highest order central places.

The k = 4 and k = 7 networks: traffic and administrative principles

Christaller also identified spatial arrangements that demonstrated other principles. He constructed a network which made it easier to travel between centres. Central places are located so that lower order centres lie along the straight-line paths between higher order centres (Fig. 1.10). This arrangement is called the **traffic principle**. Compared to the $k = 3$ network the hexagon is a little larger and re-oriented. A lower order centre is equidistant from only two higher order centres.

Fig. 1.10 k = *4 network, explanation*

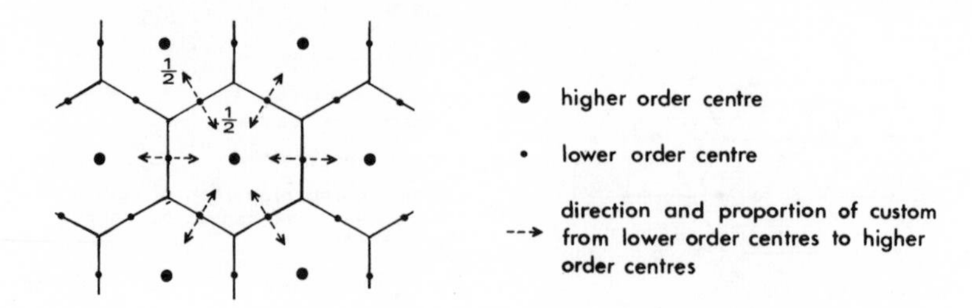

The higher order centre thus serves a half of the population of six lower order centres ($6 \times \frac{1}{2}$), plus its own (1), giving four in all (3 + 1). This is called a $k = 4$ network. In the **administrative principle** $k = 7$ since a larger and reoriented hexagon now encloses six lower order centres and a higher order one (Fig. 1.11a). Obviously it is much more efficient to administer whole centres than parts of them, as would happen in the $k = 3$ and $k = 4$ networks.

Fig. 1.11 (a) k = *7 network, explanation;* (b) k = *7 network (an alternative orientation), see p. 16*

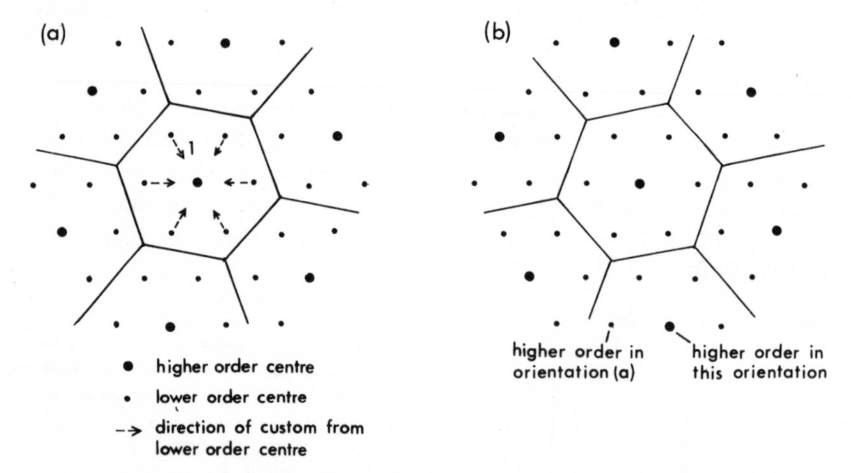

These are the basic principles and characteristics of the order that Christaller suggested. In summary, he established theoretically fixed relationships between functions of central places and sizes of market areas and between market areas and populations of central places. These yielded distinct orders of central places which dominated a given number of other places.

Author's example

Christaller assumed that the marketing principle ($k = 3$) was the main determinant of a system of central places and thus expected to find the pattern shown (Fig. 1.12).

Fig. 1.12 *The marketing principle,* k = *3, the* G-*system. (Top right sector shown in full detail.)*

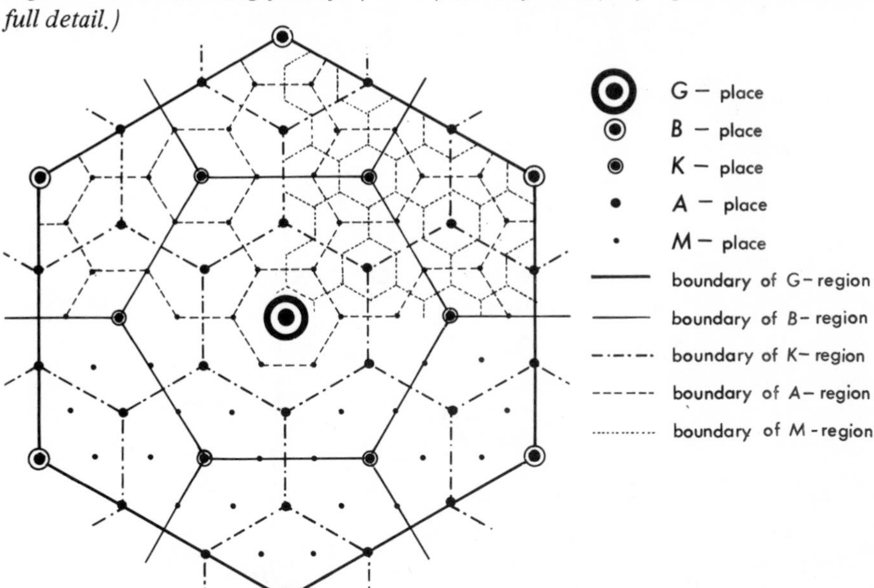

This system assumes that the largest centre is a *G*–place and is called a *G*–system. This is not the highest order of system possible, however, since above *G*–places there are *P, L, RT*, and *R*–places. Christaller regarded Paris in France as an *R*–place with Bordeaux and Lyons *RT*–places. In the case of southern Germany the highest order centre, Munich, was found to be an *L*–place. (The letters are for identification purposes only.) Christaller's expected values for such an *L*–system are shown in Fig. 1.8.

To test his ideas for southern Germany Christaller first defined a central place as possessing at least one 'central institution' which provided goods and services, for example a shop or office. He then established a method which quantified centrality. This he related to the number of telephone installations at a central place, since he

Fig. 1.13 *Classes of central places in southern Germany*

type	population (approximate)	number of telephones	centrality
H	800	5-10	−0·5-+0·5
M	1200	10-20	0·5-2
A	2000	20-50	2-4
K	4000	50-150	4-12
B	10 000	150-500	12-30
G	30 000	500-2500	30-150
P	100 000	2500-25 000	150-1200
L	500 000	25 000-60 000	1200-3000
RT	1 000 000	60 000	3000

Source: Christaller, W., *op. cit.*, p. 158

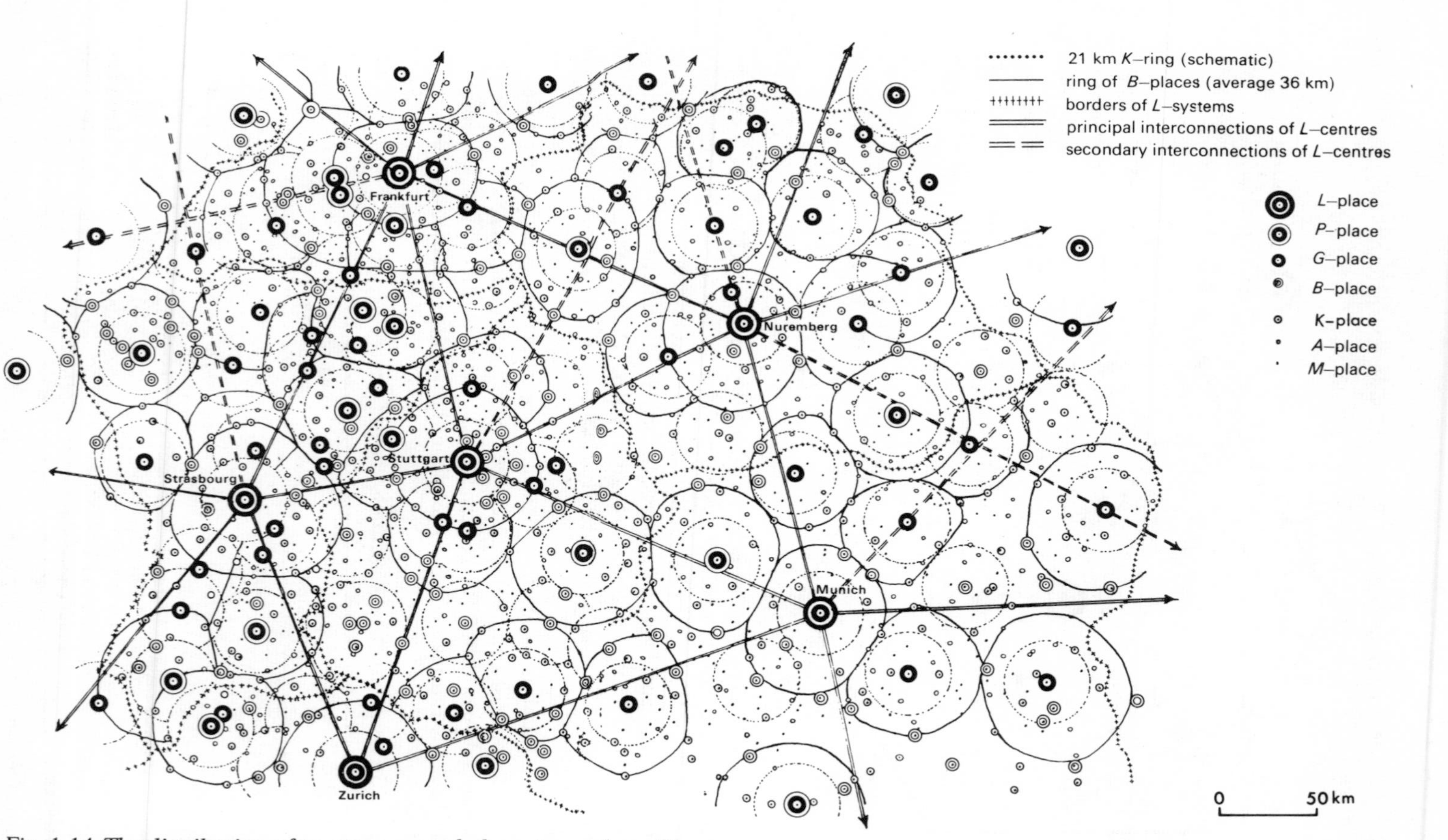

Fig. 1.14 *The distribution of towns as central places in southern Germany*

considered this a good indication of the importance of a place. He derived a measure which he called the telephone density (the number of telephone installations per person in a region). This he multiplied by the number of people in a central place, and the derived statistic he called the 'expected importance' of the place. This figure was subtracted from the 'actual importance' (the number of telephone installations at the central place) and the final 'centrality index' was a measure of how well a place was served with telephone installations in comparison with the region as a whole. Using this measure of centrality Christaller observed the classes of central places in southern Germany (Fig. 1.13).

He also determined the sizes of 'complementary regions' which corresponded to the typical sizes of the different orders of central places. Finally, he derived a map showing the actual distribution of towns as central places, each surrounded by roughly circular 'complementary regions' (Fig. 1.14).

Based on this work he concluded that the marketing principle was clearly dominant in determining the distribution of the central places in southern Germany. The traffic (k = 4) and administrative (k = 7) principles were secondary laws causing deviations. The parts of southern Germany dominated by these can be seen on the map (Fig. 1.15). Note, however, the dominance of the marketing principle.

Fig. 1.15 *The distribution of the three principles in southern Germany*

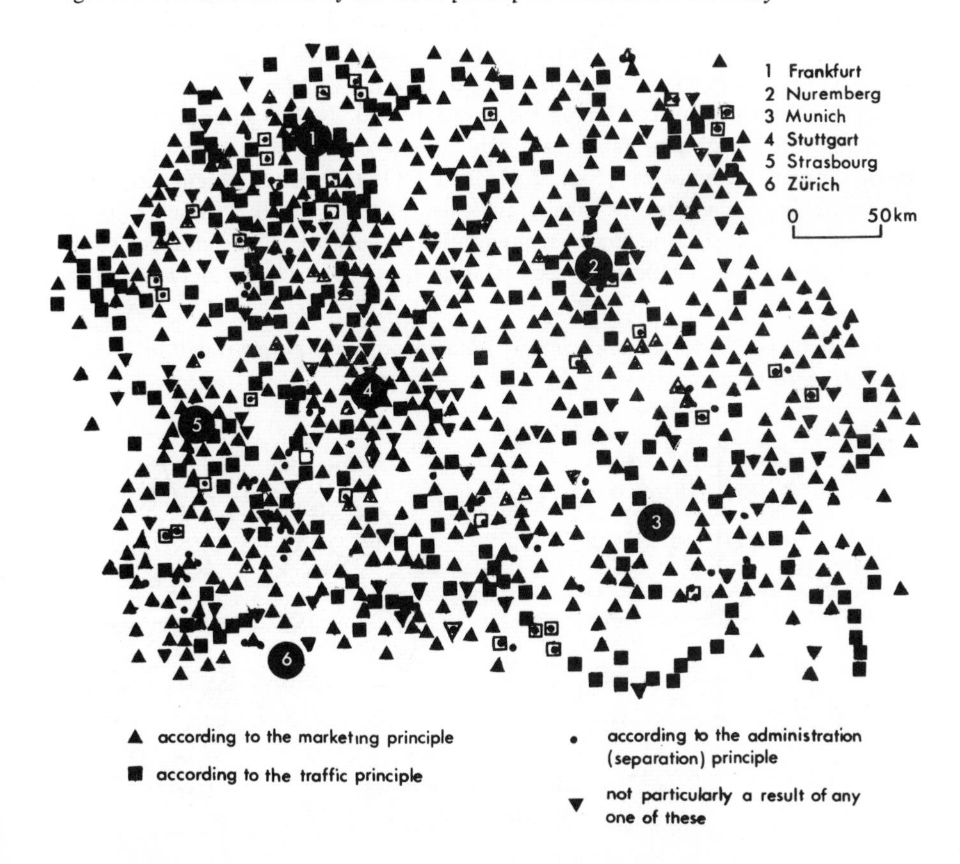

Modifications

August Lösch made an outstanding and more rigorous contribution to settlement theory. He did not assume that people were spread uniformly over the plain (a continuous even population distribution). He began the model with people living in isolated, evenly spaced farmsteads (a discontinuous even population distribution—a triangular lattice of farmsteads). In his system no supplier is allowed excess profit, that is more profit than is necessary to sustain the firm. Each good has its own distinct threshold and size of market area, which is represented by a different k function. Lösch realized that there were more k functions than the $k = 3, 4$, and 7. He constructed larger, reoriented hexagons to give $k = 9$, 12, 13, 19, and many more. The lowest order good is represented by a $k = 3$ network with the smallest market areas. The next order is represented by $k = 4$, and so on, so that there are 150 networks of different k functions representing the market areas of 150 goods. Imagine 150 sheets of tracing paper. On each is drawn the market areas of one of the goods. As each good has a different-sized market area, the size of the hexagons varies from one sheet to another. These networks are laid over the basic triangular lattice of farmsteads and centred on one, which becomes the metropolis. Since it is a central place for all 150 networks, it will sell all 150 goods.

Having selected the metropolis, Lösch followed a number of rules to determine which farmsteads would become central places on the plain. For many networks, orientation relative to the farmsteads cannot be varied. These are those requiring farmsteads to be located on the market area boundaries like $k = 3$ and $k = 4$ (Figs. 1.9 and 1.10). There is no question for these networks as to which farmsteads will become central places selling the associated goods. For some networks, for example $k = 7$, different farmsteads can become central places according to the orientation of the network (Figs. 1.11a and 1.11b). Once the orientation of the $k = 7$ network is arbitrarily chosen, the orientation of all other networks is constrained. Where there is a choice of orientation, a network will be arranged so that its central places lie in the same sectors as do those of the $k = 7$ network. Where

Fig. 1.16 (a) *The Löschian landscape;* (b) *Indianapolis and environs within a radius of 100 km*

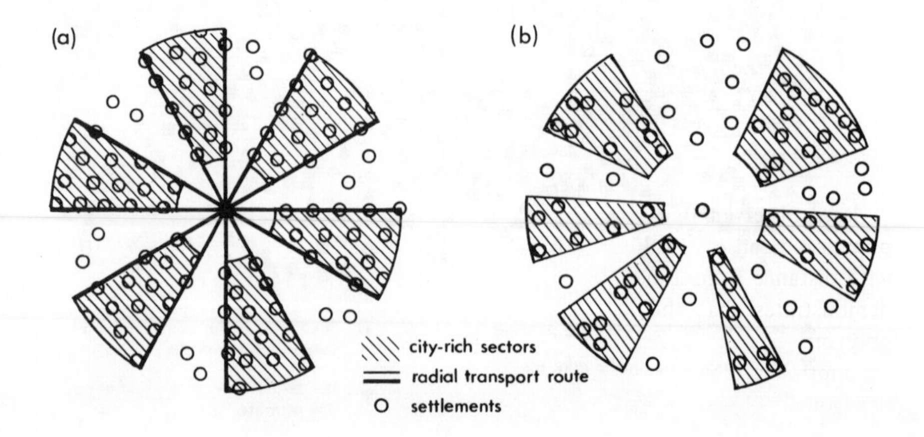

different orientations permit a choice between farmsteads within these sectors, for example $k = 49$, the place with the larger number of goods already offered is chosen. If the number of goods offered is the same, the place selling the highest order good is selected.

By overlaying and re-orienting the 150 networks in this way, the number of central places is minimized, and six city-rich sectors are found around the metropolis (Fig. 1.16a) in which many services are offered. Between these lie six city-poor sectors whose centres are small and offer fewer services. These sectors result from the above rules for orienting the networks. Lösch selected these rules because he had observed such sectors in reality (Fig. 1.16b). Between the city-rich and city-poor sectors, he located main transport routes radiating from and improving access to the metropolis. This arrangement of central places and routes is called the Löschian **economic landscape**.

A number of characteristics of this landscape are worthy of note. Although most central places provide a number of goods, they do not offer all the lower order goods below their highest order good. One centre, for example, may sell $k = 3$, $k = 4$ and $k = 19$ goods but not $k = 7, 9, 12$ and 13. Specialist centres result. Because the same set of goods is not sold in central places of a certain order, as they are in Christaller's system, in Lösch's model the populations of a given order vary and a continuous, rather than a stepped, city-size distribution results (Fig. 1.17). Another characteristic of this landscape is that central places get larger with distance from the metropolis.

Fig. 1.17 *City-size distributions.* (a) *Stepped (from Christaller's model);* (b) *continuous (from Lösch's model), logarithmic scale*

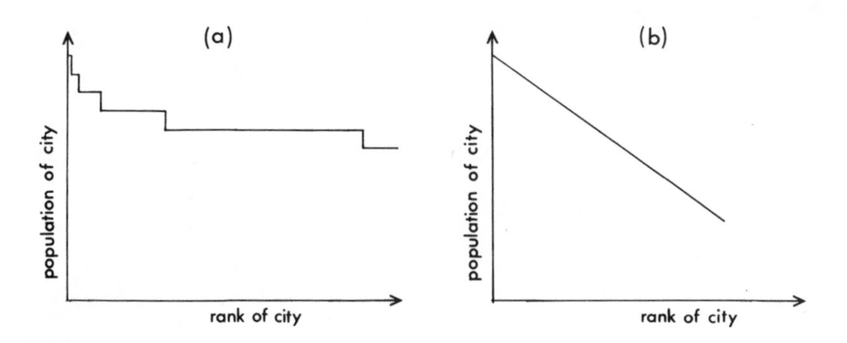

Isard observed that in both the Löschian and Christaller landscapes an uneven population density resulted. He suggested that in reality population density declines with distance from a metropolis. The modified system of market areas (Fig. 1.18) demonstrates that the neat hexagonal patterns disappear, and are replaced by polygons of varying size but with similar populations. Note that as soon as the assumption of even population density is relaxed, market areas are no longer hexagonal.

Fig. 1.18 *Population density declining with distance from the metropolis*

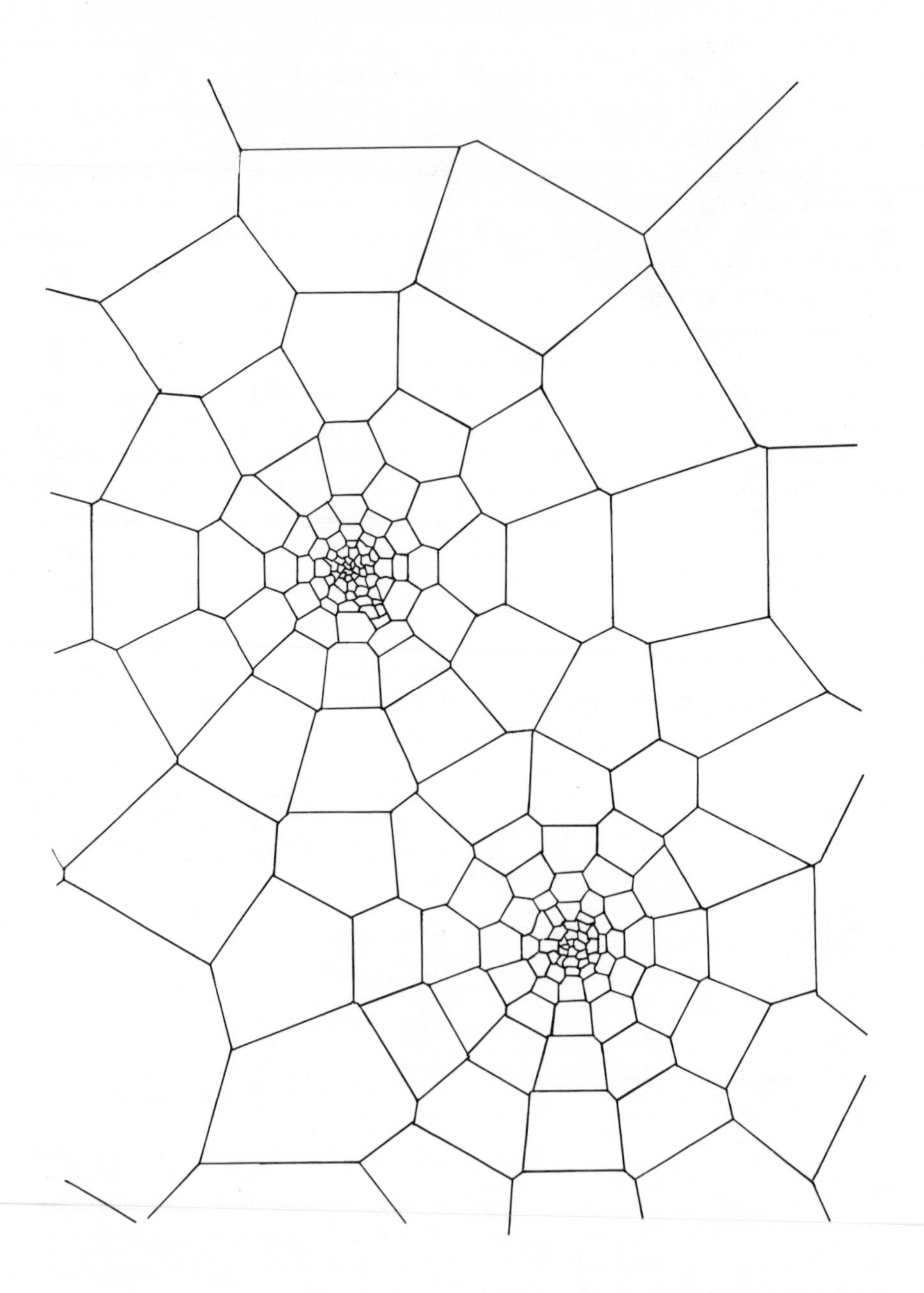

Fig. 1.19 *Threshold population levels for certain functions in a part of Oxfordshire*

		increasing order of function →				
name of village	population	church	primary school	butcher	newsagent	greengrocer
Grove	4143	3	–	1	1	1
Cholsey	3822	2	1	2	1	1
Berinsfield	3237	1	1	1	1	2
Harwell	2594	2	1	1	1	–
Sutton Courtenay	2442	2	–	1	2	[1]
Drayton	2269	2	1	1	1	
Blewbury	1609	2	1	–	–	
Brightwell cum Sotwell	1599	3	–	1	–	
Crowmarsh Gifford	1509	2	1	–	–	
Steventon	1502	2	1	–	1	
Marcham	1447	2	1	–	1	
East Hendred	1329	3	1	–	–	
Compton	1300	2	1	–	–	
East Hagbourne	1194	–	1	1	1	
Dorchester	905	2	1	1	–	
Chilton	876	1	–	–	–	
Warborough	871	–	1	–	1	
Streatley	870	–	1	–	–	
Long Wittenham	819	1	1	–	–	
Milton	731	2	–	–	[1]	
East Hanney	716	2	1	–		
Hampstead Norris	620	1	1	–		
Clifton Hampden	616	2	1	–		
Moulsford	591	1	1	–		
Culham	577	1	1	–		
South Stoke	479	2	1	–		
West Hanney	450	1	–	–		
South Moreton	419	1	1	–		
Appleford	415	1	–	–		
East Ilsley	400	2	1	–		
Aston Tirrold	373	2	–	–		
Upton	369	2	1	–		
North Moreton	369	1	–	–		
Ashampstead	365	1	1	–		
Leckhampstead	325	2	–	–		
Ardington	324	1	–	[1]		
West Hagbourne	321	–	–			
West Ilsley	320	1	–			
West Hendred	309	2	–			
Drayton St. Leonard	294	2	–			
Charney Bassett	256	1	1			
Brightwalton	255	2	[1]			
Aston Upthorpe	225	1				
Frilford	215	1				
Lockinge	198	1				
Aldworth	180	1				
Denchworth	175	1				
Newington	143	1				
Garford	104	1				
Farnborough	90	1				
Little Wittenham	66	1				
Lyford	60	[1]				

[1] observed threshold population

Note that in reality not all villages above the threshold value have the function.

Present-day examples

Very little validation of the original central place theory was done by Christaller himself outside of Germany. It has been left to other workers, especially since 1945, to test Christaller's implicit and explicit ideas for other areas. Work on the threshold population levels necessary to support certain functions has shown that there seem to be certain regularly occurring levels. Different functions therefore require different threshold populations. The table (Fig. 1.19) shows the threshold population levels necessary to support certain functions in a part of Oxfordshire. Clearly, in this area a primary school requires a minimum population of 250, whereas a newsagent requires a minimum population of 730.

A team working on the central Lancashire New Town observed the threshold populations required to support certain social facilities (Fig. 1.20). They identified four groups of social functions which have broadly similar threshold-population levels.

Fig. 1.20 *Population required to support social facilities (based on observations of existing settlements)*

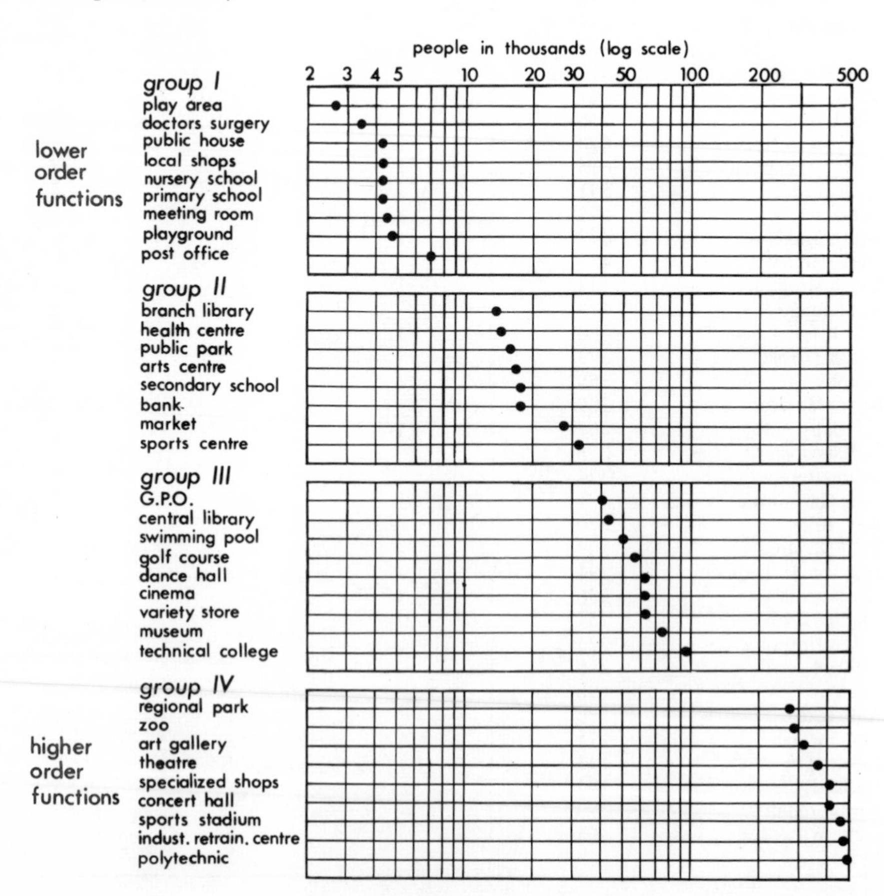

Many exceptions can exist, of course, when a high order good is found in a small village with a limited population. Often the good or service provided (for example, an antique shop) has a particular attraction for which people may be prepared to travel long distances.

The range of a good is a basic assumption of Christaller's theory which has been frequently tested. An example of this is the movement of consumers for bread and clothes to central places as shown in Fig. 1.21. Clearly, it is generally true to say that people travel shorter distances to buy low order goods such as bread, cigarettes, stamps, and newspapers which are known as **convenience goods**. But people do not

Fig. 1.21 *Shopping trips made in north Norfolk for bread and clothes*

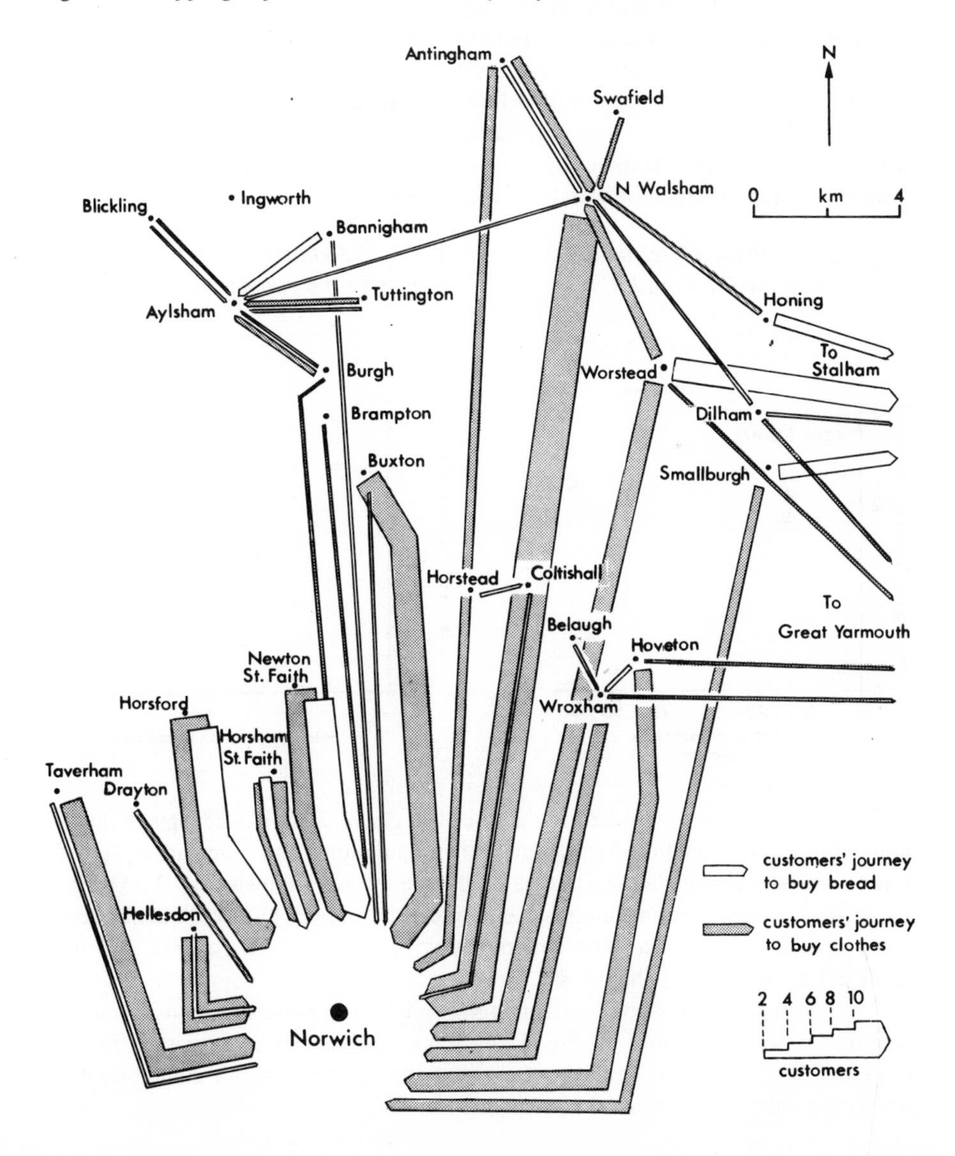

always travel to the nearest centre for such goods. This can be because of multi-purpose shopping in a large centre, the nature of bus services in an area, or simply because one person does not get on with a particular shopkeeper! Clearly in these circumstances, the assumption of minimum movement is not upheld.

One of the most disputed aspects of Christaller's theory is the suggestion that discrete (separate) orders of settlements exist (Fig. 1.17). These discrete orders are the steps on the stepped hierarchy. Trying to find evidence to support this has proved difficult. Possibly one of the most quoted efforts to identify a stepped hierarchy is that of Berry and Garrison in a study of thirty-three central places in Snohomish County in Washington State, U.S.A. They analysed the hierarchy of functions provided by the towns to discover if the centres fell into groupings according to functional significance. They discovered that in general there was a reasonable relationship between population size and functional importance (Fig. 1.22), and that four centres were particularly poor in service provision in relation to their size. Finally, they found that three reasonably distinct groups (A, B and C) emerged when the settlements were analysed according to the total number of activities or functions. Statistically it was found that the variations between these groups were greater than the variations within them.

Fig. 1.22 *Population size/functions relationship for Snohomish County*

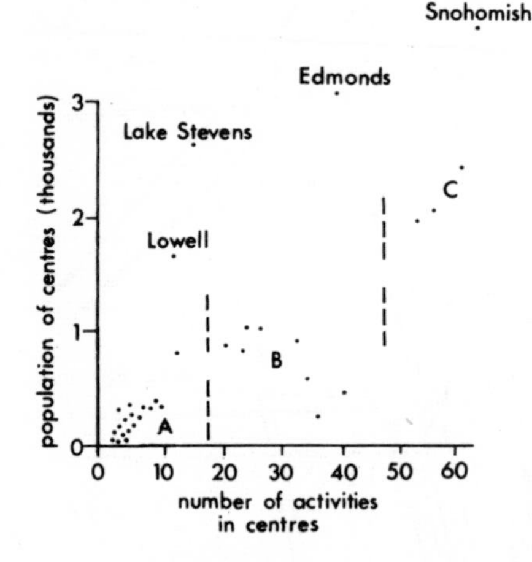

Fig. 1.23 *Relationship between trade area and total population served (Iowa)*

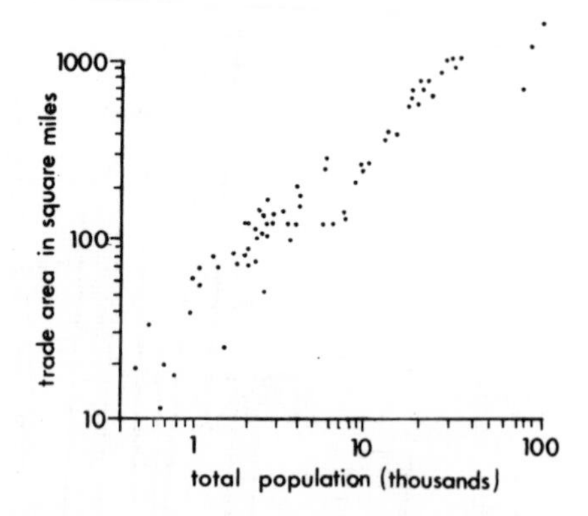

The basic problem of identifying so-called discrete levels when graphing the population/rank, functions/rank, functions/population, and population served/trade area relationships is well illustrated by the example shown (Fig. 1.23). Here the difficulty of identifying levels is clearly great. Because of observed distributions, many research workers feel that a hierarchy with a continuous sequence of settlement size is more usual (Chapter 4).

Underserved and overserved settlements (in relation to population) are a frequent occurrence and are shown in Fig. 1.24. Many reasons can be suggested for the residuals. X could be an historic centre or tourist centre, whereas Y could be a very new community or a commuter settlement.

Fig. 1.24 *Underserved and overserved settlements (idealized pattern)*

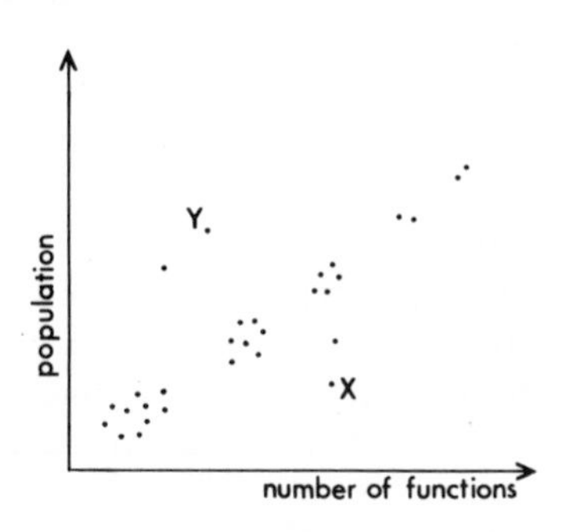

Much research has also been conducted on the spatial implications of Christaller's work. Brush and Bracey made a comparative study of rural service centres in south-west Wisconsin and southern England. Though these two areas are unlike in population density, urbanization, and transportation, three orders of service centres were distinguished in both. The average distance between the highest order centres is about 13 km, the middle order centres 5–6 km, and the lowest order centres 3–4 km. The fact that this lowest order of central places in both countries developed at about 4 km intervals suggests that the need to get to a local trade centre by cart or foot and back in a day was the original determinant of the spacing.

Certain extensions of Christaller's ideas have been made. Skinner's work on marketing and spatial structure in rural China shows that a hierarchical structure closely corresponds in some places to a $k = 3$ system, in others to $k = 4$. However,

Fig. 1.25 *Hierarchy of shopping centres in south Leicester*

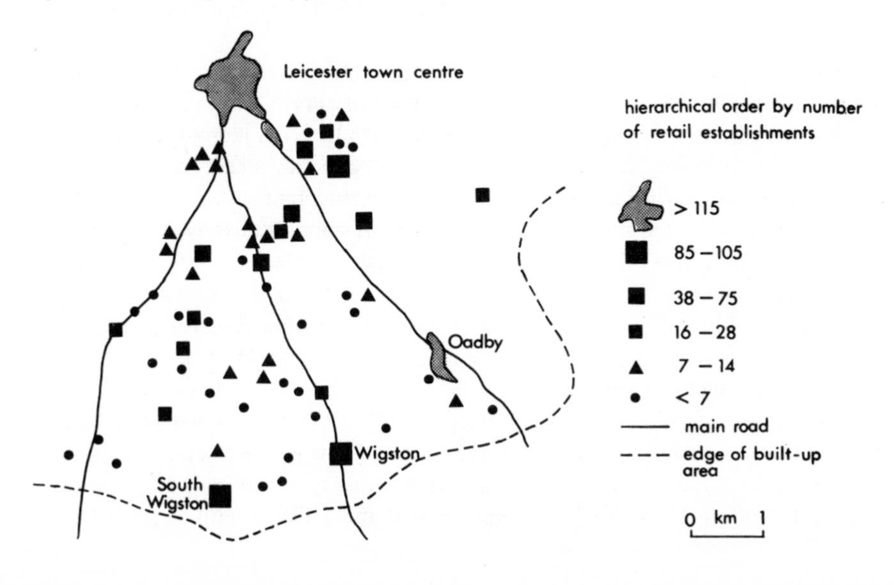

this system is unusual since merchants, in order to achieve at least the threshold population, are itinerant between the centres. Customers are not prepared to travel very far for the goods (short range of a good). If the merchants offer their wares in one place all the time, they will not achieve the threshold to remain in business. By moving to different market places over time, the threshold level can be attained. Similarly, in Britain, circuses, street fairs, and ice-cream salesmen are itinerant and often follow a set route and timetable.

Christaller's theory has also been applied to service centres within cities. It has been found that a hierarchy of shopping centres often occurs within cities. The example of south Leicester (Fig. 1.25) clearly demonstrates that there is a great range in size and functions of the many centres. The spacing of such centres does not fit Christaller's theory because of greater mobility, unequal ease of transport, and uneven population density within cities.

Problems and applicability

The examples have shown that some of the ideas of Christaller are upheld in the real world. The overall spatial organization that is described is, however, rarely found, since his argument has some logical inconsistencies, and reality is more complex than the simplifying assumptions allow.

The logical inconsistencies concern the distribution of population and ease of transport. Although the theories of Christaller and Lösch at first assume even distributions of population, the resulting spatial models clearly display uneven distributions of population. The market areas of similar size that had the same number of people within them at the beginning of the analysis contain different-sized populations at the end. The resulting uneven population distribution will modify the location of central place activities. Similarly, although transport is assumed to be equally easy in all directions, Christaller's $k = 4$ network and Lösch's radial routes between city-rich and city-poor sectors modify the costs and ease of movement over the plain. The location of the central places and market areas will again be modified.

Some of the assumptions would not be expected to reflect reality. Without a uniform plain the neat pattern of hexagons will not appear. Physical barriers often lead to linear transport routes and lines of central places, as along the coal-mining valleys of South Wales. The pattern of land-ownership may affect transport routes, for example, the township and range system in the midwest of the U.S.A. is associated with a grid system of roads. Even on this approximately uniform plain, hexagonal market areas do not result. They remain an ideal pattern which reality can only approach. Similarly, the neat relationship between the number and size of settlements is blurred in reality, since as regions are bounded, for example, by coastlines, unbounded plains do not exist. Thus some market areas are truncated by boundaries, yielding smaller central places than the model would predict. The distinct orders of towns may also be blurred in reality (Chapter 4), since Christaller's theory does not include some of the functions of towns that create employment and population. For example, manufacturing industry is ignored. Its location is unlikely to follow Christaller's assumption that those places with industrial firms requiring large markets also contain establishments of all other industrial concerns with smaller market requirements. Lösch's specialist centres are much more realistic for the location of industry. Yet neither theory includes the effect of the location of raw materials, both theories assume a uniform plain. Since Christaller's analysis, a whole set of services has evolved to serve industry rather than households, for example, market research firms and consultancies. The distribution of these services is based on the distribution of industries which is certainly not even. Their market is often concentrated in a few large cities rather than continuously distributed over space. The predominant movement is thus inter-city rather than city–hinterland.

The set of assumptions about the behaviour of suppliers and consumers is not very realistic. The organization of retailing, for example, has changed. Multiple stores such as Tesco, Safeways, Boots, and Marks & Spencer occur as well as independent concerns. A multiple may be able to support the running of a few of its outlets at a loss for a short period in the hope that eventually a threshold market will be realized. Consumers, with their increased mobility, do not always visit their nearest store. Suppliers are thus unable to command a **spatial monopoly**, and market areas overlap. Competition becomes other than spatial as suppliers become more uncertain as to their market. Suppliers attempt to lure customers by the price, quality, and variety of goods offered and the services provided, such as credit facilities. Some of these factors have also been combined with the convenience of shopping under one roof, typified by the French hypermarkets. Multi-purpose shopping often results in the low order centres being by-passed for low order goods, thus leading to their decline.

Even the relationship between population size and number of functions is not always clear. The mobility of people leads to some towns being overendowed with functions, given their population. Such resorts as Bournemouth, Blackpool, and Brighton are classic examples of this. Retailers in Britain also seem slow to react to changes in population distribution. Thus the provision of facilities in new commuter centres or New Towns may lag behind the expansion of population, for example, Skelmersdale in Lancashire. Although Christaller discussed dynamic factors such as population change and technical progress, it is not very clear how his central place system would evolve. Much depends, for example, on the direction and timing of any colonization that may have taken place.

The distribution, size, and functions of central places are also influenced by the government and planning agencies. They control development, as demonstrated in the rejection of the proposed Haydock Park regional shopping centre between Liverpool and Manchester and the granting of permission for centres at Brent Cross in north London and Yate to the north-east of Bristol. They influence the siting of new facilities by establishing New Towns such as Peterlee in Durham, and help to enlarge towns like Nottingham with its two central regional shopping centres. They also decide where to locate their own offices, which are central institutions in Christaller's theory. In the case of the national government, these are by no means distributed according to Christaller's principles.

Despite these distorting factors, it might be said in summary that Christaller's ideas are more applicable to retailing, while Lösch's model is better suited to manufacturing industry. Consequently Christaller-type settlement patterns are more likely to be found in non-industrial or rural regions like much of Iowa, while elements of the Löschian landscape are more likely to be observed in industrialized areas. Both models predict the relative location of settlements. The authors were aware that the absolute or exact location of centres would be influenced by physical factors such as relief, drainage, and water supply. It is the effect of these factors that traditional settlement geography has illustrated so well.

Conclusion

The Christaller and Lösch systems remain ideals which, in their entireties, are difficult to observe. Parts of the theories do fit reality. Even just as ideals, though, the theories are useful because reality can be compared with them; where theory and reality diverge, an area of research can be pinpointed to discover the reason for the divergence. Their main contribution to settlement geography has been their identification of the order which is reflected in the integrated system of central places and market areas. Before their work, the town and its hinterland were usually treated in isolation from other towns and hinterlands. Certainly the hierarchical spatial organization of the economic system had not been observed. Some have attributed even greater significance to central place theory, nominating it as geography's finest intellectual product. Certainly the spatial organization of the economic system has become a central part of geographical study.

The theories have stimulated much work on retailing and consumer behaviour, not only between settlements but also within them. Such work has permitted geographers to advise on the planning of settlements and retail centres and has given geographers a commercial role in market research. Although settlements are not exclusively central places, it is still useful to study them as such. For an overall model of settlements, the subject awaits a better theory which will include many of the distorting factors that have been identified.

Bibliography

Berry, B.J.L., *Geography of Market Centres and Retail Distribution* (Prentice-Hall, 1967)

Berry, B.J.L., Gardiner Barnum, H., and Tennant, R.J., 'Retail Location and Consumer Behaviour', pp. 362–84 in Smith, R.H.T., Taaffe, E.J., and King, L.J., (eds.), *Readings in Economic Geography* (Rand McNally, 1968)

Berry, B.J.L., and Garrison, W.L., 'The Functional Bases of Central-Place Hierarchy', pp. 218–27 in Mayer, H.M., and Kohn, C.F., *Readings in Urban Geography* (University of Chicago Press, 1959)

Brush, J.E., and Bracey, H.E., 'Rural Service Centres in Southwestern Wisconsin and Southern England', pp 210–17 in Mayer, H.M., and Kohn, C.F., *op. cit.*

Christaller, W., *Central Places in Southern Germany*, translated by C.W. Baskin (Prentice-Hall, 1966)

Isard, W., *Location and Space Economy* (Wiley, 1956)
Lösch, A., *The Economics of Location* (Yale University Press, 1954)
Scott, P., *Geography of Retailing* (Hutchinson, 1970)

Essay questions

1. What factors affect the relative size and spacing of towns and cities? (Cambridge, 1974)
2. How would central place theory help in planning the settlement structure of a newly developing area? (Oxford and Cambridge, 1973)
3. (a) Describe the main features of Christaller's central place model.
   (b) Discuss the extent to which it is helpful in interpreting geographical patterns in any specific region you have studied. (Joint Matriculation Board, 1976)
4. Discuss the problems of defining central place hierarchies in rural areas. (Southampton University)

Chapter 2

Agricultural land use: von Thünen's model

Introduction and link

Following the analysis of the relative location and size of settlements, the agricultural land use around the settlements will now be examined with the aid of the ideas of Johann Heinrich von Thünen. The works of Christaller and von Thünen show many similarities. Both writers emphasize the importance of distance and transport costs. Just as Christaller's model provides a counterbalance to the traditional explanation of settlement location based on the physical factors of site and situation, so von Thünen's emphasis on economic factors counteracts the use of mainly physical factors to explain agricultural land use. The methods by which the two authors proceed are also alike. They use a similar set of simplifying assumptions about the behaviour of man and about the physical environment. With these assumptions they formulate their basic models which are then modified as the assumptions are relaxed to conform more to reality.

Like Christaller, von Thünen (1783–1850) also lived in Germany. At the age of twenty-seven he acquired the estate of Tellow near Rostock in Mecklenburg which he operated for forty years until his death. Most of the data used in explaining his theory were obtained by him through practical experience, including detailed cost accounting on his estate. His was the first theory of the location of agricultural production.

Main aim

The main aim of von Thünen's analysis was to show how and why agricultural land use varies with the distance from a market. He had two basic models:

1. The intensity of production of a particular crop will decline with the distance from the market. **Intensity of production** is a measure of the amount of inputs per unit area of land; for example, the greater the amounts of money, labour, and fertilizers that are used, the greater the intensity of agricultural production.
2. The type of land use will vary with the distance from the market.

Assumptions and principles

Von Thünen employed certain assumptions which simplify the complex real world.

1. An 'isolated state' (no links with the rest of the world) with one city at the centre of an agricultural area.

2. The city is the sole market for the surplus production from the agricultural area, and the agricultural area is the sole supplier to the city. At the city all farmers receive the same price for a particular crop at any one time.
3. This agricultural area is a uniform plain over which soil fertility, climate, and other physical factors do not vary. There are no physical barriers to movement across the plain.
4. All farmers act as economic men; this means that they aim to maximize their profits and have full knowledge of the needs of the market.
5. There is only one form of transport (in those days, horse and cart).
6. The cost of this transport is directly proportional to distance.

The basic principle underlying the two models is **economic rent**. Later workers have called it **locational rent**. Locational rent is the difference between the total revenue received by a farmer for a crop grown on a parcel of land and the total cost of production and transport of that crop. The revenue received is based on the price of the crop offered at the market, which is determined by supply and demand. All farmers receive the same price, however, at any one time. Production costs are also assumed to be the same for all farmers on the uniform plain. Transport costs increase with distance from the market. The greater the transport costs, the smaller the difference between revenue and total costs, so the smaller the locational rent. The locational rent of a parcel of land, therefore, decreases with the distance from the market (Fig. 2.1). For a farmer at A, revenue and costs will be equal and production not worthwhile. He is said to be on the **margin of cultivation**. At A the locational rent of a unit of land is zero.

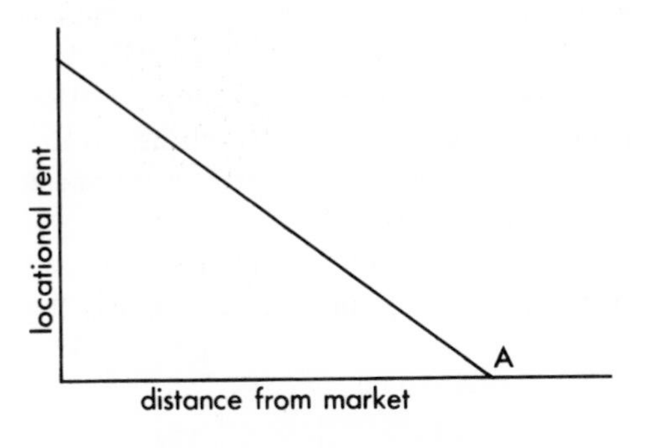

Fig. 2.1 *Locational rent and distance from market for one crop*

It is important to note that locational rent is not the same as actual rent. Locational rent is what a farmer can afford to bid for the parcel of land.

Model 1

The model of intensity, in a simplified form, is as follows. Two farmers, Giles and Brown, wish to cultivate the same crop. Giles's farm is situated close to the city, while Brown's is located some distance from the city. They will both receive the same market price for their crop, but the difference between Brown's total revenue and costs will be less than that for Giles, since Brown will pay higher transport costs to the market. The locational rent is thus higher for Giles than Brown for the same intensity of production.

Fig. 2.2. *Variations in locational rent with intensity of production*

farmer	farmer's distance from market (km)	type of farming	cost of production (inputs)	yield (tonnes)	total transport costs (yield × distance × cost per tonne/km)	total costs (of inputs + transport)	total revenue (yield × market price per tonne)	locational rent (total revenue – total costs)
Giles	1	intensive	2000	80	80	2080	4400	2320
		extensive	1000	50	50	1050	2750	1700
Brown	30	intensive	2000	80	2400	4400	4400	0
		extensive	1000	50	1500	2500	2750	250

(Price at market = 55 per tonne, transport cost = 1 per tonne/km)

Giles may increase the intensity of his production by applying more inputs to his land, and so increase crop yield. Although as more labour and fertilizers are applied to the land the yield increases, it may not increase in proportion to the amount of inputs. Whereas in the example (Fig. 2.2), inputs increase by 100 per cent (from 1000 to 2000), yield increases only by 60 per cent (from 50 to 80). The return for a given unit of input may thus decline as more inputs are applied. This is called **diminishing returns**. Although with larger yields Giles's transport costs increase, he is still able to derive greater returns for more intensive production simply because he obtains a greater revenue for the total crop (Fig. 2.2). At a greater distance from the market Brown cannot afford to intensify his production because the returns he receives from higher yields do not outweigh his greater transport costs to market. More extensive cultivation is better for Brown since it can be done at lower cost, making his returns greater (Fig. 2.2).

From this illustration it can be seen that the intensity of production of one crop will decline with distance from the market. The diagram (Fig. 2.3) shows the

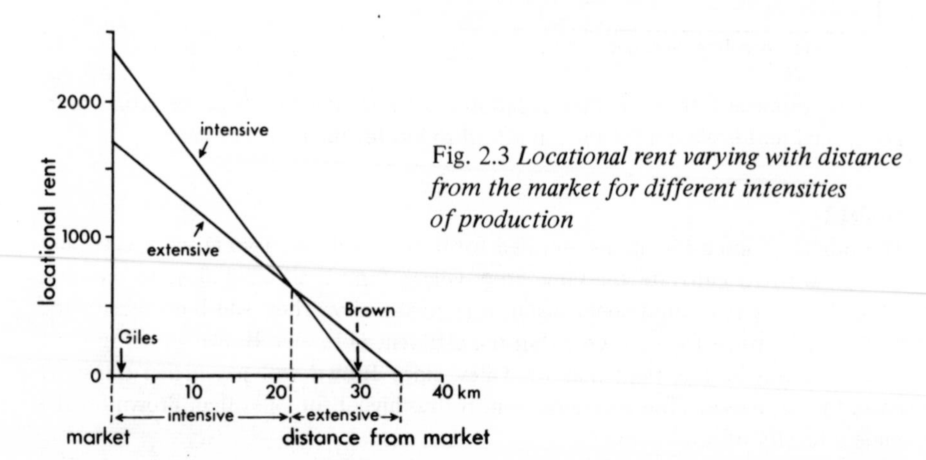

Fig. 2.3 *Locational rent varying with distance from the market for different intensities of production*

locational rents of the two farming systems, one intensive and the other extensive. The system with the greater locational rent will be adopted.

Model 2

Von Thünen's second model examines the location of several crops in relation to the market. Their location is determined by their market prices, transport costs, production costs, and yields per hectare. Transport costs vary with the bulk and perishability of a product. The crop with the highest locational rent for the unit of land will always be grown, since it gives the greatest returns, and all farmers attempt to maximize profits. Two crops may have the same production costs and yields but different transport costs (per tonne/kilometre) and market prices. If A is more costly to transport per tonne/kilometre and it has a higher market price, A will be grown closer to the market than B (Fig. 2.4). The locational rent for A decreases

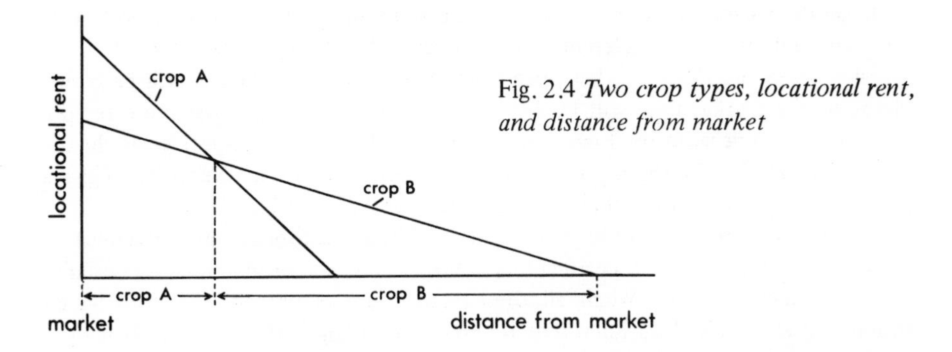

Fig. 2.4 *Two crop types, locational rent, and distance from market*

more rapidly than that of B because of A's higher transport costs. As the market price of A is greater than B, the total revenue is higher at the market for A than B. Thus, at the market the locational rent of A is greater than B, because production costs are the same and no transport costs are incurred. If the market price of B were greater than that of A, A would not be grown at all.

Fig. 2.5 *Locational rents of two crops at different distances from market*

crop	distance from market (km)	transport costs per tonne/km	yield (tonnes) per unit of land	total transport costs	production costs per tonne	total production cost	total costs	market price per tonne	total revenue	locational rent
C	5	2	10	100	20	200	300	40	400	100
C	10	2	10	200	20	200	400	40	400	0
D	5	2	5	50	20	100	150	45	225	75
D	10	2	5	100	20	100	200	45	225	25

Transport and production costs per tonne are the same.

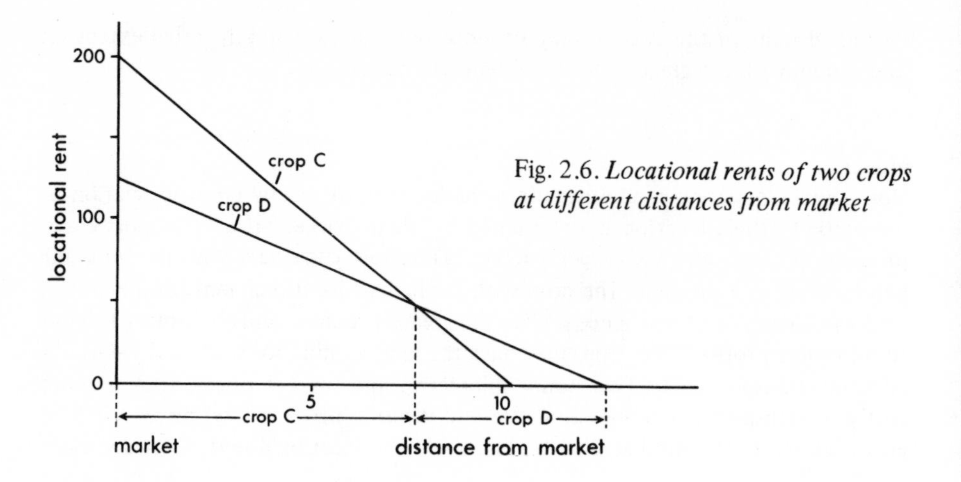

Fig. 2.6. *Locational rents of two crops at different distances from market*

In another case two crops may have the same production and transport costs per tonne/kilometre but different market prices and yields per unit of land. If C has a higher yield and lower market price than D (Figs. 2.5 and 2.6), it will be grown closer to the market than will D. The locational rent of C decreases more rapidly than that of D because the higher yield means higher total transport costs. In the case shown (Fig. 2.5), the higher yield of C offsets its lower market price to give a greater total revenue for C than D at the market. With production costs the same, the greater total revenue for C means it has a higher locational rent at the market.

In reality, market price, perishability, bulk, yields, and production costs usually vary between products. When all these factors are combined, the crop which produces the highest locational rent for the unit of land will be grown. However, the locational rent will have to be paid for in the form of land prices or land rent. If the farmer does not grow the crop with the highest locational rent, he still has to bear the high land charges. He is not, therefore, maximizing his profits and is liable to run at a loss.

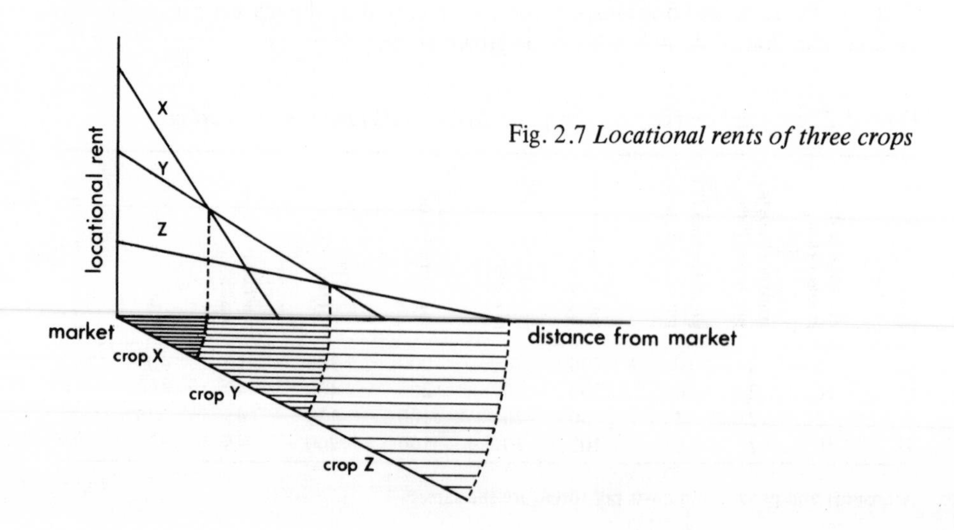

Fig. 2.7 *Locational rents of three crops*

An example of the combined impact of these factors on the locational rents of three crops is shown in the diagram (Fig. 2.7). It also displays the distance at which each crop will be grown from the market. In reality both the type and the intensity of production may vary, and thus, as in von Thünen's example below, models 1 and 2 are combined. The reader may find it helpful to use the following formula to calculate the locational rent of a crop:

$$LR = Ym - Yc - Ytd = Y(m - c - td)$$

where LR = locational rent per unit of land
Y = yield per unit of land
m = market price per unit of commodity
c = production cost per unit of commodity
t = transport cost per unit of commodity
d = distance from the market

Author's example

Von Thünen's classical example incorporated the ideas of the two models, showing how intensity of production and type of land use vary in the *isolierte staat* (isolated state). Remember the author was writing in the 1820s.

Having set out his assumptions and principles, von Thünen suggested that in theory the pattern shown in Fig. 2.8a would result. The production of fresh milk and vegetables was concentrated in the zone (1) nearest the city, because of the perishability of such products. Here cattle were kept in stables throughout the year. The fertility of the land was maintained by means of manuring, and, if necessary, additional manure was bought in the city and transported short distances to the farm.

The second belt (2) was used for the production of wood, a bulky product in great demand in the city as a fuel. Von Thünen showed, on the basis of his empirical data, that forestry yielded a higher locational rent since its bulkiness meant relatively higher transport costs.

Beyond the forest belt were three zones where rye was an important market product. The difference between the zones was in the intensity of cultivation. As the distance from the market increased so the intensity of rye production decreased with a consequent reduction in yields. In the first of these three outer zones (3) farmers employed a six-year crop rotation. Rye occupied one-third of the land and the rest was given over to potatoes, barley, clover, and vetch. Potatoes, like rye, were sold in the city. Vetch was used both as a green fodder and to help maintain soil fertility. Cattle were kept in stables for most of the year. There was no fallow land, and manuring maintained soil fertility.

In the next zone (4) the farming was less intensive. Farmers used a seven-year crop rotation in which rye occupied only one-seventh of the land. There was one year of rye, one of barley, one of oats, three of pasture, and one of fallow. The products sent to market were rye, butter, cheese, and occasionally live animals to be slaughtered in the city. These products did not perish so quickly as fresh milk and vegetables and could, therefore, be produced at a considerably greater distance from the market.

Fig. 2.8 *The spatial outcome of von Thünen's model:* (a) *the simple case,* (b) *the more complex case*

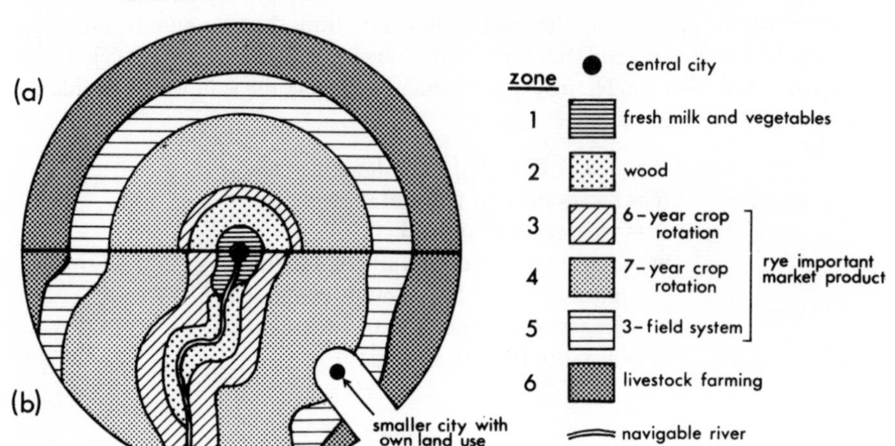

In the most distant of the zones supplying rye to the city (5) farmers followed the three-field system. This was a rotation system whereby one-third of the land was used for field crops, another one-third for pasture, and the rest left fallow.

The furthest zone of all (6) was one of livestock farming. Because of the distance to market, rye did not produce so high a rent as the production of butter, cheese, or live animals (ranching). The rye produced in this zone was solely for a farm's own consumption. Only animal products were marketed.

Finally, von Thünen incorporated two examples of modifying factors in his classic model (Fig. 2.8b). The effect can clearly be seen of a navigable river where transport was more speedy and cost only one-tenth as much as on land, together with the effect of a smaller city acting as a competing market centre.

Even the inclusion of only two modifications produces a much more complex land-use pattern. When all the simplifying assumptions are relaxed, as in reality, a complex land-use pattern would be expected.

Present-day examples

It is useful to examine present-day examples on three scales: farm, village, and continental.

The farm and village can be the sources of labour as well as the markets or initial collection points for the crops. Where they are the sources of labour, the overall intensity of production may be expected to decrease with distance from the farm or village because it takes time and effort to move from the home to the field. Transport costs of labour, in this case, increase from the farm or village outwards. This is due to the frictional effect of distance which is particularly noticeable in regions where transport is primitive.

Farm scale

Manor Farm and Buildings Farm, which are run as one unit, are at Marcham, 13 km to the south-west of Oxford (Fig. 2.9). The rearing of young cattle, which need a great deal of attention, is the most intensive activity of the farms and is carried out in fields next to the farmhouses. Wheat and barley are cultivated in the remaining fields. Superficially, distance seems the key variable explaining this pattern.

However, there are other considerations which affect the present pattern of farming here. Wheat, for instance, is grown at Manor Farm in the south since the soil there is considerably heavier and damper. The main reason for this continuing to be arable, apart from the low rainfall, warm summers, relatively flat land, and large fields, is that it has always been an arable farm. Since the present owners are new, this **inertia factor** or reluctance to change could soon be swept away. In the future, too, the farm buildings at Buildings Farm are likely to be used only for storage, and most of the active farm work will be based on Manor Farm. This could mean that cattle will no longer be kept in the field adjoining Buildings Farm. Certainly distance is an important, possibly the most important, factor on this farm, but there are several other contributory factors.

There can be no doubt about the importance of distance in the example of crofting, a fast declining form of subsistence farming in the highlands of Scotland. The contrast between the extensive husbandry of the rough grazings and the intensive cultivation of the arable plots next to the crofter's cottage is very marked. This is an excellent example on the farm scale of the farm being the main market for the products and the result being a version of von Thünen's system. However, this is increasingly unusual in British farms, since so many factors other than distance have an effect on the land-use pattern.

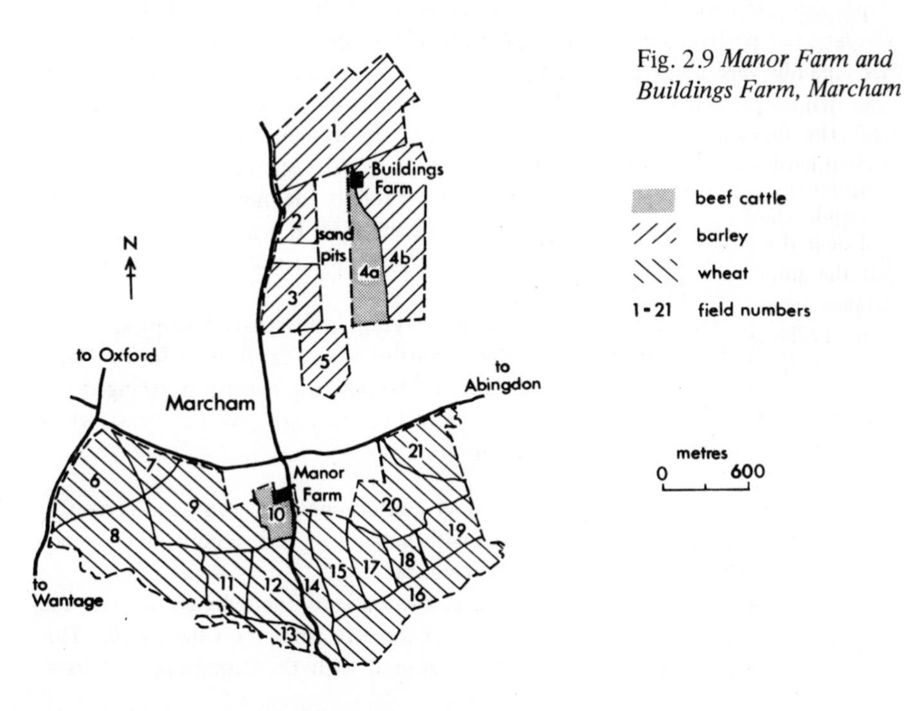

Fig. 2.9 *Manor Farm and Buildings Farm, Marcham*

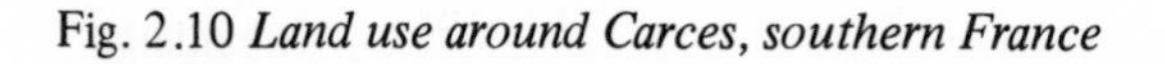

Fig. 2.10 *Land use around Carces, southern France*

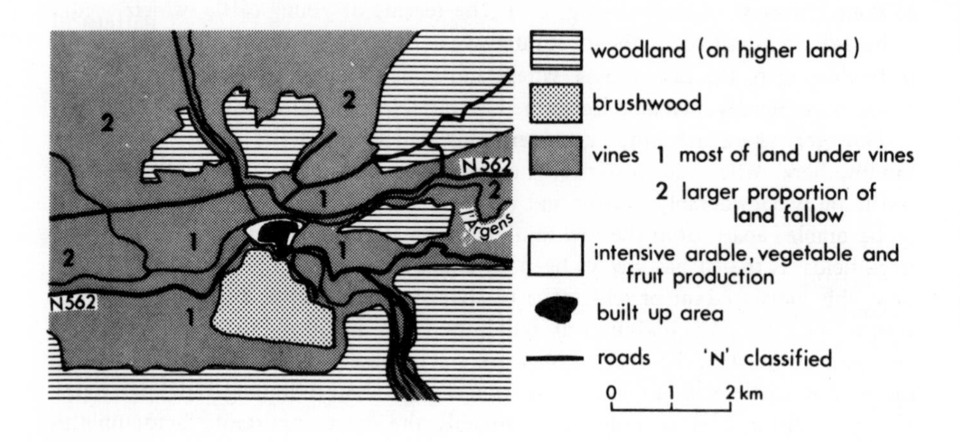

Village scale

Many present-day villages in both the Mediterranean and less-developed areas do seem to illustrate certain of von Thünen's principles. This is especially true where the means of transport is limited and the market is the village itself.

Carces, in Haute Provence, France, is in a vine-growing area (Fig. 2.10). The grapes are taken to the co-operative in Carces where they are processed into wine. The land-use pattern consists of small plots of kitchen gardens next to the village. Here mainly vegetables are grown, while much of the remaining area is under the vine. The farmers live in the village and travel mostly on foot to the fields. The kitchen gardens are tended by both the men and the women. However, the physical environment has an effect on the land-use pattern. The steepest, driest, and least accessible vineyards have been abandoned, and it is only the most accessible, flattest land near the l'Argens which continues to be cultivated. It is noticeable in this area that the amount of farm land and the intensity of production both decrease with distance away from the village and its farmers.

A similar pattern can be observed in varying forms in the tropical world. Prothero, in studying land use at Soba in northern Nigeria, showed how a Hausa village illustrates such a pattern (Fig. 2.11). The land-use pattern is arranged in a series of largely concentric zones, best developed on the north, west and east, where the greater part of the village land is located.

1. Zone A, within the village walls, is under continuous cultivation and is heavily manured. Tobacco is most important with patches of guinea corn, okra, sugar-cane, and peppers, in that order of importance.
2. Zone B is an area of almost unbroken cultivated land, immediately outside the village, extending up to a maximum of a kilometre from the village walls. This land is continuously cultivated and is manured with the droppings of horses,

donkeys, sheep, goats, and Fulani cattle. Guinea corn and cotton are the major food and cash crops followed by tobacco and groundnuts.

3. Zone C extends from three-quarters to one and a half kilometres in width, and here there is a system of land rotation. Farms are cleared and cultivated for three to four years and then the land reverts to fallow for at least five years. The crop types are similar to zone B but cotton is rather more important.
4. Zone D, the outermost land-use zone, lies within three to five kilometres of the village and dense bush growth is dominant. Cultivated land is made up mainly of the farmland of peripheral hamlets, where, on a smaller scale, the A, B, C zones are repeated.

This case study suggests that a decreasing intensity of cultivation with increasing distance also occurs in and around tropical villages, where the villages are both the markets and the sources of labour and manure. However, it should be pointed out that even here the physical environment has a role to play. For example, in part of zone A there are the 'fadamma' areas where the river floodplain is inundated annually, and silt maintains the fertility. Here more tobacco and sugar-cane are grown.

In the past, zonal patterns have been observed around some British villages, for example the early infield-outfield system in highland Britain. However, nowadays it is difficult to identify zones around villages. This is partly because of a great improvement in transport, so that many more markets are accessible and partly because many farms have been located outside villages since the enclosure movement.

Fig. 2.11 *Land-use zones at Soba, northern Nigeria*

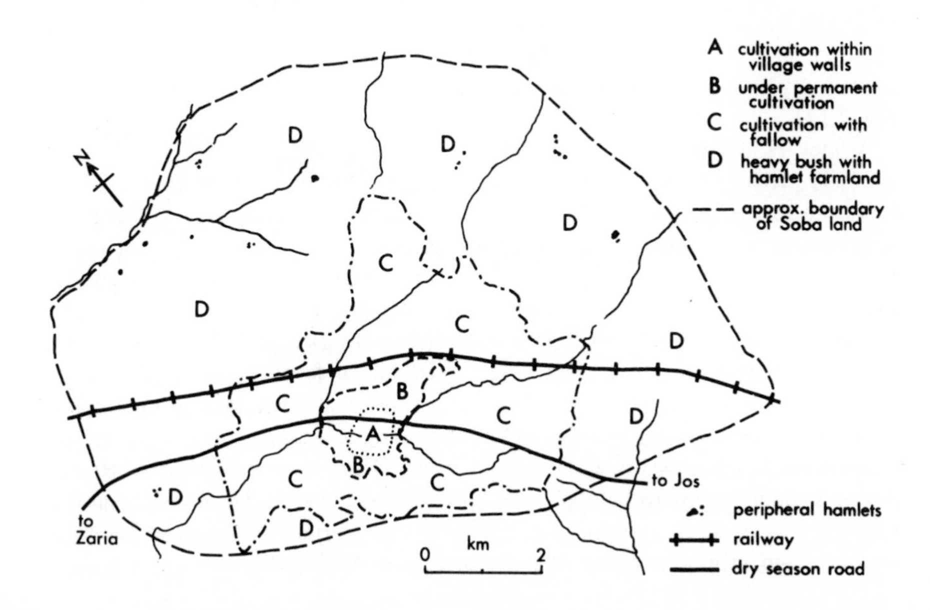

Fig. 2.12 *Zones of production around a theoretical isolated city in Europe*

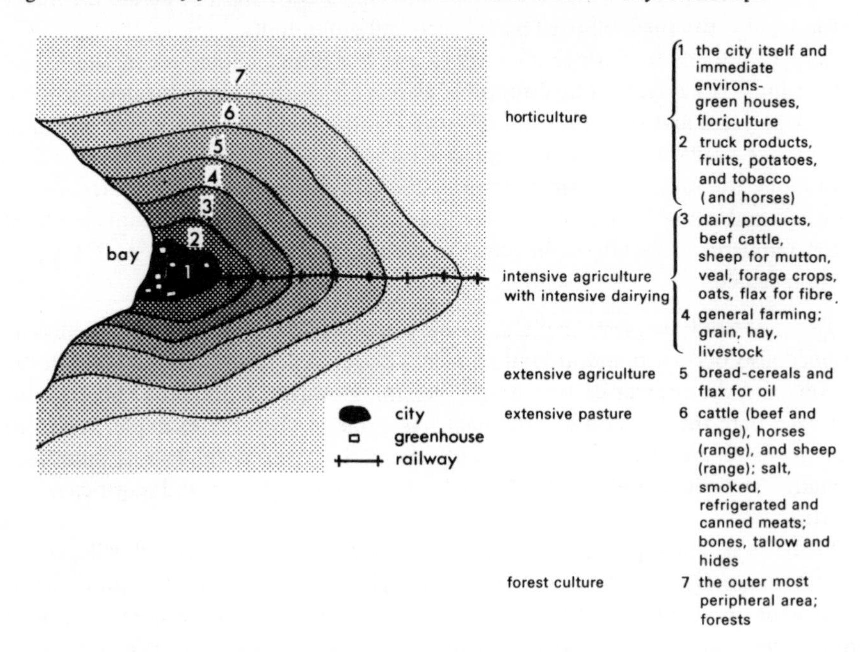

The continental scale

It was observed as early as 1925 by Jonasson that in Europe and North America, zones of agricultural land use were arranged about the industrial centres. 'In both these regions the most intensive development of agriculture is in the hay and pasture region in which the industrial centres are situated, about these are arranged concentrically the successive grades of land use – grain growing, pasturing, and forestry.' Jonasson, in fact, proposed a model distribution of land use around a theoretical, isolated city in Europe, bearing a considerable resemblance to von Thünen's model (Fig. 2.12).

A later validation of Jonasson's ideas appeared in 1952 when van Valkenburg and Held produced a map of the intensity of agriculture in Europe (Fig. 2.13). It shows the productivity of the land per acre on the basis of eight very widely raised crops: wheat, rye, barley, oats, corn, potatoes, sugar-beet, and hay. For each crop, the average yield per acre for Europe as a whole is taken as an index of 100, and the specific yield in each country is calculated accordingly. The outstanding fact is that the Netherlands and Belgium lead in intensity, with Denmark, Switzerland, and England closely approaching them. The application of fertilizers in such areas is a major factor, as are the selection of seed and careful crop rotation. If one regards the major market of Europe for agricultural products as north-east France, the Netherlands, Belgium, south-east England, north Germany and Denmark, then von Thünen's model seems to be applicable on a continental scale. However, it is not as simple as this since, to mention just one factor, the periphery of Europe has much less useful agricultural land (the Alps, Pyrenees, and Apennines).

Fig. 2.13 *Intensity of agriculture in Europe (the index of 100 is the average European yield per acre of eight main crops; 1937 political boundaries)*

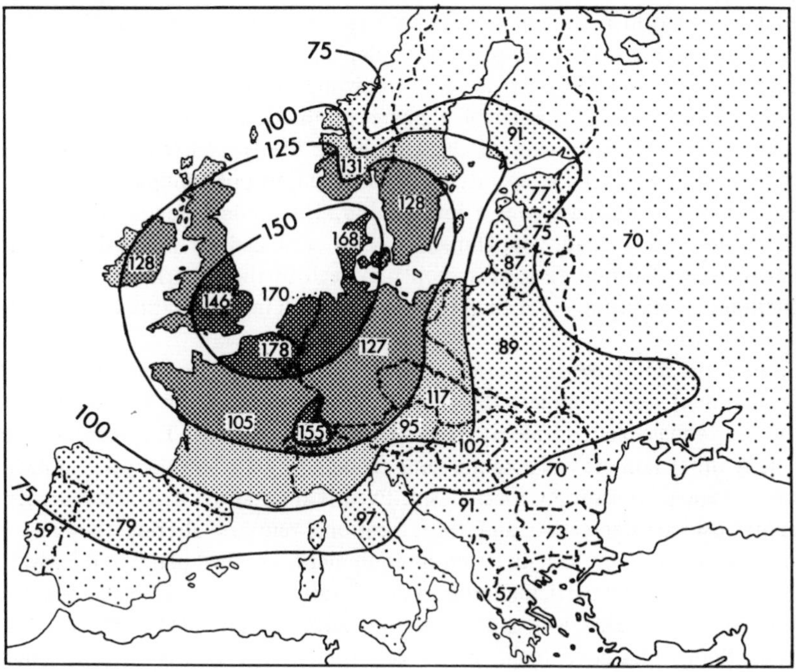

Problems and applicability

Although examples may be found which reflect some of von Thünen's principles of land use, it should not be surprising that von Thünen's actual land-use pattern does not occur. Many factors have changed since 1826, in particular, the type and relative cost of transport. Obviously many of von Thünen's simplifying assumptions do not apply in the real world.

The main alterations in factors affecting land use derive from man's changing use of resources and his increasingly rapid development of technology. For example, timber is now little used for fuel, so it no longer commands such proximity to the market. London may now be served from Devon by milk trains with refrigerated containers. The improvement in transport and storage technology has lowered transport costs relative to production costs, so production is possible much further from the market, and each of von Thünen's original rings may be very much wider. Yet larger rings are rarely distinguishable, even if a single market may be identified, for within a particular theoretical ring, production may be concentrated in certain areas where such physical factors as climate and soil fertility are especially favourable. These areas within the ring, rather than the whole ring, may specialize in the product of the ring. This leads to the emergence of regions, rather than rings, characterized by a particular type of agricultural land use. Thus transport costs and therefore distance from market have become relatively less important, and consequently the expected spatial outcome has changed.

In the real world farmers do not behave as von Thünen assumed. They do not act as economic men. They are often not independent of one another. Co-operative production, such as Californian truck farming and Danish dairying, has developed since von Thünen's day. It has enabled greater production at lower production costs per unit. This increased scale of production in the specialized areas often also results in lower transport costs per item, because the transport company is guaranteed a large volume of business over a long period. This again extends the theoretical width of the rings. Indeed, von Thünen may be criticized for not realizing that an increased scale of production of a crop may lead to the lowering of the costs of production and transport, and thus to a modification in the locational rent and the land-use pattern.

Farmers do not have the perfect knowledge of economic men. They do not know what next year's weather will be when deciding which crops to sow. Pessimists and optimists may plant different crops in the same situation. They can only guess how many other farmers will sow the same crop and thus affect the price at harvest-time by means of the supply mechanism. Even if they know that prices are rising, transport costs are decreasing, and, thus, locational rents are altering, they may still not change crops. They have invested in equipment, physical plant, and know-how in the production of a particular crop. A conservative element, which is reflected in a disinclination to take risks and adopt innovations, is reflected in the pattern of land use. Sometimes government policy accentuates this conservatism by granting subsidies and guaranteeing prices. Indeed, the effect of costs of transport to market may be nullified by a marketing body such as the Milk Marketing Board in Britain, which gives the same price at all farms despite their distance from the market.

It is unreasonable to criticize von Thünen for not foreseeing the increasing governmental impact on the economy. Even in his day, though, he would have recognized that once his state ceased to be isolated, trading policies in the form of free trade, import tariffs, and restrictions might affect the pattern of land use.

As the examples and this section show, there are many factors influencing land use, most of which vary over time. Von Thünen understood this and, in particular, foresaw the effect of the relative lowering of transport costs. Von Thünen's model can no longer be used by itself to explain agricultural land use, but the importance of the major principle that it identifies, that is, locational rent, must not be underestimated.

Conclusion

Von Thünen's work is useful in two main ways. It focuses attention on economic factors, particularly transport costs and distance to market, factors which in the past geographers have subordinated to those of the physical environment when attempting to explain land-use patterns. It also introduces the concept of locational rent into geography. This concept is useful in studying urban, as well as rural, land use (Chapter 5). The rigid assumptions of the model have also indirectly led to more research emphasis on the ways that farmers make decisions, the information they possess, and their willingness to innovate. With this knowledge a greater understanding of rural land use is gradually being acquired. For the geographer, von Thünen's work with all its limitations still provides a useful framework for organizing village and farm studies. As with many models, the residuals, or parts unexplained by the model, often prove to be of greatest interest and lead the student on to greater understanding.

Bibliography

Chisholm, M., *Rural Settlement and Land Use* (Hutchinson, 1965)
Found, W.C., *A Theoretical Approach to Rural Land-Use Patterns* (Arnold, 1971)
Hall, P., (ed.), *Von Thünen's Isolated State* (Pergamon, 1966)
Tarrant, J.R., *Agricultural Geography* (David & Charles, 1974)

Essay questions

1. Explain how 'the friction of distance' can affect the distribution of agricultural activity. (Oxford and Cambridge, 1975)
2. Outline briefly von Thünen's theory of agricultural location. How far is it true of the rural land use of an area or areas you have studied? (Cambridge, 1974)
3. With reference to an area you have studied in the field, discuss the pattern of agricultural land use and the factors which have, in your opinion, most strongly affected it. (Cambridge, 1973)
4. 'Profit maximization remains the single most useful simplifying assumption for the spatial analysis of farming patterns.' Discuss. (University College, London)

Chapter 3

Industrial location: Weber's model

Introduction and link

Following the analysis of the location of central goods and services by Christaller and Lösch, and the location of agricultural land use by von Thünen, an examination of the location of manufacturing industry is required to complete the discussion of the location of economic activity. Alfred Weber's theory forms the basis of this discussion. Weber, a German economist, wrote his book *Theory of the Location of Industries* in 1909. It was translated into English in 1929 and has since become a standard reference on the subject. Like Christaller, Lösch, and von Thünen, Weber was interested in discovering order from an apparent chaos, particularly since industry seemed to him to be the 'substance' of what were then new agglomerations of people. In the same way as von Thünen, he deduced laws of location from a set of simplifying assumptions. Although many of the assumptions are similar to those used by von Thünen and Christaller, his uniform plain does have an uneven distribution of raw material deposits. The plain suggested here, therefore, is closer to reality than that assumed by Christaller and von Thünen. Again, as with von Thünen, transport costs form the basis of the explanation. Weber, though, is determining the location for the minimum cost of production of a given item, whereas von Thünen is deciding the best agricultural land use for a given location.

Main aim

Weber aims to explain the location of industrial activity in terms of three economic factors, namely transport costs, labour costs, and agglomeration economies. His explanation is based upon finding the least-cost location for production.

Assumptions and principles

Weber made three explicit assumptions that were retained throughout his analysis:

1. There is an uneven distribution of natural resources on the plain. Thus the raw materials, fuel, and water needed for industrial production may be found only in given locations.
2. The size and location of centres of consumption of the industrial products are given. The markets are thus points on the plain.

3. There are several fixed locations of labour where given wage rates operate. Labour is immobile and unlimited at these locations.

   There are other assumptions which are implied in his work.
4. The area has a uniform culture, race, climate, and political and economic system.
5. The entrepreneurs seek to minimize the total cost of production.
6. Conditions of perfect competition are assumed, whereby resources and markets are unlimited at their given location and no firm may obtain a monopolistic advantage from its choice of location.

   Some other assumptions are made for the description of his pure theory.
7. Costs of land, building, equipment, interest, and depreciation of fixed capital do not vary regionally.
8. There is a uniform system of transport over a flat surface.

Weber maintains that there are three regional factors which affect the costs of production. These are the cost of **raw materials**, and the cost of **transporting** raw materials and products, and the cost of **labour**. The cost of materials varies, for example, according to the nature of the deposits and the difficulty of mining them. He suggests that this variation should be reflected within the costs of transport of the materials. So his general regional factors affecting production are reduced to transport costs and labour costs. He identifies another local factor called **agglomeration** or **deglomeration economies**. The first are the savings to the individual plants that result from their operating in the same location. These may result from the common use of such activities as auxiliary industries, financial services, and public utilities. In a single-firm location, these processes and services have to be carried out or borne by the firm at greater cost. Agglomeration economies also include **linkages** between firms, where there are flows of goods between the plants, the development of a specialist labour force, and savings owing to the bulk purchasing of materials and large-scale marketing of products. Weber suggests that many of these economies may be gained by the increased scale of production of one firm as well as by the clustering of several. Deglomeration economies involve the weakening of the agglomeration economies and, especially, the increase in the cost of land owing to such a clustering of firms.

His analysis is divided into two major sections:

1. The identification of the point of minimum transport costs.
2. A discussion of the circumstances under which production will be attracted away from this point owing to advantages gained from cheaper labour or agglomeration.

The point of minimum transport costs

The simplest case for the least-transport-cost location involves one raw material source (R) and one market (M). For this, labour costs are assumed to be equal over the plain. The chosen source is the most advantageous of those providing the raw material. Fig. 3.1 shows the cost of transporting the material needed for one unit of product at various distances from the material source, while the equivalent costs of transporting a unit of product to the market is also shown. Another set of lines are

Fig. 3.1. *The construction of isodapanes: one market, one raw material case with transport costs proportional to distance and no weight loss. Optimum location either at R or M, or if no extra handling charges anywhere along the line between R and M*

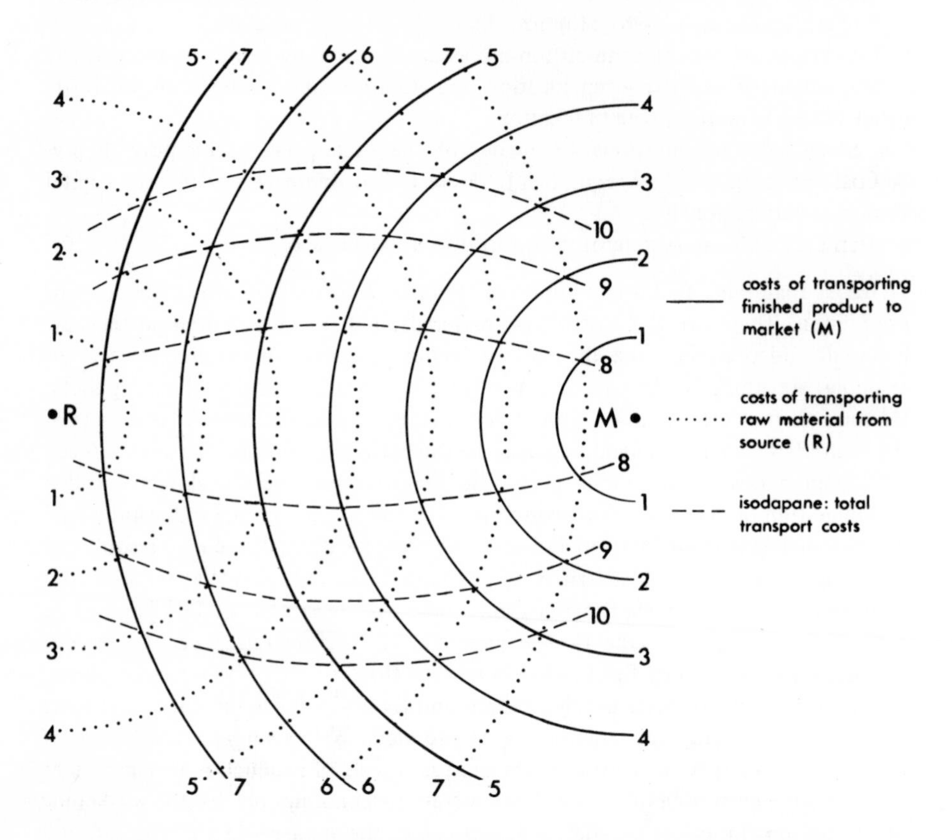

shown which join locations where the total transport costs (transporting both material and product) are equal. These lines are called **isodapanes**. Clearly the point of minimum total cost of transport lies within the isodapane of lowest value. In this case it can be at R or M, or anywhere along the line between them.

In this simple example, transport costs are directly related to distance. In Weber's analysis they are also influenced by the weight of the material and product. The greater the weight of material to be moved, the greater are the transport costs. The least-transport-cost location is the point where the total tonne-kilometres of material assembly and product distribution is at a minimum. **Ubiquitous materials** which are those found everywhere, such as water, do not need to be transported, and plants using mostly these tend to locate closer to the market. The location of plants which employ mostly **localized materials** depends upon the amount of weight lost from the materials in production. Only part of some raw materials is used in production. The rest is waste. For example, iron has to be extracted from its ore. Such materials are called **weight loss** or **gross materials**. Materials which are totally used in production are called **pure materials**. Weber constructed an index to differentiate between industries where there was much or little weight lost in production. This **material index** =

$$\frac{\text{the total weight of localized materials used per product}}{\text{the weight of the product}}$$

For industries using pure materials, the index equals 1, as there is no weight lost in production. Where there is substantial weight lost, the material index is much higher than 1. For these industries the cost of transporting materials is much higher than that of the product. The least-transport-cost locations will tend towards the material sources rather than the market. Industries with a material index of 1 or close to 1 are located close to the market, since the cost of transporting the product is much greater than the cost of transporting any one of the pure materials from its source. The type of production measured in terms of weight-loss thus affects the location of a plant.

In the simple illustration (Fig. 3.1) there is only one material source. Where there are two, a **locational triangle** results (Fig. 3.2). The resolution of the least-transport-cost location depends on the relative weights of the products and the two raw materials used (Fig. 3.2i, ii, iii). In the illustrated case, production is close to R_1, since the weight loss is greater for this material.

Fig. 3.2 *Locational triangle using two raw materials, R_1 and R_2*

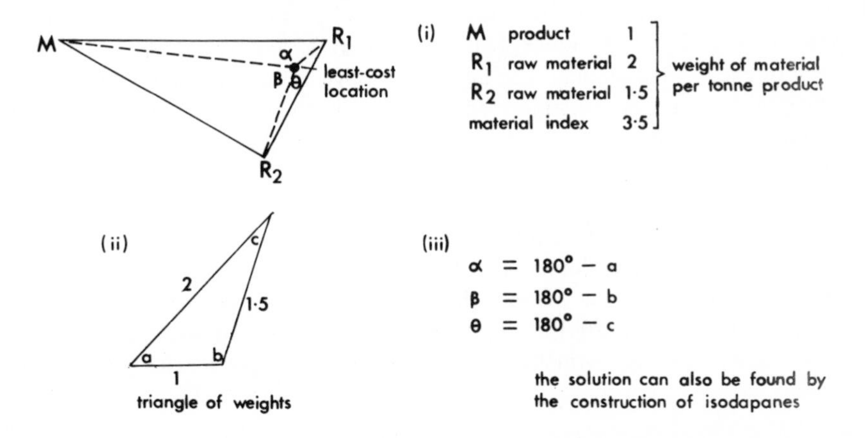

Weber moved closer to reality by introducing many material sources, transport costs based on costs per unit distance which involve factors other than weight, more than one transport system, and the location of a whole industry rather than one plant. The basic principles of location already described still applied.

The deflecting effect of labour costs

Having obtained the least-transport-cost location, Weber introduced the factor of labour costs. He asked whether the savings derived from moving to a location of cheaper or more efficient labour would more than offset the increase in transport

Fig. 3.3 *Deflecting effect of labour costs: critical isodapane*

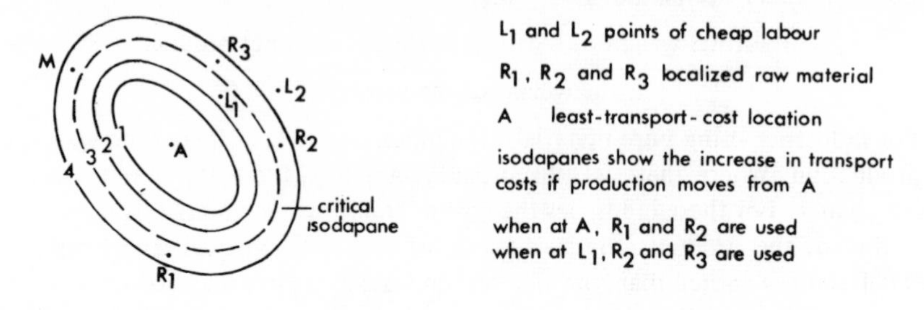

costs that would result from leaving the least-transport-cost location. Isodapanes, the lines of equal total transport cost, are again constructed (Fig. 3.3). In this example the isodapane values show the difference in transport costs per product involved in locating other than at the least-transport-cost location. The savings on a single product derived from using the cheaper labour at L_1 and L_2 are estimated as £3. L_1 lies between the isodapanes of £2 and £3 extra transport costs. It would be profitable to move to L_1 since the savings on labour exceed the extra transport costs. The move to L_2, however, would be unprofitable since the cheaper labour would not offset the extra transport costs of over £4. To simplify the procedure, the isodapane with the value of the labour savings is noted (Fig. 3.3). Weber called it the **critical isodapane**. If the cheaper labour is located within the critical isodapane, it is profitable to move. If it is outside it, then it is not. A relocation to the site of cheaper labour may then involve a change in the sources of raw materials as other sources may become more advantageous in the new location (for example substituting R_3 for R_1).

The deflecting effect of agglomeration economies

The treatment of the agglomeration factor follows a similar logic. The savings derived from the clustering of, say, three firms are estimated at £10 per product for each of the firms. The critical isodapane with the value of £10 extra transport costs is drawn for each firm from their least-transport-cost locations (Fig. 3.4).

Fig. 3.4 *Deflecting effect of agglomeration economies*

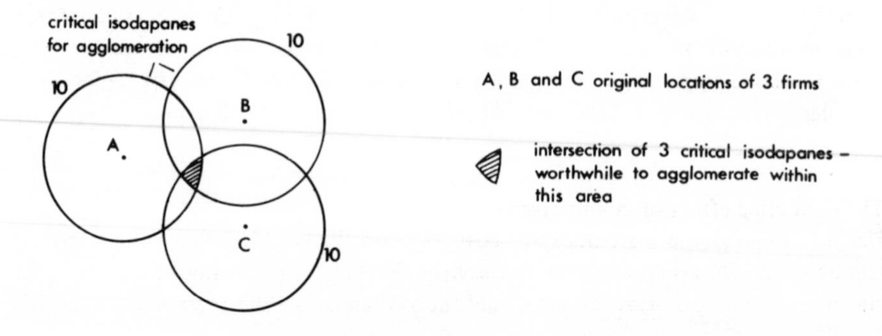

It is profitable to agglomerate only within the area delimited by the intersection of all three critical isodapanes (Fig. 3.4 shaded area). It is not economic to cluster outside that area. If the critical isodapanes did not intersect, it would not be profitable to agglomerate.

These are the basic principles of Weber's analysis. He went on to show the combined effect of the three factors – transport costs, labour costs, and agglomeration economies – on the location of a set of industries which produces the industrial part of an economic landscape.

Author's example

The essence of Weber's theory can be summarized in tabular form as shown in Fig. 3.5. Here eight types of industry are distinguished according to the differing influence of factors which affect their location. Note that industry B is the equivalent of the case illustrated in Fig. 3.1, and industry E is that of the locational triangle shown in Fig. 3.2. If, however, the two gross materials used in type E experienced very unequal weight loss in manufacture, the industry would be located at the material with the greatest weight loss.

Fig. 3.5 *The main types of locational orientation according to Weber*

	locational factors						orientation					
type of industry	ubiquitous materials	'pure' materials	'gross' materials	labour	agglomeration	deglomeration	materials	intermediate	market	labour	agglomeration	deglomeration
A	1+								*			
B		1					?	?	?			
C	1+	1+							*			
D			1				*					
E			2					*				
F	←	unspecified	→	√						*		
G	"	"	"		√						*	
H	"	"	"			√						*

* definite locations + 'or more' materials ? equally viable locations

Present-day examples

A variety of research workers have applied aspects of the Weberian theory to the study of modern industry. Wilfred Smith, for example, in his work in 1955 on the location of industry, tested Weber's weight-loss hypothesis against reality. As Smith observed, 'Without question some industries fulfil Weber's requirements.' For example, in the extraction of raw sugar in a sugar-beet factory, the final product

Fig. 3.6 *The location of sugar-beet factories in relation to beet-producing land in England and Wales*

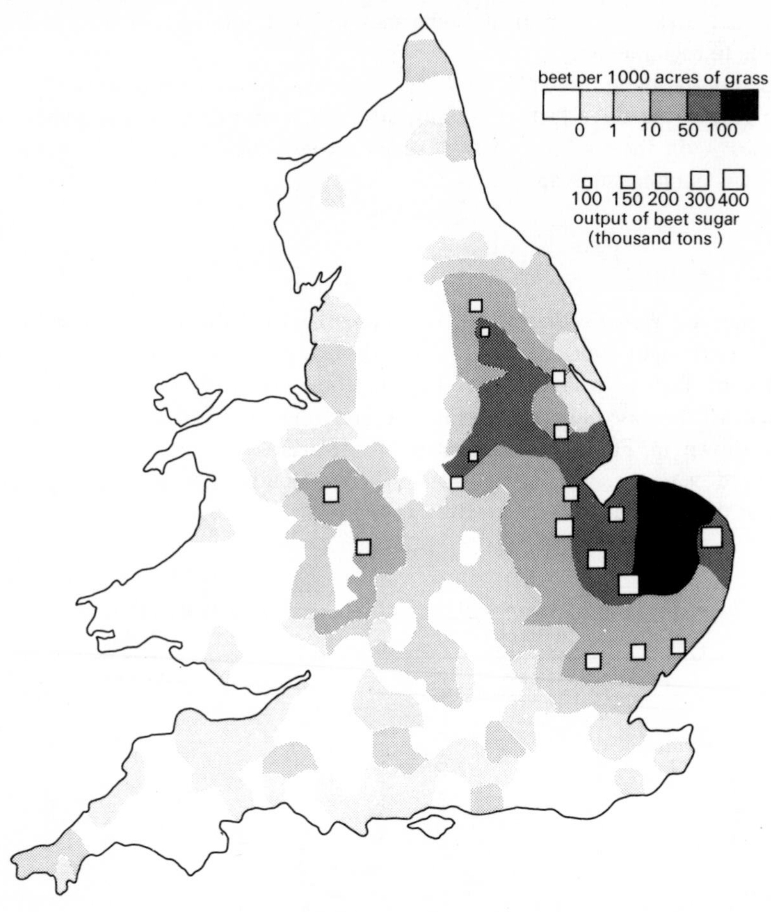

is one-eighth the weight of the materials (beet, coal, and lime) used in the extractive process. As would be expected, therefore, the location of sugar-beet factories is very closely tied to beet producing land (Fig. 3.6).

Similarly, but to a lesser extent, such industries as the manufacture of pig iron and the production of cheese and other milk products, have high material indices and are usually found at the location of their raw materials. These Smith suggested could be called **primary industries**, since the raw materials are handled direct from mining or from farming. This initial processing involves the greatest loss of weight. Smith suggested that port industries, such as grain milling, fish curing, and oil refining, were similar in that production occurs at the country's nearest points of access to the raw materials.

The main statistical work which Smith undertook was with reference to sixty-five industries for which data were collected from the 1948 census of production. He concluded that the material index certainly isolated the extreme cases of industries located at the raw material source or the market, but was less useful for the majority

Fig. 3.7 *A sequence of industries connected with steel*

industry	weight of finished product as per cent of weight of materials	weight of material per operative (tons)
blast furnaces	27	1447
steel mills	81	117
tube mills	84	38
chain, nail, and screw mills	74	15
textile machine shops	50	5
motor-vehicle manufacturing shops	inadequate evidence	7

of industries in the middle range. He decided that coal should be omitted as a raw material since he classed it as a fuel. He considered the material index a rather blunt tool of analysis and went on to examine other indices that might be helpful in distinguishing types of industrial location.

Finally, Smith showed by reference to the location pattern of a particular sequence of industries all using one material, steel (Fig. 3.7), that raw material locations are less relevant the more elaborately manufactured a material becomes. The sequence clearly displays 'the full range of locational shift from a location tied to raw material to a location wholly independent of raw material'. Smith concluded by suggesting that there was a need to develop new analytical tools capable of handling the many modern industries not related to raw materials.

Isard and Cumberland, in studying New England as a possible location for an integrated iron and steel works, relied implicitly on many of Weber's ideas. Indeed, they eventually decided that the only meaningful way of analysing the location of the iron and steel industry was to adopt a Weberian type of analysis backed by

Fig. 3.8 *Transport costs required per net ton of steel for certain steel centres serving the Boston market*

location	transportation costs ($)			total
	ore	coal	finished products	($)
Fall River — Labrador ore	4·56	6·01	4·60	15·17
Fall River — Venezuelan ore	3·68	5·63	4·60	13·91
New London — Labrador ore	4·56	5·79	6·80	17·15
New London — Venezuelan ore	3·68	5·42	6·80	15·90
Pittsburgh	5·55	1·56	15·20	22·31
Cleveland	3·16	3·85	15·20	22·21
Sparrows Point	4·73	4·26	12·40	21·39
Buffalo	3·16	4·27	12·60	20·03
Bethlehem	5·56	5·06	10·60	21·22
Trenton	3·68	4·65	10·40	18·73

Source: Isard, W., and Cumberland, J.H., 'New England as a possible Location for an Integrated Iron and Steel Works,' *Economic Geography*, vol. 26 (October, 1950), p. 249

economic data. One of their conclusions was that Fall River and New London (two possible New England steel sites) certainly seemed best suited to serve the central and eastern New England market. However, these two sites came under severe competition from Trenton, New Jersey, when the western and southern New England market was considered. Eventually this conclusion was related to a quantitative analysis of transport costs to the possible market centres in New England. Fig. 3.8 is one example of the many tables they produced.

Kennelly, writing about the location of the Mexican steel industry, used various aspects of Weber's theory in addition to other theoretical contributions. He concluded that the Mexican steel industry was well located, his analysis stressing transport costs. Kennelly found the isodapanes a particularly useful technique; and he found the basis of the theory, transport orientation, especially applicable to the Mexican steel industry situation. However, he did point out the weaknesses of the material index, which places too much emphasis on the relative weight of materials and not enough on their relative location.

Recent additions to industrial location theory

David Smith made a significant contribution to location theory by introducing **space-cost curves** and **spatial margins of profitability**. Smith used the isodapane technique and developed cost contour maps as a result. His space-cost curve was a cross-section of such a cost contour map. The least-cost location on this curve is the lowest point. Fig. 3.9 shows one example of a space-cost curve. The importance of this approach is that the margins of profitability can be identified spatially. The least-cost location (at 0 in Fig. 3.9) is difficult to find and rarely chosen, but satisfactory locations within these margins (between A and B in Fig. 3.9) are more common. Industrialists who are content with choosing satisfactory, rather than optimal, locations have been called **satisficer men** rather than economic men.

Lösch devised the first general theory of location with demand as a major spatial variable. Given Lösch's assumptions, there were no variations in production costs. His emphasis was on locations where profit was greatest, that is where total revenue exceeded total cost by the greatest amount. Thus maximum profit was the goal, rather than least costs as in Weber's model. Lösch devised an economic land-

Fig. 3.9 *A space-cost curve*

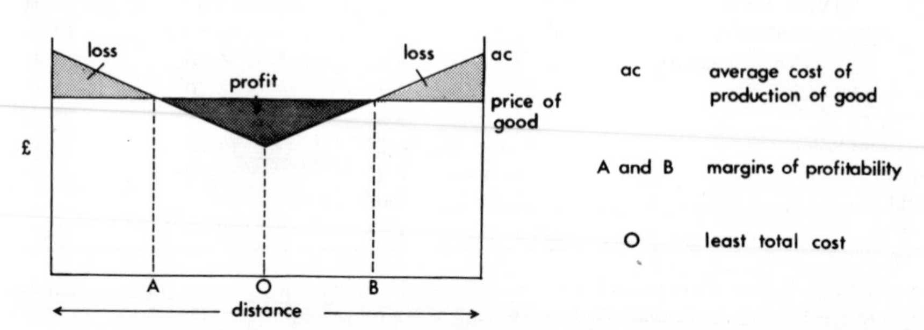

Fig. 3.10 *The location of two ice-cream salesmen on a beach*

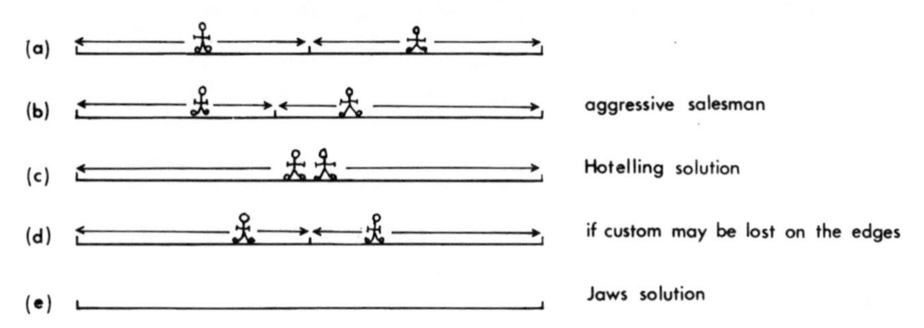

scape (Chapter 1) in which individual locations were interrelated. The weaknesses of his theory are its overemphasis on demand, its neglect of any spatial variables in cost, and its great abstraction from reality. However, Lösch never aimed at producing a realistic theory, just a framework of analysis.

Isard sought to create an overall theory based on the fusion of the frameworks of von Thünen, Lösch, and Weber. He linked location theory with other branches of economic theory, particularly through the **substitution principle**. Greenhut summarized the substitution approach to location theory as follows: 'The extent to which labour can be substituted for capital or land and *vice versa* is basically the same problem as the selection of a plant site from among alternative locations.' For example, given two equally advantageous sites for a factory, one may have cheaper land, the other cheaper labour. By locating on the cheaper land site, an entrepreneur would be substituting cheap land for cheap labour. Both locational and economic theory have as one objective the optimal allocation of resources.

As a response to some of the weaknesses in traditional least-cost theory a **locational interdependence** school of thought developed. In this approach the spatial pattern of plants and market areas results from spatial variations in demand and the need to consider the location of competing firms. Each firm is seeking to supply the largest possible market area taking into account the actions of both consumers and competitors. Hotelling, who is often associated with this school of thought, envisaged a duopoly whereby two sellers, for instance of ice-cream, compete to supply an identical product to customers who are evenly distributed along a seaside beach and will visit the nearest ice-cream salesman. In Fig. 3.10a each salesman commands half the beach, but this permits an aggressive salesman to move towards the centre of the beach and capture part of his competitor's market (b). Hotelling suggested that the stable solution would be when the ice-cream sellers were standing back to back in the centre of the beach, each serving one-half of the market (c). However, this assumes that people on the edges of the beach do not decide against buying ice-cream because of the greater distance they have to travel. If they do, the salesmen will move equal distances away from the centre to counteract this (d).

Greenhut attempted to integrate ideas of least cost and locational interdependence. To a great extent he succeeded by taking maximization of total profit (not maximizing revenue or minimizing costs) as the basis for the optimum location. The theory was comprehensive and included the following factors:

1. Cost factors of location (transport, labour and processing costs).
2. Demand factors of location (locational interdependence of firms, or attempts to monopolize certain market segments).
3. Cost-reducing factors, for example nearness to suppliers of raw materials or capital.
4. Revenue-increasing factors, for example sales gained from proximity to buyers.
5. Personal cost-reducing factors, for example good relations with suppliers and bankers.
6. Personal revenue-increasing factors, for example existing good contacts with customers.
7. Purely personal considerations, for example entrepreneur's preferences for place of residence.

At the same time, the importance of the market as a location factor attracted greater interest, in particular from Harris who studied the localization of industry in the U.S.A. Harris suggested that economic activities were increasingly related to the market and gave the example of steel, an industry at first primarily connected with raw materials, yet now increasingly dominated by the market. Harris explained that one-half of the retail sales in the United States were made in the American industrial belt which extends from St. Louis and Milwaukee in the west to Washington and Boston in the east. His map transformation of retail sales in the United States (Fig. 3.11) supported his point.

Fig. 3.11 *A market view of the United States*

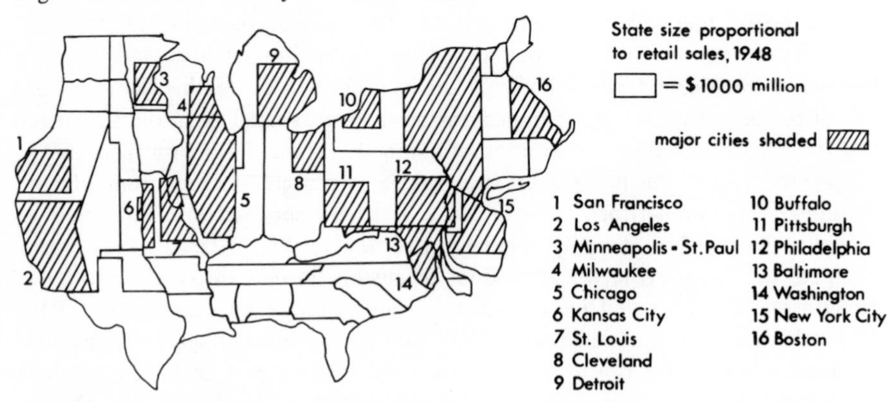

The technique of **market potential** was used by Harris as an abstract index of the intensity of possible contact with the markets.

$$\text{Market potential } P_i = \sum_{j=1}^{n} \frac{M_j}{d_{ij}} = \frac{M_1}{d_{i1}} + \frac{M_2}{d_{i2}} + \frac{M_3}{d_{i3}} \ldots + \frac{M_n}{d_{in}}$$

where the market potential (P) at point i is the summation (Σ) of n markets (j)

Fig. 3.12 *Distribution of market potential for the United States, based on retail sales in 1948 and on land transport only. The points for which calculations were made are indicated by dots*

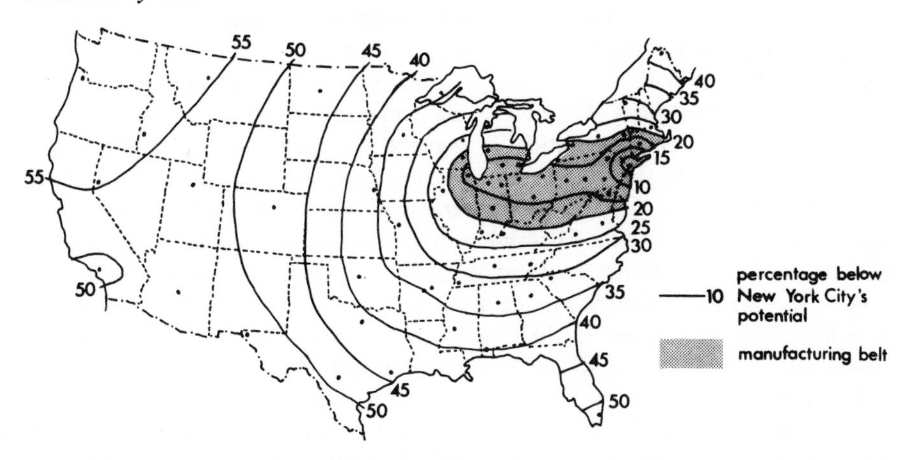

accessible to the point (i) divided by their distance (d_{ij}) from that point. Retail sales on a county basis were the data giving the values for M. Transport cost was used as a measure of (d) distance. P was worked out for all points (cities) on the map (Fig. 3.12); and based on these values, lines of equal market potential were drawn to produce a market potential surface. The map shows the surface in a two-dimensional form, with the lines of equal market potential being similar to contour lines for this imaginary three-dimensional surface with its peaks and troughs. The value for each line was expressed as a percentage of the city with the highest value, New York (the peak of the surface). Harris concluded by suggesting that the existence of the manufacturing belt was the dominating and self-perpetuating factor in industrial location in the United States.

A final change of emphasis in studies of industrial location concerned the process of decision-making. The usual assumption of economic man, an all-knowing, super-rational individual, began to be challenged. Decision-makers do not have all the knowledge and ability to make the optimal decisions. This realization led Simon to suggest that satisficer man was a more realistic alternative to economic man. This fits in with David Smith's space-cost curves where most locations are satisfactory but not optimal. This is also related to Greenhut's concept of psychic income where the entrepreneur gains non-financial satisfaction from setting up in a particular location, for example good climate and recreational amenities. This has meant in recent years an increase in interest in the behavioural approach to decision-making.

Problems and applicability

Many of the limitations of Weber's theory have been illustrated in the preceding discussion. As is shown by the analyses of later researchers, many factors have changed since Weber wrote. Transport innovations have greatly reduced the cost of transport, and technological innovations now allow a more efficient use of resources.

Labour mobility has increased. The organization of industry is more complex, and governmental influence on location is much more important. Despite this, Weber's principles still apply to the location of certain industries, as shown by Wilfred Smith.

Weber's concern only with point markets and his assumption that any one plant serves only one market seem rather unrealistic today. Lösch employs areal, rather than point, markets in his model and thus, with the use of only ubiquitous materials, the emphasis is on finding the point of maximum profit rather than that of least cost. For this the relative position of competitors becomes an important consideration as demonstrated by the locational interdependence school. Even when localized materials are used nowadays, transport costs are relatively much less, scales of production are greater because of technological advance, and the provision of many markets is possible. A location central to these markets or close to the peak of the market potential surface is characteristic of many modern industries. Here they have easy access to their customers so as to discover their needs and provide after-sales service, as well as to sell the finished product.

Market orientation has been accentuated by increased complexities in freight-rate structures (Chapter 7), leading to higher relative costs for transporting finished products than raw materials. The increased efficiency in the use of resources has also added to the trend of market orientation, because the weight of resources required has decreased and the transport costs of the product have become more related to the value added in production than to product weight. Examples of such high value-added industries are pharmaceuticals and machine tools. Indeed Weber's emphasis on weight loss is rather narrow for, as well as the value added, other factors have been identified (Fig. 3.13).

Weber's assumption that labour is immobile is not entirely realistic, although the existence of areas of unemployment and labour shortages within a country offer some justification for it. Strong ties to family, friends, and home area, together with a lack of funds, often explain this situation and lend support to Weber's assumption. However, the spatial mobility of labour is sometimes very obvious, as illustrated by the movement of the unemployed in the Depression of the 1930s. Often mobility between industries from one type of job to another in the same area is inhibited because of the need for retraining and the reluctance to give up the

Fig. 3.13 *How the characteristics of raw material and product affect location*

factor	location	example
bulk loss	material	compressing cotton into high density bales
bulk gain	market	manufacturing containers
perishability loss	material	canning food
perishability gain	market	baking bread
fragility loss	material	packing goods for shipment
fragility gain	market	coking of coal
hazard loss	material	microfilm recording
hazard gain	market	manufacturing explosives

Source: after Hoover, E.M., *An Introduction to Regional Economics* (Knopf, 1971), p. 47

skills of the previous occupation. Flexibility and retraining, however, are becoming more prevalent as the industries based on long-established skills become less important.

The increased complexity of industrial organizations, as the single-product, one-factory, private firm is replaced by the multi-product, international corporation, also makes it more difficult to apply Weberian principles to modern practices. These corporations have numerous factories and offices. Manufacturing may be located in countries with cheap labour, like Taiwan, while research and development projects of the manufacturing process are carried out in advanced centres like the United States and Britain. Location, however, may be just a part of a much more complex equation determining production. The goals of large organizations appear to be survival and growth. These are likely to be reflected in moves to increase their share of markets and to integrate their production both horizontally and vertically, rather than in attempts to minimize costs or even to maximize profits. For example, the availability of buildings within the margins of profitability (Fig. 3.9), at the time of the need to locate a branch plant, may allow the early penetration of a market which would be lost if time were taken to find the least-cost location. The availability of vacant cotton textile mills, for example, has recently been an important factor attracting industry to parts of Lancashire.

Finally, as with the location of agricultural production and central place goods and services, government influence on industrial location has grown. Grants, buildings (perhaps initially rent free), and financially aided moves are examples of governmental incentives to industry to move to development areas like north-east England. At the same time industrial expansion above a certain scale may be restricted in the advanced areas by not issuing development certificates. In non-capitalist countries like the U.S.S.R. the role of the government and political factors are all important in the location of industry.

Weber did not ignore the type of economic and political system operating, but it is unlikely that he could have anticipated that governmental incentives, controls, and ownership would be an accepted part of most industrial economies. His work has been particularly important in highly planned, non-capitalist economies where his ideas are attractive since they do not involve the concept of profit. Here his principles have been applied to locate plants rather than to explain their location.

Conclusion

Weber's contribution to understanding the distribution of industrial activity is immense. Like all research it has its limitations. It does not explain many of the changes on the industrial scene that could not have then been foreseen. His three major factors, though, still have a very important influence on location, although for much of present-day industry the impact of transport costs is rather overstressed. His work has not yet been superseded by that of other authors; rather they have added important principles which, taken together with those of Weber, help to explain a much more complex industrial world.

At the end of this chapter it is worth commenting on the theories (Chapters 1,

2, and 3) that have been proposed to explain the distribution of economic activity. Christaller, von Thünen, and Weber all have their limitations when explaining their particular parts of the economic landscape. When their models are combined, they still leave great gaps in our understanding of the whole system. However, they have demonstrated that some order may be discerned in seeming chaos and that certain major principles underlie that order. They all emphasize the importance of distance and transport costs in giving spatial order and organization to economic activity. Undoubtedly much is owed to these authors for the present understanding of the distribution of economic activity. It is likely to be a long time before any overall theory is proposed or accepted.

Bibliography

Estall, R.C., and Buchanan, R.O., *Industrial Activity and Economic Geography* (Hutchinson, 1961)

Greenhut, M.L. *Plant Location in Theory and Practice* (University of North Carolina Press, 1956)

Hoover, E.M., *The Location of Economic Activity* (McGraw-Hill, 1948)

Hotelling, H., 'Stability in Competition', *Economic Journal*, vol. 39 (1929)

Isard, W., *Location and Space Economy* (Wiley, 1956)

Karaska, G.J., and Bramhall, D.F., *Locational Analysis for Manufacturing: A Selection of Readings* (M.I.T. Press, 1969)

Lösch, A., *The Economics of Location* (Yale University Press, 1954)

Smith, D.M., *Industrial Location* (Wiley, 1971)

Smith, R.H.T., Taaffe, E.J., and King, L.J., (eds.), *Readings in Economic Geography* (includes articles by W. Smith, Harris, Kennelly, Isard and Cumberland) (Rand McNally, 1968)

Weber, A., *Theory of the Location of Industries*, translated by C.J. Friedrich (University of Chicago Press, 1929)

Essay questions

1. Discuss the factors which lead to the concentration of a great variety of industry in large industrial areas. (Cambridge, 1974)
2. How does location theory help to explain industrial patterns and why may it be only partly successful in doing so? (Oxford and Cambridge, 1974)
3. The diagram below illustrates Weber's 'locational traingle'. The triangle is equilateral, and at its apices are two localized raw materials (R_1 and R_2) and the market for an industry's product (M). X is at the mid-point of one of the triangle's sides.

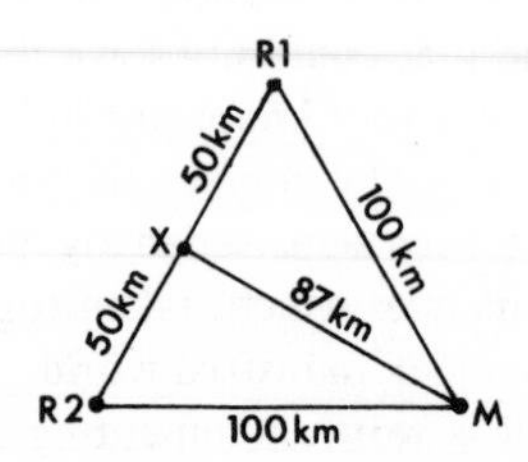

(a) Refer to the diagram. The basic assumptions of the Weber model apply. An industry produces a product, each unit of which contains equal weights of raw materials R_1 and R_2; and sells this product at market M. Explaining your reasons fully, state the location (either R_1, R_2, X or M) at which the industry enjoys the lowest transport costs in each of the following cases:

(i) both raw materials are 'pure', i.e. lose no weight during manufacture;

(ii) both raw materials lose 50 per cent of their weight during manufacture;

(iii) raw material R_1 is pure, but raw material R_2 loses 50 per cent of its weight during manufacture.

(b) Illustrate the principles of the Weber model by discussing the factors which influence the location of the following industries:

(i) *either* the milling of flour *or* sawmilling;

(ii) *either* the baking of bread *or* the manufacture of furniture. (Joint Matriculation Board, 1976)

4. Assess the contribution of Alfred Weber to the formulation of a theory of the location of manufacturing industry. (Manchester University)

Chapter 4

Modifications to central place theory and the rank-size rule

Introduction and link

In the light of the preceding chapters on agricultural and industrial location, it is worth while re-examining central place theory as an explanation of the relative location and size of towns. In particular, an alternative view to Christaller's stepped hierarchy of city sizes (Fig. 1.17a), the rank-size rule, is reviewed.

The last chapter indicated that settlements perform functions other than those of central places. They might form part of an industrial agglomeration like the Lancashire textile area. In this case, the settlements are located close to one another so that the whole industry may be more easily organized and so that goods may be passed from one town to another for different industrial processes. These agglomeration economies (Chapter 3) counteract the tendency of locating as far from other settlements as possible in order to maximize the market areas for central goods and services. The even spacing of Christaller's theory is distorted. Weber's theory also introduced particular resource locations on to the uniform plain. The establishment of industries with high material indices (great weight-loss of material during production) on or near some of these resource locations also distorts Christaller's scheme.

Even the outcome of von Thünen's analysis (Chapter 2) affects the settlement pattern. Zones of intensive agriculture are likely to have higher population densities than those of extensive production. This leads to different densities of central places in various zones. The lowest order centre in a sparsely populated area performs fewer functions than one in a densely peopled area. This is because its increased market area does not fully compensate for the lower density. There is, therefore, lower demand. Fewer thresholds are attained, and thus fewer goods are sold. Therefore, the numbers employed, and consequently the total population, are smaller. The relation between order, size, and number of functions is not the same in the two zones. Because of the variation in the type of agriculture, the demand for machinery and services in the zones is also likely to vary, so there are other reasons why similar order centres in the different zones may perform different functions. These complications suggest that, in a modern industrial society, the spacing and size of settlements may not conform to the Christaller model.

The search for order in the location and size of settlements still continues. A number of authors have examined the size distribution of settlements which describe in graphical form the relationship between the number and size of settlements. Their method has been very different from that of Christaller, von Thünen, and

Weber. Rather than making a set of assumptions, deriving a theory, and testing it against reality, they have observed the sizes and number of settlements in various countries and have noticed a common characteristic which has been called the **rank-size rule**. Having once observed this order in the real world, they then sought to explain it. A relationship which is observed on most occasions is called an **empirical regularity**. The rank-size rule is such an empirical regularity. It was first observed by Auerbach in 1913, but was popularized by Zipf in books published in 1941 and 1949. Since then, many writers have attempted to explain it. The discussion here follows a slightly different format from the previous chapters, since the establishment of the rule was not deduced from a series of assumptions. The rule is outlined, and possible explanations are described. Present-day examples closely fitting the rule are illustrated. Deviations from the rule, which are possibly more interesting, are then observed.

Main aim

A series of authors have attempted to find regularities concerning the characteristics of settlements in various countries. They have attempted to fit a graphical description to the size distribution of cities which would apply to the situation in many countries.

The rank-size rule: description, examples, and explanation

The settlements within a defined area are ranked in descending order according to the sizes of their population. The rule suggests that the size of a particular town can be predicted by observing its rank and the size of the largest city in the area. The town's population is derived by dividing the largest city's population by the town's rank. Thus the second-ranked city should have a population one-half the size of the first-ranked, while the tenth-ranked city should be one-tenth of the size of the first-ranked. This relationship may be simply described by the formula:

$$p_r = p_1 \times \frac{1}{r} = p_1 r^{-1}$$

where p_1 is the population of the city ranked 1 and p_r is the population of the city ranked r. For example, if the largest city's (rank 1) population is 600 000, what is the population of the second largest (rank 2)?

$$p_2 = 600\,000 \times \frac{1}{2} = 300\,000$$

This relationship can also be described in graph form (Fig. 4.1) by plotting a city's rank against its population, according to the rule. In Fig. 4.1a the relationship is plotted using arithmetic scales for the axes. A curve results. If the logarithms

Fig. 4.1 *The rank-size relationship for cities*

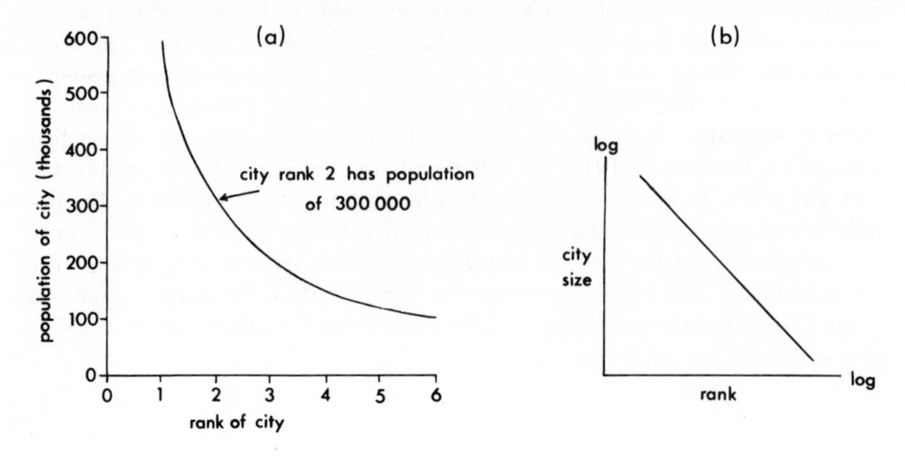

(base 10) of population and rank are plotted on this graph a straight line will be produced. The formula can then be rewritten

$$\log p_r = \log p_1 - \log r$$

To save the effort of looking up the logarithms from tables special graph paper has been constructed which has logarithmic scales on its axes. The ranks and populations can be plotted directly on to this, and according to the rule a straight line will result (Fig. 4.1b). This is the form in which some of the examples are shown (Figs. 4.5 and 4.6).

Fig. 4.2a shows the frequency distribution of towns of different sizes that would occur if the rule applied. The essence of the rank-size rule can be seen from this graph. There are few cities with large populations and many with small populations. As the size of settlements decreases, the frequency of them increases. The cumulative

Fig. 4.2 *The rank-size rule.* (a) *Frequency and city size;* (b) *cumulative percentage frequency and city size (logarithmic scales)*

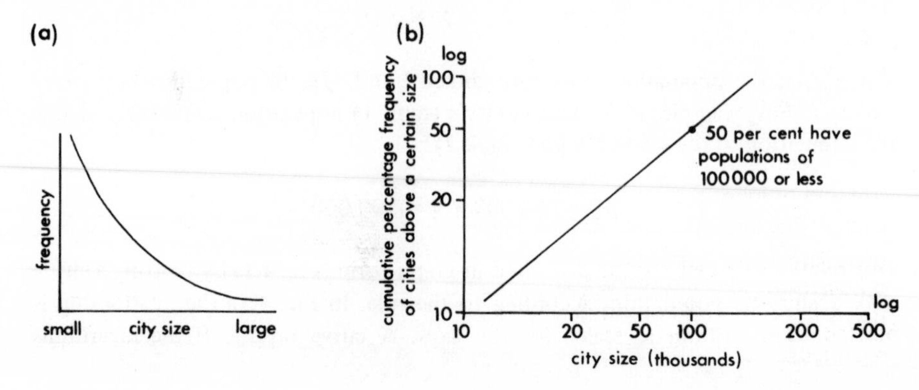

Fig. 4.3 *The log-normal city-size distribution:* (a) *frequency,* (b) *cumulative percentage frequency (log-probability scales)*

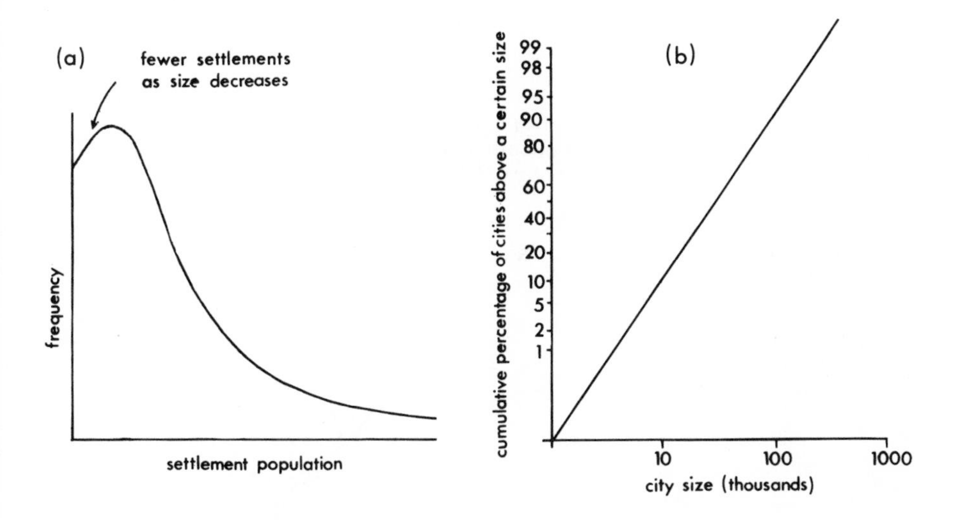

percentage frequency and population is also shown (Fig. 4.2b). In this example 50 per cent of the towns have 100 000 people or fewer.

There has been an amendment to the rule which allows a more flexible relationship between the size and rank. The relationship on the log graph paper is still a straight line but the slope may vary. This can be written as:

$$p_c = p_1 c^{-q}$$

where q can take on any value. In the rank-size rule proper, q is 1. In Fig. 4.7, for example, the slope for Switzerland is much steeper than that for Belgium, showing that a smaller percentage of Switzerland's towns are under 100 000.

Unfortunately there are many graphical descriptions which may be fitted to the size distribution of cities. One such is the so-called log-normal distribution (Figs. 4.3a and 4.3b). In order to obtain a straight-line relationship which describes the log-normal distribution, the cumulative percentage frequency and the population have to be plotted on log-probability paper (x axis a logarithmic scale and y axis a probability scale, where the scale is compressed around 50 per cent and extended for low and high percentages). Figs. 4.7 to 4.10 are plotted on log-probability paper. The log-normal distribution is very similar to the rank-size distribution; indeed, it is often confused with it. However, it suggests a very different relationship between size and number of settlements for very small towns (compare Figs. 4.2a and 4.3a). Unlike the rank-size rule, a point is reached on the log-normal distribution where there are fewer settlements as the size of settlements decreases. This has been shown to be the case for hamlets in Sri Lanka and rural France. For larger towns there is little difference between the two descriptions and they can almost be regarded as the same.

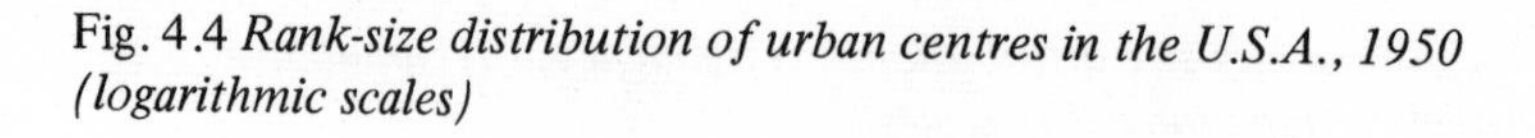

Fig. 4.4 *Rank-size distribution of urban centres in the U.S.A., 1950 (logarithmic scales)*

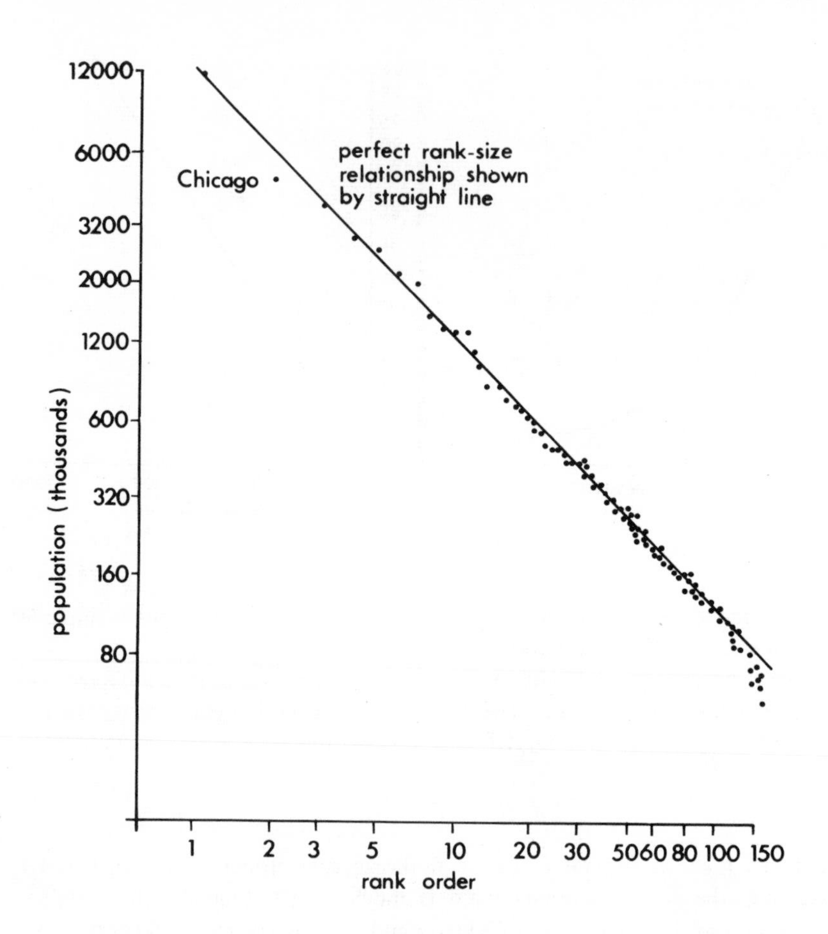

Present-day examples fitting the rule

The rank-size distribution of modern American cities complies to a great extent with the rank-size rule (Fig. 4.4). Note, however, that Chicago is smaller than expected, but that in general the rule fits. This is the case over a long period of time for the U.S.A. (Fig. 4.5) and also for towns and cities in England and Wales (Fig. 4.6).

opposite (top): Fig. 4.5 *Rank-size distribution of urban centres in the U.S.A., 1790–1950 (logarithmic scales)*

opposite (bottom): Fig. 4.6 *Rank-size distribution of urban centres in England and Wales, 1801–1911 (logarithmic scales)*

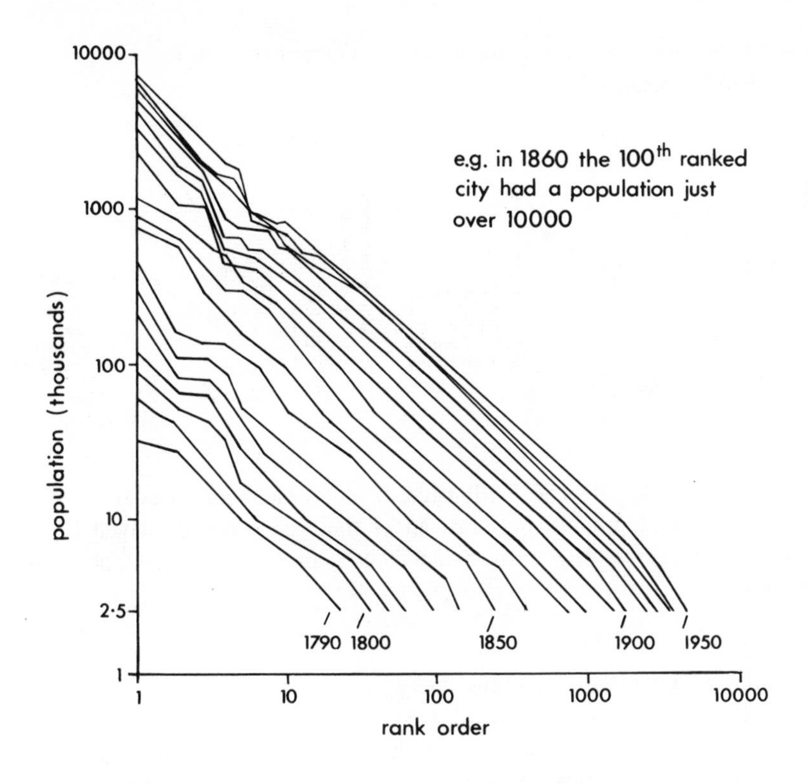
e.g. in 1860 the 100th ranked city had a population just over 10000
population (thousands)
10000
1000
100
10
2·5
1
1790 1800
1850
1900 1950
1
10
100
1000
10000
rank order

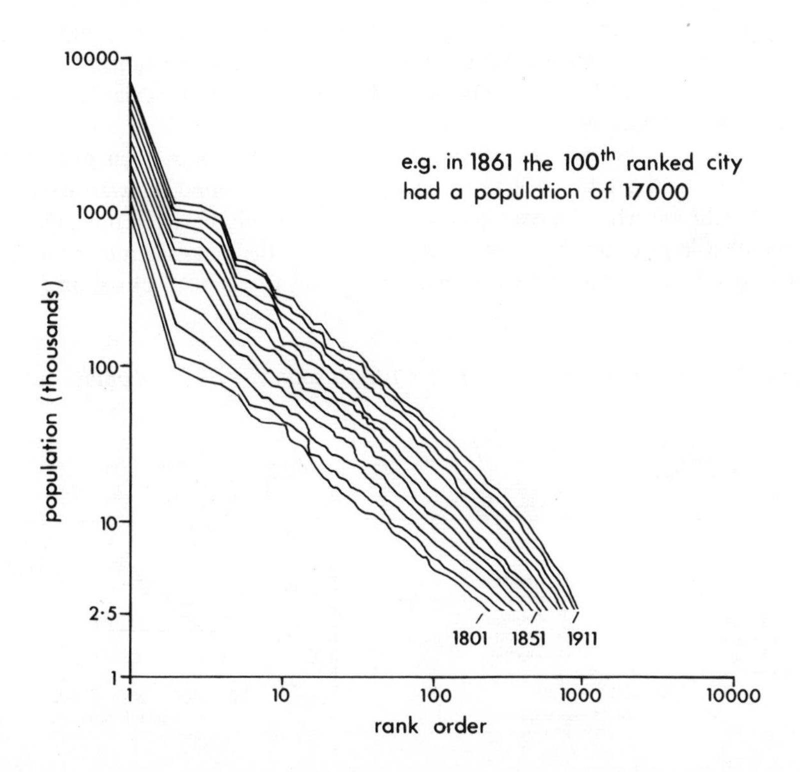
e.g. in 1861 the 100th ranked city had a population of 17000
population (thousands)
10000
1000
100
10
2·5
1
1801 1851 1911
1
10
100
1000
10000
rank order

Fig. 4.7 *Log-normal city-size distributions for thirteen countries (log-probability scales)*

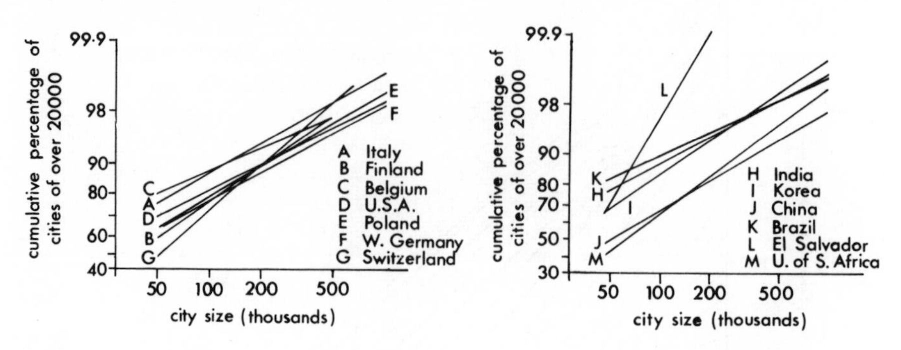

Berry studied the city-size distributions of thirty-eight countries at varying levels of economic development, and thirteen of these countries displayed log-normal city-size distributions. The thirteen included lesser and more developed countries (Fig. 4.7).

Present-day examples not fitting the rule

Urban primacy is the most noteworthy exception to the rank-size distribution. It is where the difference in size between the largest city and other large cities is much greater than is predicted by the rank-size rule or the log-normal distribution. This means that, for example, the size of the second city is much less than half the size of the largest city. In Berry's study, fifteen of the thirty-eight countries displayed primate city-size distributions (Fig. 4.8). For example, Montevideo is clearly a primate city for Uruguay.

There seem to be few generalizations one can make about such primate distributions as to the type of country in which they are found. Stewart came to a similar conclusion when he examined the size relationship between the largest city and the next-largest city for seventy-two countries. If the rank-size rule applied, the second-ranked cities would be half the size of the first-ranked cities. In fact, he

Fig. 4.8 *Primate city-size distributions for fifteen countries (log-probability scales)*

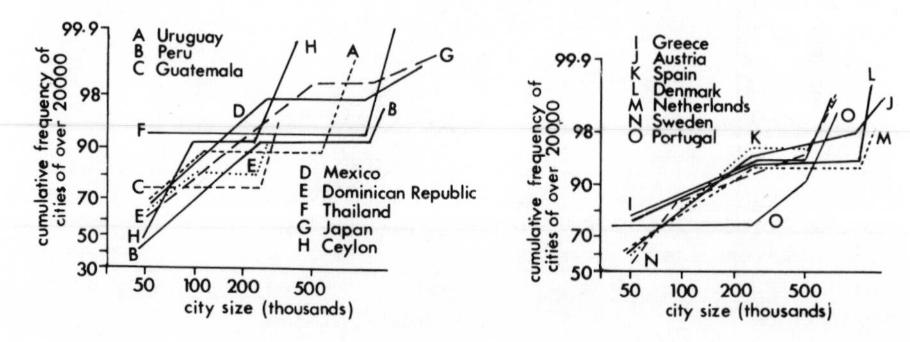

Fig. 4.9 *Berry's model of the evolution of city-size distribution (log-probability scales)*

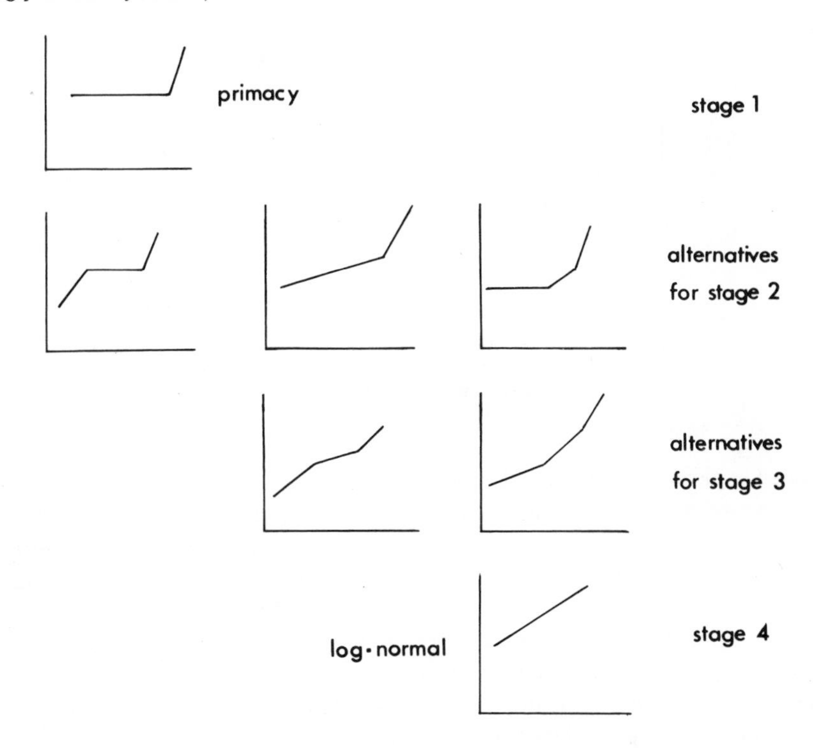

observed that the second-ranked city characteristically was approximately one-third the size of the first-ranked. Stewart discovered few generalities about these seventy-two countries other than that in larger countries the second-ranked city tended to be more than one-third the size of the first-ranked. In many countries, then, the rank-size rule may not be applicable to the very largest cities.

Berry has proposed a simple graphic model of the evolution of city-size distributions changing from considerable primacy to a log-normal situation (Fig. 4.9). It is suggested that as a country becomes more economically, socially, and politically developed, then its city-size distribution becomes more log-normal. This, Berry suggests, is an equilibrium state towards which many countries, for example Israel (Fig. 4.10), are moving. The evidence available to support this general theory, however, is not altogether convincing. Berry suggests, though, that primacy is the simplest city-size distribution and is found in particular situations. Where, for instance, countries have been, until recently, politically or economically dependent on some foreign power, there is a tendency for primate cities to occur. These tend to be the cultural and economic centres, the chief port, and the focus of national consciousness and feeling. An example is Buenos Aires. Similarly, countries which once had control of extensive empires, for example Austria and Spain, tend to have primate cities.

Fig. 4.10 *Change in the city-size distribution of Israel, 1922–59 (log-probability scales)*

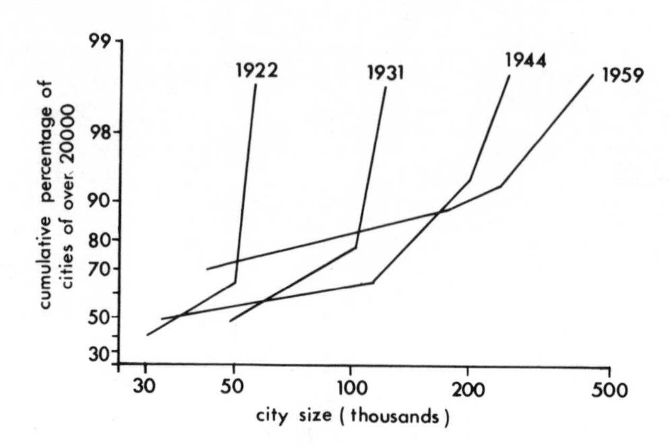

Suggested explanations of the rank-size rule

There have been many attempted explanations of the rank-size regularity. Some researchers have tried to relate it to Christaller's central place theory by suggesting that the populations of a given order of centre fluctuate around the norm for that order. The fluctuation is due to variations in the **activity ratio** (the ratio between number employed and total population) in towns of the same order. The stepped hierarchy (Fig. 1.17a) would then be transformed. However, the preceding discussion has identified so many distorting factors of central place theory, even without a flexible activity ratio, that the isolation of one factor seems of little value.

Another set of explanations suggests that the rank-size relationship results from the balancing out of conflicting forces. Zipf, for example, suggests that the two opposing forces of diversification and unification produce the regularity. Diversification leads to a large number of small places, each located near resources, thus minimizing the transport costs of raw materials to the people. Unification leads to the population being concentrated in a few large places with the raw materials being transported to the people, rather than the people to the raw materials, thus minimizing the movement of people. It is interesting to observe that in these forces there are elements of both Weber's and Christaller's thinking. It is not clear, however, how the conflict of these forces is resolved into the precise form of the rank-size rule.

A rather better attempt is also based on minimizing costs and maximizing efficiency. It is suggested that very large cities are much more costly to society than smaller ones because proportionally more infrastructure (for example, roads, rail, power, public utilities, health, and education) must be provided and maintained. These are called diseconomies of scale. Yet certain functions, like stock exchanges and merchant banking, are performed more efficiently in very large cities than in smaller ones. Overall costs could be minimized and efficiency increased, if the urban population was contained in a few larger cities, which could perform these functions efficiently, and in many smaller cities, which are less costly to society. This, of course, is the rank-size situation with few large cities and many small ones.

Fig. 4.11 *Proportional growth of cities related to their size:* (a) *no relationship,* (b) *smaller cities growing faster, and greater variance of growth rates*

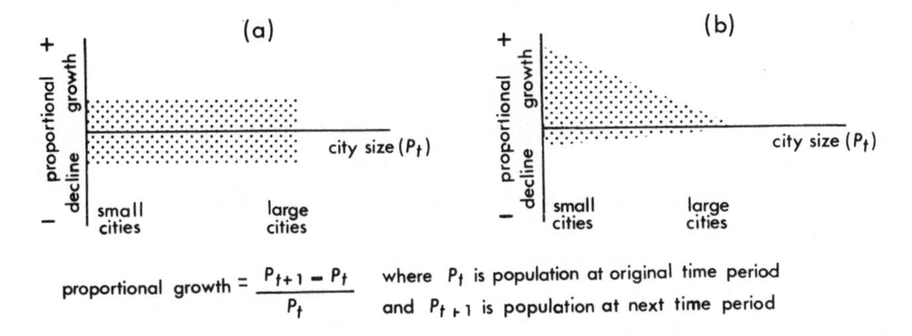

The explanation has been explicitly demonstrated elsewhere, but the mathematics are too complex to be included here.

Researchers have noticed that the sizes of cities are not the only characteristics to approximate the rank-size rule. The distribution seems to fit the size and sales of firms, the population of countries, personal incomes, and the numbers of species in biological genera. Some suggest that it is not the characteristics of the phenomena themselves that may yield an explanation of the fit but the characteristics of their growth. For example, if cities grew in such a way that their proportional growth was not related to their size (Fig. 4.11a), the resulting city-size distribution would fit the log-normal curve. Recent research has attempted to determine whether cities grow in this way. Robson has shown that from 1861 to 1901 the relative growth of towns in England and Wales bore little relationship to their size. Yet from 1901 to 1911 this was not the case, because the growth of large cities was proportionally less (similar to Fig. 4.11b). He also analysed the changing ranks of cities over time.

Other research is considering the elements of city growth: natural increase and migration. For example, it is examining the extent to which migrants are from the countryside, thus increasing the total urban population, and the extent to which they are from other towns, thus changing only the distribution of the same total urban population. Any explanation of growth within a system of cities has to examine these questions. It is towards an explanation of this growth, rather than the rank-size rule, that most of this research is now focused.

Problems and applicability

The fitting of different lines to city-size distributions seems a little sterile when there are so many possible explanations of each line, and when it is realized that the definition of city sizes is rather arbitrary. There are many cities where the built-up area extends outside the administrative boundaries of the city and where many city workers live beyond the edge of the built-up area. Just where to delimit the city is not very obvious.

The delimitation of the area enclosing all the cities to which the rank-size rule is to be applied can also be rather arbitrary. Different distributions may result from different demarcations of the area to be studied. The inclusion or exclusion of a very large city, for example, will very much affect the analysis. Since so much depends on the size of the largest city in the rank-size rule, this may be a crucial decision.

These problems indicate that it is better to use the rule for comparative purposes and to examine the set of cities in many other ways. There is nothing in the size distribution, for instance, to show how the cities are located in space. The spatial organization, so important in central place theory, is missing. In the examples, some of the comparative purposes and useful extensions to the graphical analysis have been introduced.

More general work on the growth of cities has numerous applications, not least important being contributions to policies on the number, size, and location of new towns in a country where the urban population is increasing.

Conclusion

This chapter has shown a different, perhaps less satisfactory, approach to modern geography. The identification of empirical regularities does demonstrate order, but the regularities must be framed in such a way as to enable a satisfactory explanation which will further our understanding. This cannot be said of the rank-size rule. It has been included in this book only in order to demonstrate a different approach and to focus attention on the varying forms of city-size distribution and the growth of cities.

Bibliography

Berry, B.J.L., and Horton, F.E., *Geographic Perspectives on Urban Systems* (Prentice-Hall, 1970)
Robson, B.T., *Urban Growth: An Approach* (Methuen, 1973)
Stewart, J.Q., 'The Size and Spacing of Cities', *Geographical Review,* vol. 48 (1958)
Zipf, G.K., *Human Behaviour and the Principle of Least Effort* (Cambridge University Press, 1949)

Essay questions

1. With reference to specific examples explain briefly what you understand by the rank-size distribution of cities. Describe how you would investigate the topic. (Cambridge, 1973)
2. Suggest reasons for changes in the urban rank-size relationship over time. (Manchester University)
3. Explain what is meant by the urban rank-size rule. How widely and with what reservations can it be applied to empirical studies of urban systems? (Manchester University)

4. The following graphs show the rank-size distribution of urban settlements in six European countries. Population (in thousands) is plotted on the vertical axis and rank on the horizontal axis, both axes being logarithmic.

   What do these graphs tell you about the urban characteristics of these countries? (Oxford and Cambridge, 1975)

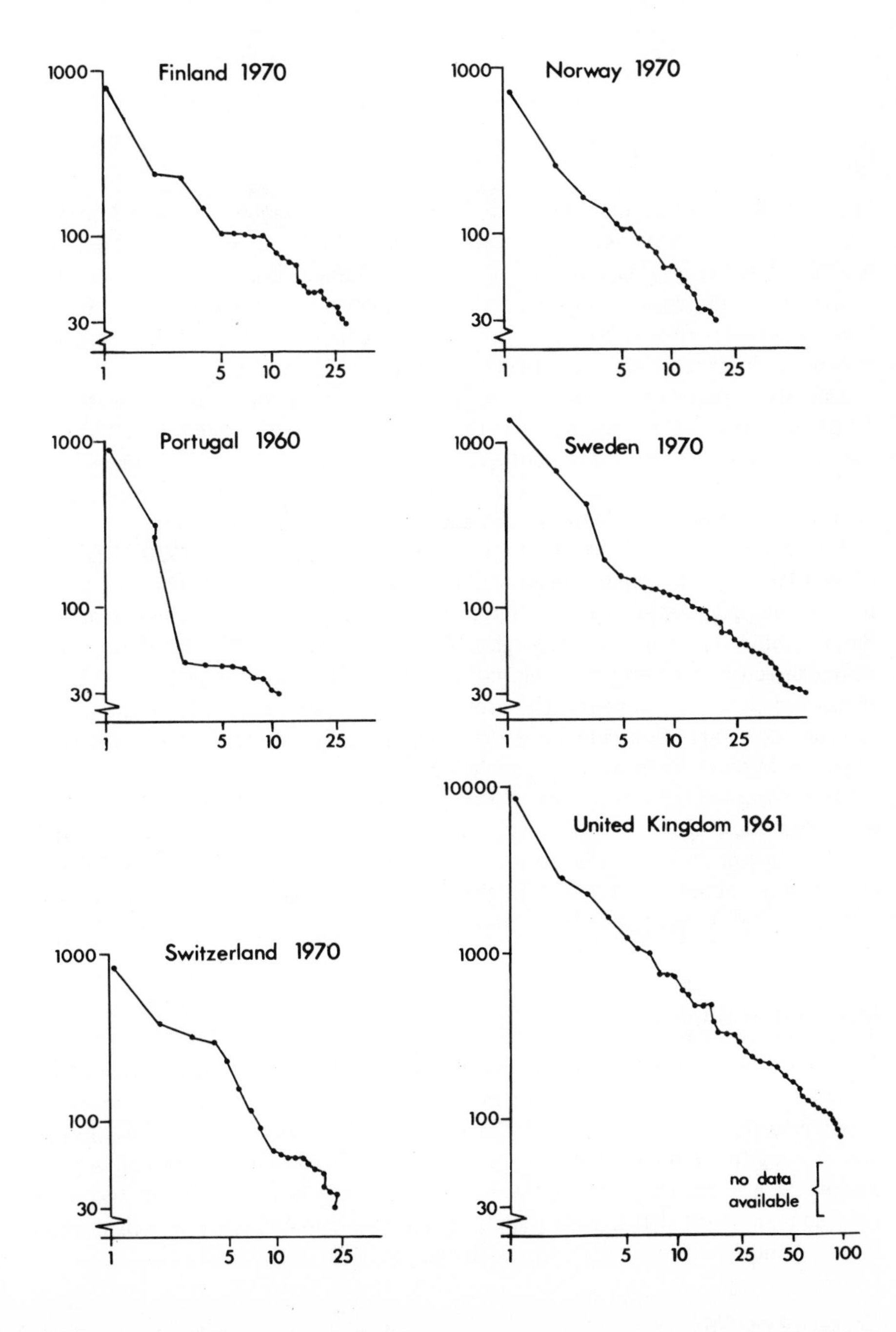

Chapter 5

The internal structure of the city

Introduction and link

In the models of Christaller, von Thünen, and Weber (Chapters 1, 2 and 3, respectively), settlements (markets) are treated as points. In this chapter that assumption is removed as the internal structure of cities is examined. The great growth of cities in the twentieth century has meant that cities cover very extensive areas. Within these urban areas, important spatial variations of economic and social characteristics have been observed which researchers have sought to describe and explain.

One city, in particular, seems to have attracted the attention of many researchers. To geographers, Chicago means more than the gangster city of the prohibition era. Models based on its internal structure abound and have been applied to many other world cities. This chapter discusses the assumptions and principles of two of these models, and outlines later work which adds to and modifies their findings.

E.W. Burgess, a sociologist, proposed his model of cities in the 1920s. His main interest lay in identifying the areas of Chicago where major social problems existed. In previous chapters, economic factors have been prime explanatory variables. Burgess, however, employed ecological factors to explain the spatial variations within the city. In ecology the emphasis is on the interrelationships between living things and their environments. The ecological factors were analogous to the factors of invasion, competition, and succession used in biology to explain the distribution of plants. In short, he substituted people for plants!

Homer Hoyt, a land-economist, was also based in Chicago. His main concern was to explain the distribution of rents within the city. He emphasized, to a greater extent than Burgess, economic factors like access to major transport routes. Many of the other authors mentioned in the text and bibliography have also studied within Chicago. They include Harris and Robson.

Main aim of Burgess's theory

The aim of the Burgess model was to offer a generalized description of the residential structure of one city at one point in time and to see how ecological processes determined that structure. In particular he studied the impact of a city's expansion and the way that residential mobility can affect the social characteristics of an area. Essentially he aimed at a descriptive model of Chicago in the 1920s. At the same time he maintained that it would apply to the then contemporary American city, though he never expected any one city to exemplify perfectly the theory.

Assumptions and principles

Few assumptions within the Burgess model are explicit. Other authors attempted to make them so. The assumptions implied were:

1. Cultural and social heterogeneity (great variation in characteristics) of the population.
2. Commercial-industrial base to the economy of the city.
3. Private ownership of property and economic competition for space.
4. Expanding area and population of the city.
5. Transportation is equally easy, rapid, and cheap in every direction within the city.
6. The city centre is the main centre for employment and near this centre space is limited; competition for this space is high, and therefore it is most valuable. The opposite is true of peripheral areas.
7. No districts are more attractive because of differences in terrain.
8. No concentrations of heavy industry.
9. No historic survival of an earlier land-use pattern in any district.

Many of the principles used by Burgess were derived from the work in plant ecology being conducted at the University of Chicago at the time. The analogies made with these processes included: **invasion of natural areas** by competing groups; **competition** between the invaders and invaded; **dominance** of the area by the invaders causing their **succession** to the area. When applied to relationships between groups of people and areas in cities these were called **urban ecological processes**.

The main process operating in his model was the tendency for the people living in an inner zone to invade and eventually succeed to the next outer zone. The energy to maintain this dynamic system was the continuing growth of the city's population by means of immigration to the centre.

Author's example

Fig. 5.1 shows, according to Burgess, 'an ideal construction of the tendencies of any town or city to expand radially from its central business district'. **Zone 1** is the **central business district** (C.B.D.), or 'Loop', the usual description of Chicago's downtown. The C.B.D. is the main centre for the retailing of goods and services, and contains the major financial and commercial offices. **Zone 2** is the **area in transition** which is being invaded by business and light manufacturing. It is the zone of invasion, consisting primarily of sub-divided houses occupied by newcomers to the city. **Zone 3** is inhabited by the workers in industry who have escaped from zone 2, an area of deterioration. **Zone 4** is the residential area of high-class apartment buildings or of exclusive districts of single-family dwellings. **Zone 5** is beyond the city limits and is the commuter zone, consisting of suburban areas or satellite cities within a 30- to 60-minute ride of the C.B.D.

Having outlined his theory Burgess then considered the case of Chicago. Within or close to the C.B.D. was 'hobohemia' where formally homeless itinerant men resided. The slums in the zone of transition were crowded to overflowing with

Fig. 5.1 *Burgess's model of urban areas*

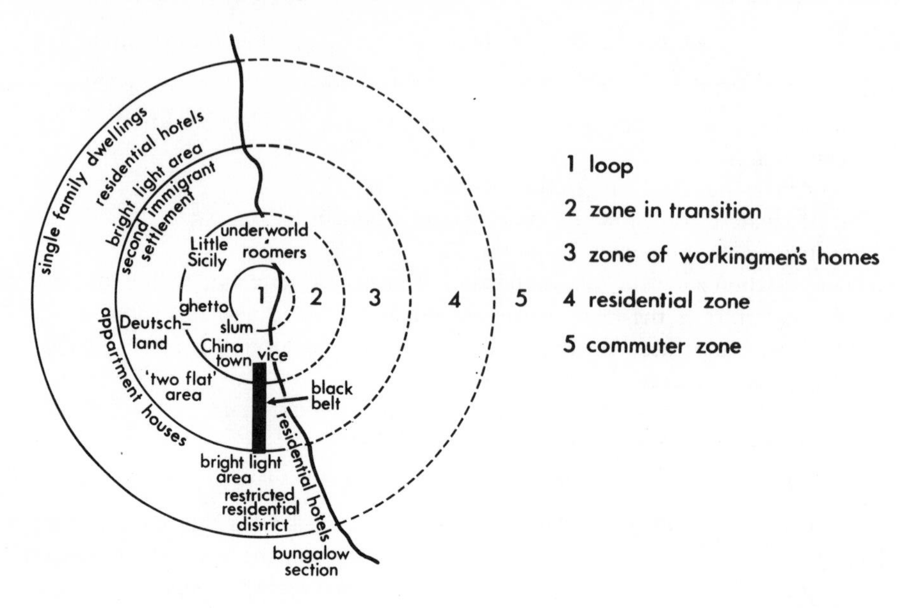

immigrant colonies: the ghetto, Little Sicily, Greektown, Chinatown. Zone 3 was an area into which sons and daughters of the original immigrants moved, making this an area of secondary immigrant settlement, an escape from the slums. Yet the inhabitants of the area, in turn, looked to the 'Promised Land' beyond, to its residential hotels, its apartment-house region, its 'satellite loops', and its 'bright light' areas. These 'natural areas' form distinctive and homogeneous, yet small, parts of each major zone, and 'give form and character to the city', according to Burgess.

Main aim of Hoyt's theory

Hoyt's original work in 1939 was a large-scale empirical analysis of 142 cities in the United States. For each city, maps were plotted portraying eight housing variables. Of these, the maps of the rental variables have since attracted most attention. Based on these observations, Hoyt began to theorize upon the structure and growth of American cities. His **sector theory** has since become well known (Fig. 5.2a).

Assumptions and principles of Hoyt's theory

Hoyt used the same implicit assumptions as Burgess except for assumption 5 concerning transport. He suggested that the key determinant of the housing pattern in cities was the choice of residential location made by the wealthy who could afford the highest rents. The sectoral location and extension of high-rent areas

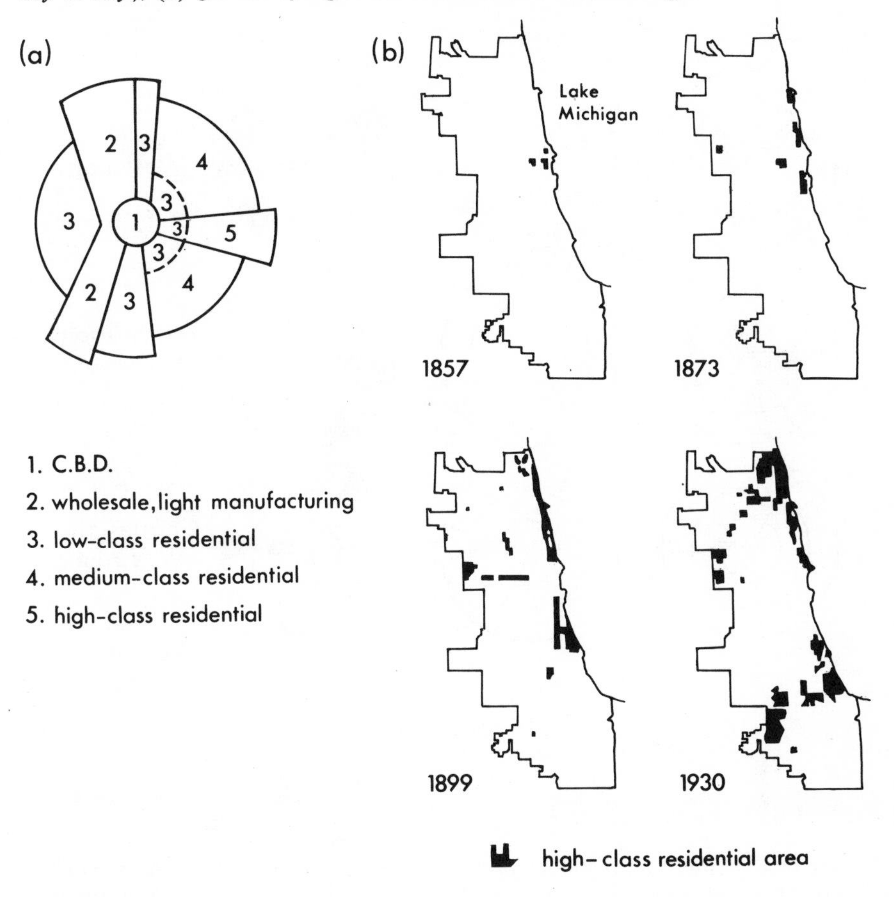

Fig. 5.2 (a) *Generalized model of a city (the arrangement of sectors may vary from city to city);* (b) *growth of high-class residential areas in Chicago*

tended to be related to established lines of travel especially along routes of fastest transport for ease of commuting into the C.B.D.; to waterfronts not used by industry; and to high ground, open country, and the houses of community leaders. He observed that high- and low-rental areas repelled one another.

Author's example

The maps of Chicago (Fig. 5.2b) show the semblance of a sectoral pattern of high-class residential areas and their extension in sectors along the lake shore and lines of fast transportation. The diagrams of three other American cities (Fig. 5.3) suggest that the sectoral pattern and growth of fashionable residential areas is not confined to Chicago. Note that in each of the three instances the higher-class population has moved out of the formerly fashionable inner-city areas. The houses in these areas have since filtered down to lower-income people.

Fig. 5.3 *Sectoral pattern and growth of fashionable residential areas (shaded) in three American cities*

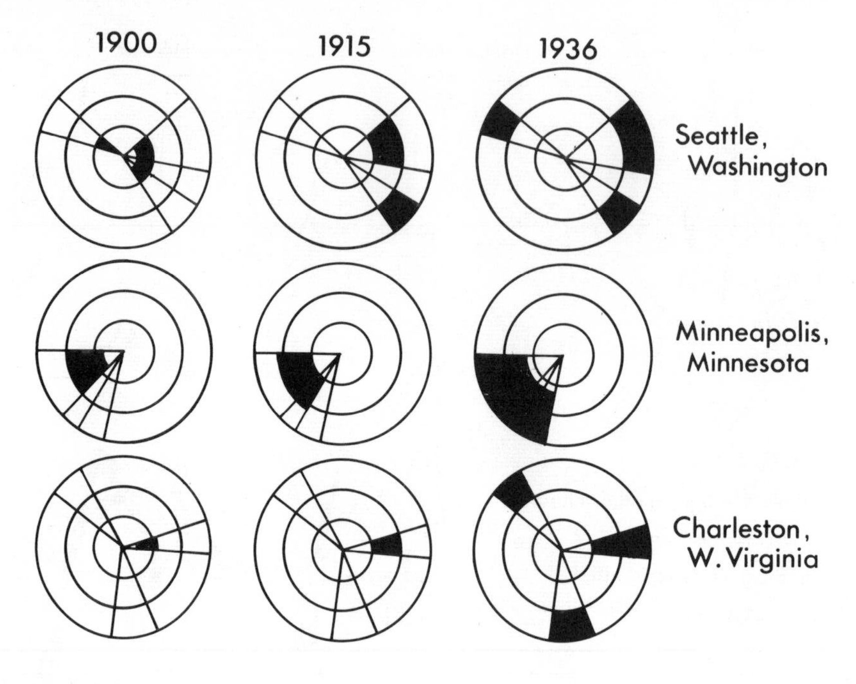

Present-day examples

Testing of the Hoyt sector model has rarely been conducted using Hoyt's variables. Robson (Fig. 5.4) and Jones found evidence of sectors in Sunderland and Belfast, respectively. No worker has found an example of a city where only a sectoral pattern is clearly present. Perhaps the best example illustrating how Hoyt's ideas can be relevant was in a study by P.J. Smith of Calgary. He first rejected concentric rings as being an oversimplification of Calgary's urban form. Later when he was analysing land-value maps of the city, he found that important sectoral variations emerged. Five sectors were identified, one of which was the critical high-cost housing wedge. The essential dynamics of Calgary's growth, in particular the outward progression of certain land-uses along radial lines of transportation, bear a marked resemblance to Hoyt's model. However, several low-value residential areas emerged on the periphery in the 1930s, thus distorting the ideal pattern.

For Calgary in the 1930s Hoyt's model is a reasonable description of the form of the town. Since then (Fig. 5.5) it has become less relevant as certain modern elements have appeared. Dormitory towns with low-cost housing have been built on cheap land; small industrial nuclei have grown up south and north-east of the city; major public developments such as the university and airport have appeared; and suburban shopping and commercial centres have developed.

Fig. 5.4 *The general pattern of social areas in Sunderland*

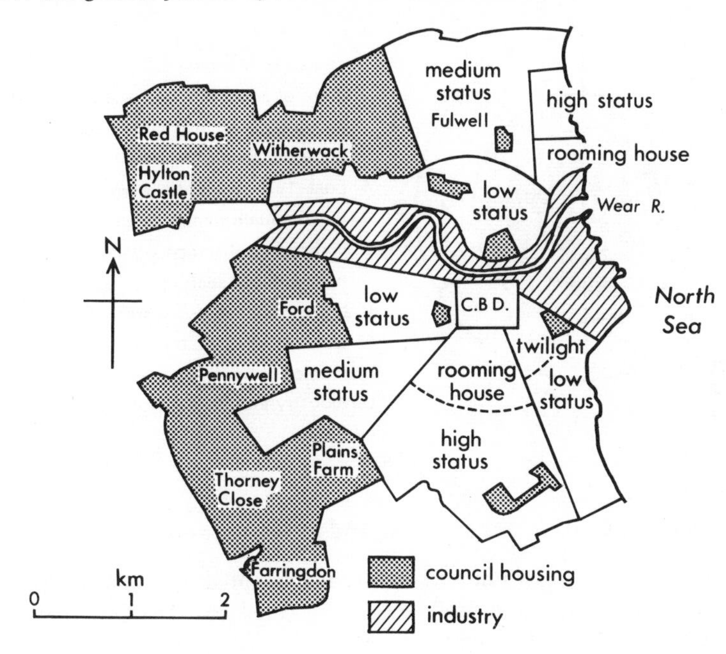

Fig. 5.5 *Generalized land-use pattern of the Calgary metropolitan area, 1961*

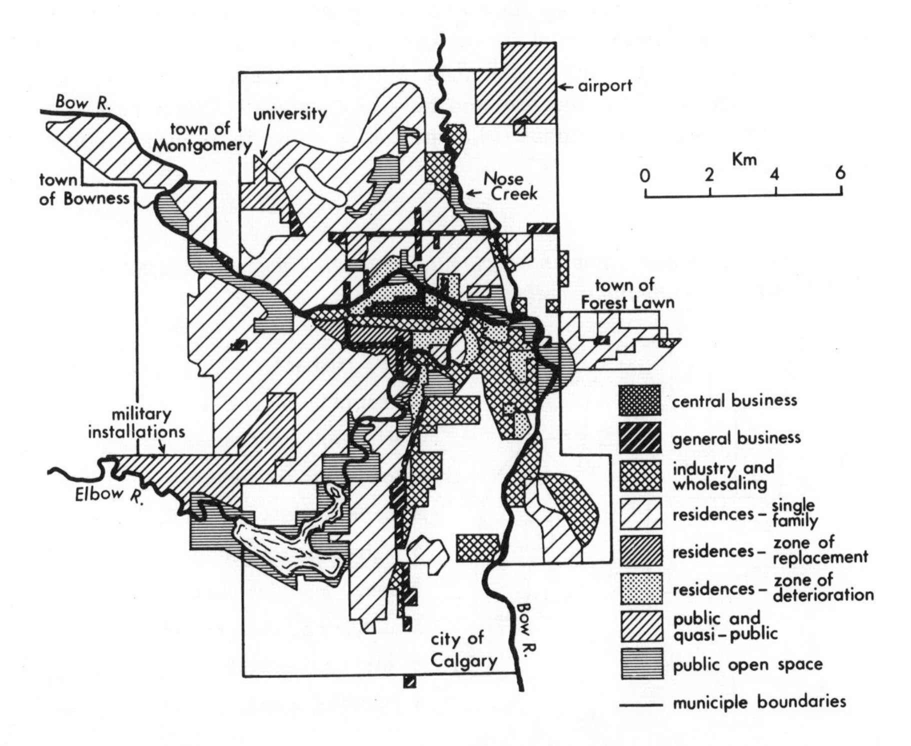

Fig. 5.6 *A model for a typical medium-sized British city*

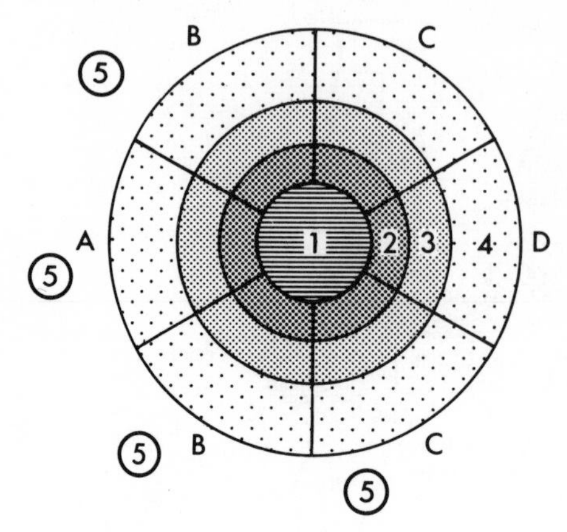

1 city centre
2 transitional zone
3 zone of small terrace houses in sectors C and D, larger bye-law houses in sector B, large old houses in sector A
4 post-1918 residential areas with post-1945 development mainly on periphery
5 commuting distance villages'
A middle-class sector
B lower-middle class sector
C working-class sector (and main municipal housing areas)
D industry and lowest working-class areas

Attempts to incorporate the Burgess and Hoyt models

A conscious fusing of the two models has been attempted by Mann. He evolved a structure for a typical medium-sized British city (Fig. 5.6). The hypothetical city has one centre; allows commuting from separate villages outside it; and assumes a prevailing westerly wind, localizing the best residential area on the western fringe of the city on the opposite side from the industrial sector.

Harris and Ullman also used the models of Burgess and Hoyt. They added the idea that in many cities the land-use pattern is built not around a single centre but around several discrete nuclei (Fig. 5.7). Sometimes these nuclei have existed for years, such as villages incorporated by a city's growth. Others have formed in recent times, such as new industrial estates acting as foci for suburban residential development.

Fig. 5.7 *The Harris and Ullman multiple-nuclei model. The diagram represents one possible pattern among innumerable variations*

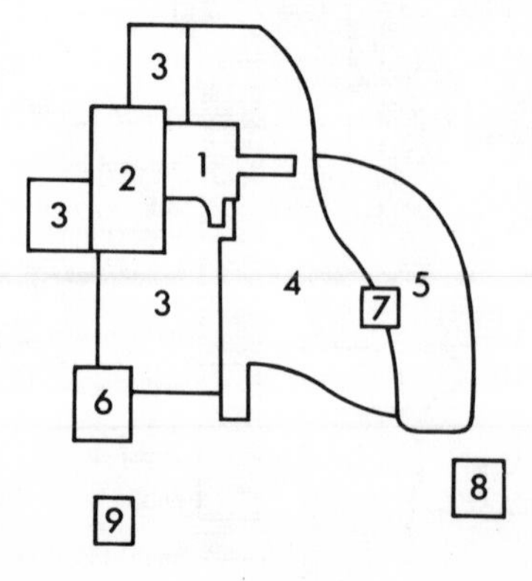

district
1 central business district
2 wholesale, light manufacturing
3 low-class residential
4 medium-class residential
5 high-class residential
6 heavy manufacturing
7 outlying business district
8 residential suburb
9 industrial suburb

The emergence of these separate nuclei is a response to four major factors:

1. Certain activities require specialized facilities, for example a port district needs a suitable waterfront.
2. Similar functions group together because they profit from juxtaposition, for example office districts (Weber's agglomeration economies).
3. Certain unlike activities are detrimental to each other, for example heavy industry and high-class residential development repel one another, as suggested by Hoyt.
4. Certain activities cannot afford the high rents of the most desirable sites, for example a modern one-storey factory cannot afford the high rents that office functions are prepared to pay for central sites.

Other simple models of urban structure

Population density

A very simple descriptive model of city structure has been constructed from observations of the population densities of many cities. As with the rank-size rule (Chapter 4), an empirical regularity was observed. Like Burgess's model, it was also based on distance from the city centre.

The density of population has been observed to decline with distance from the city centre. The form of the decline is shown in Fig. 5.8. This can be written as

$$d_x = d_0 e^{-bx}$$

where d_x is the population density at distance x from the city centre,
d_0 is the interpolated (estimated) population density at the city centre,
e is the base of Naperian logs = 2·718, and
b is the density gradient.

Fig. 5.8 *Negative exponential decline of population density with distance from the city centre*

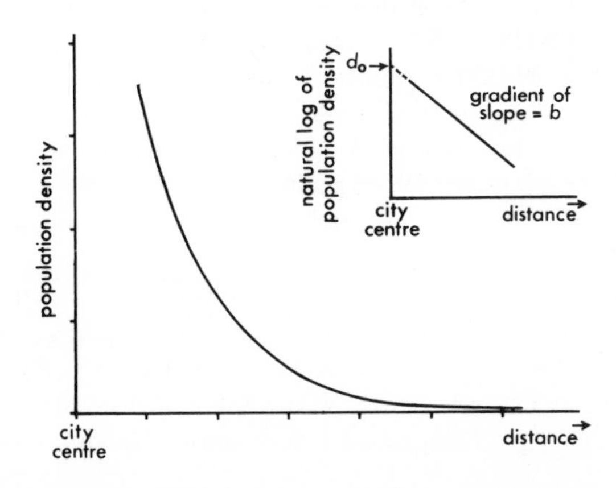

Fig. 5.9 *Decline of population density with distance for London, 1801 to 1941*

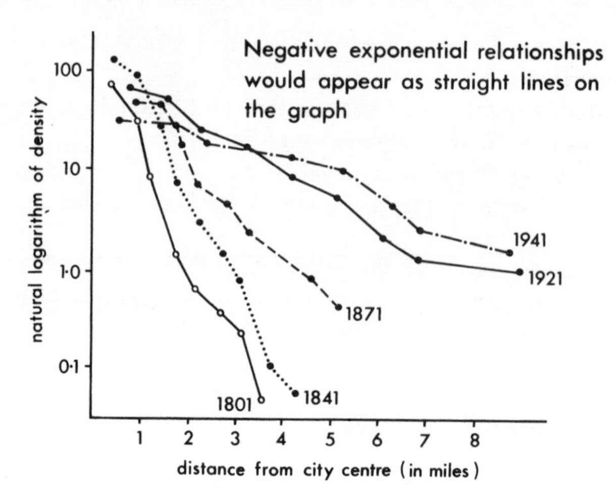

If the above equation is written with natural logarithms (*ln*), it appears as

$$ln\, d_x = ln\, d_0 - bx$$

So if the natural logarithm of population density is used on the graph, the relationship can now be drawn as a straight line with b being the gradient of that line. The relationship is described as a **negative exponential decline of density with distance** (since e^{bx} has a positive exponent and e^{-bx} a negative exponent). An example of the population densities of London at various times is shown in Fig. 5.9.

Although it is not always clearly stated, most authors use gross density, that is, the number of people per unit area, rather than net density, which is the number of people per unit of residential area. The former obviously includes all land uses in the city.

Attempts to explain this form, as was true of the rank-size rule, are somewhat unsatisfactory. Explanations usually involve a balance of two desires, one for access to the city centre for employment, the other for abundance of living-space. Those who can afford to pay commuting costs can therefore live on larger areas of land (that is, at lower densities) on the periphery of the city.

The model is more useful for making comparisons between cities than for giving clues to the explanation of the form of one particular city. Comparisons show that larger and younger cities have gentler gradients. This is because in larger cities there are more commercial, industrial, and administrative activities competing for urban space and in most younger cities, the higher densities of old cities are not socially acceptable.

Changes in the density curve over time also depict the growth of cities. The area of maximum density moves outwards from the city centre as the commercial core expands and redevelopment of old central housing occurs (Fig. 5.10). This leaves a density crater in the city centre, which the model does not predict. The peak density also typically declines as it moves outwards, while densities rise on the

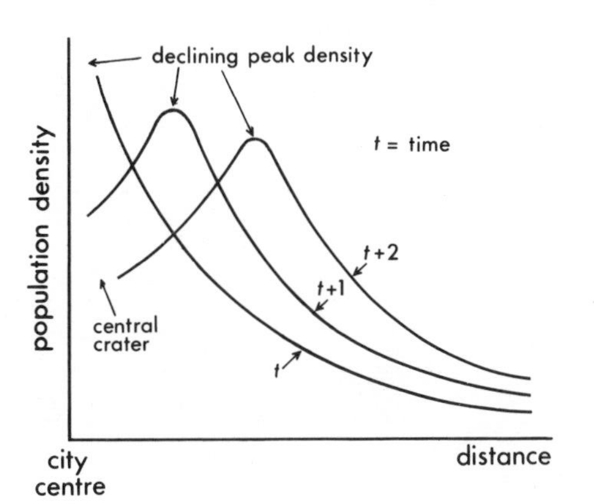

Fig. 5.10 *Changes in population densities in a city through time*

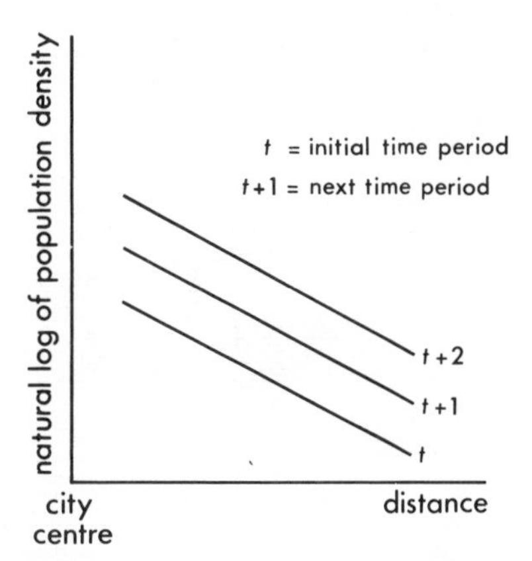

Fig. 5.11 *Postulated changes in population densities in a non-western city through time*

periphery as the city population increases. It has been suggested that this process does not operate in non-western cities, rather that densities increase while the gradient remains the same (Fig. 5.11). However, elements of the 'western' process are being found in so-called 'non-western' cities such as those of Iran.

This model describes only the night-time distribution of population and, like Burgess and Hoyt, assumes a single centre of employment. Most modern cities now have more complex patterns of population density around nuclei of employment similar to those suggested by Harris and Ullman.

Land values

A further model of urban structure involves land values. Like population density, land values have been observed to decline with distance from the city centre. The model is similar to von Thünen's model of agricultural land use (Chapter 2), since it is based on **locational rent** or **bid-rent**. It suggests that the highest bidder will obtain the use of the land in a free market. The person willing to pay most will be the one who will obtain the greatest returns from the site. In many cities the central position is prized most. It is occupied by high order retail functions, like department stores which need to be central to their market, and offices which need to be easily accessible to the labour pool. The market and labour pool are most accessible from the centre because public and private transport systems are focused there. Industrial and residential uses place less value on centrality. Fig. 5.12 shows the locational rents that different activities will bid for locations at various distances from the centre. Just as in von Thünen's initial model, rings emerge that are characterized by certain land uses.

This analysis shows the basic patterns of commercial and residential land use suggested by Burgess. It also helps to explain the population density model. Those who can afford commuting costs can buy a larger amount of land on the periphery for the same money as a smaller unit nearer the centre.

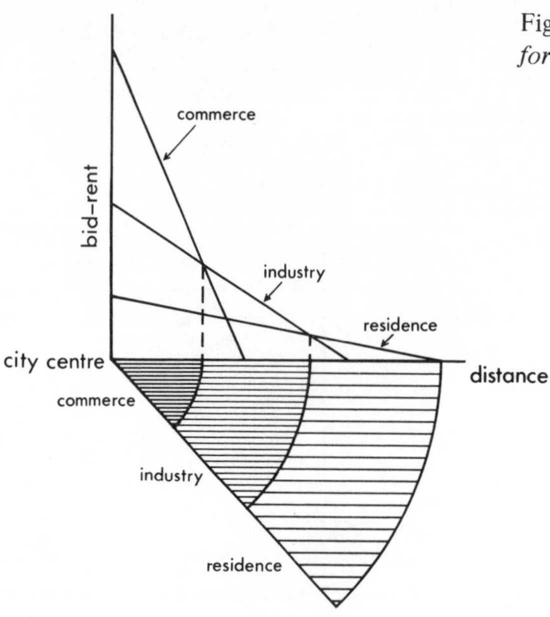

Fig. 5.12 *Idealized bid-rent curves for three land uses in a city*

In larger cities there are minor business nuclei in addition to the central business district as Harris and Ullman found. These sites are likely to be more highly valued than those surrounding them and will form minor peaks in the land-value surface (Fig. 5.13). For example, in London such minor peaks are Hendon, Croydon, and the new Brent Cross shopping complex. Easy access to these and other amenities, like recreational and educational facilities, also add to the value of some locations within the city.

Modern analyses of residential structure

The population density and land-value models do not differentiate between the types of people living within the city as do the models of Burgess and Hoyt. Modern analyses of the social structure of the city have concentrated on finding basic factors which differentiate between areas on the basis of the characteristics of their residents, and on observing the way that these factors vary within the city. Three basic factors have been distinguished, namely **socio-economic status, family life-cycle**, and **ethnic character**. A household's socio-economic status is related to its income, and the occupation and education of the head of the household. The family life-cycle is best illustrated by some of its different stages: a young, childless, married couple, a couple with young children, one with teenage children, one where any children have left home, and lastly a retired couple. Finally, ethnic status is related to race, nationality, and religion. The spatial variation in the character of residential areas is best summarized by the distribution of these three factors.

It is worth while mapping the spatial distributions of these factors. Maps show that the pattern of socio-economic status is mainly sectoral. Thus Hoyt's sectors of high-, middle-, and low-income families are seen to occur in modern

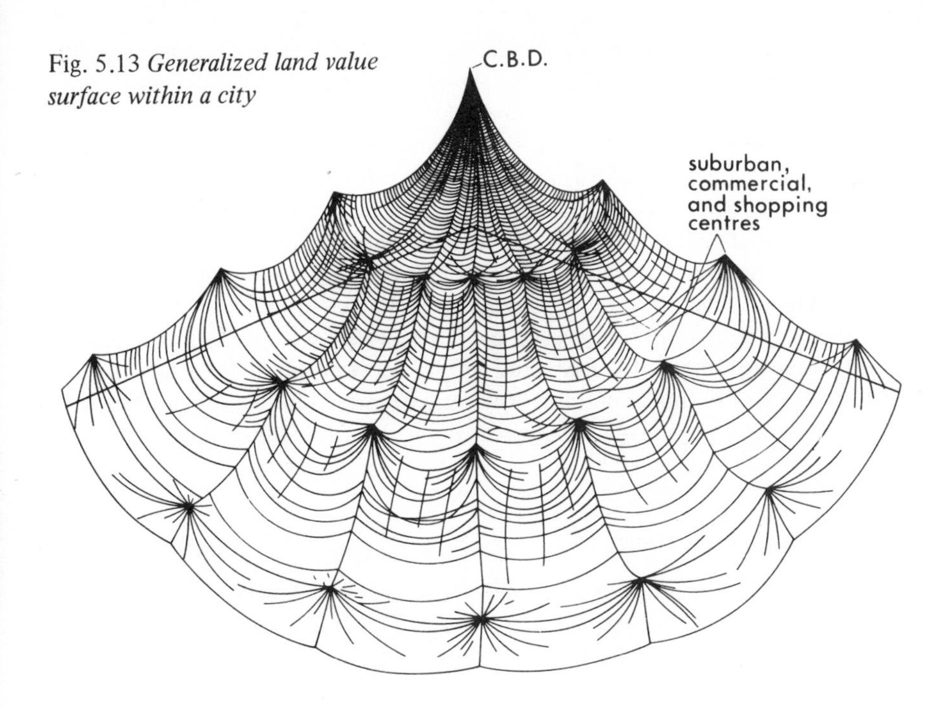

Fig. 5.13 *Generalized land value surface within a city*

cities. Family life-cycle varies zonally, with the older households generally living more towards the city centre than the younger ones. Households of particular ethnic characteristics tend to cluster in one or more areas near the city centre, rather than in any zone or sector. These are the ghettoes. They tend to grow outwards along one sector. So there is evidence of both sectoral and zonal patterns, as is shown for modern-day Chicago (Fig. 5.14).

Fig. 5.14 *Residential areas of the Chicago metropolis showing two basic factors: socio-economic status and family life-cycle*

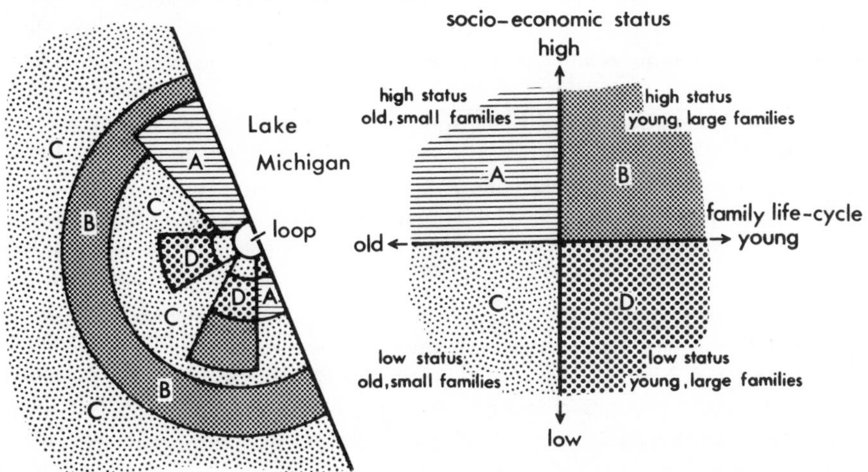

In British cities the pattern is complicated by the existence of council housing. The impact of the three factors, however, still persists. In many European cities, though, the ethnic factor is of minor importance.

These analyses demonstrate how similar people tend to attract one another. This produces distinctions between areas. Over time it has been shown that many areas retain their character, as people moving into the area exhibit similar characteristics to those of the existing population. Other areas change character, sometimes spectacularly, as Hoyt's **downward filtering process** takes place with deteriorating housing being occupied by people of lower economic status. Occasionally in cities where property is in very short supply and centrality is valued, old but structurally sound housing near the centre may be bought by richer people and the status of the area begins to rise. Examples of this process, called **upward filtering** or **gentrification**, may be seen in London in Pimlico, Chelsea, and parts of Islington.

Problems and applicability

One of the major limitations of both the Burgess and Hoyt models is their emphasis on only one set of processes, which they suggest produce the structure of cities. The ecological processes of Burgess and the more economic ones of Hoyt need at least to be combined for an overall explanation, since both the invasion of areas by lower-status people (Burgess) and the filtering down of property (Hoyt) have been observed in reality. The first is more a push factor as people are repelled by the characteristics of the invaders or by the changing value of property which reflects the characteristics of the invaders. The second is more a pull factor on higher-status people as better areas become available in other parts of the city. Contrary to the theories there is also evidence of upward filtering or gentrification. Other processes have also been observed which do not involve a change in the character of the area. Some central high-class areas have persisted through time, neither being invaded nor filtering down. Beacon Hill in Boston is an often-quoted example. The prestige of living in the area continues to attract high-class people, although eventually invasion or downward filtering usually takes place. Burgess's and Hoyt's processes are typical of growing western cities. Such processes, especially invasion, are not so prevalent in cities with static or declining populations. Very different models are required for non-western cities.

The models are also less applicable today since many changes have taken place within western cities. Their outward growth has led to the coalescence of cities, producing new forms such as the conurbation and megalopolis (originally identified on the eastern seaboard of the U.S.A., extending from Boston to Washington). These forms are obviously more complex. Even the single city has experienced changes as increased mobility owing to the car has allowed many centres of employment to grow outside Burgess's central business district. Planning control of office building in city centres has also led to the growth of suburban office centres, such as Croydon. Simple models of the city, like Burgess's concentric zones, and the descriptions of population density and land values have to be amended to incorporate these multi-nuclear cities. New building types have also given the city a more three-dimensional form. For example, high-rise luxury apartment blocks like the John Hancock building in Chicago have permitted the rich to live in homes with plenty of floor space, yet close to their employment in the city centre. Neither of the two basic models allows for this.

The simple spatial patterns of the two models are therefore more difficult to discern. Some have even likened the residential structure of cities to a mosaic. More recent authors have distinguished both sectoral and zonal elements in the mosaic, though these have been of the three basic factors which summarize the spatial variation in residential structure rather than of the structure as a whole. At the same time it has been realized that physical features like rivers, lakesides, and coastlines themselves promote a sectoral pattern, as does the barrier effect of radial transport lines such as railways. The age of buildings also tends to be zonal. These factors may be as important in producing zonal and sectoral patterns as those outlined by Burgess and Hoyt. Two basic spatial relationships may be observed, however. High-class residential areas and industry do repel one another, the political power of the rich being recognized now as one of the forces that keeps the two types of area apart. Secondly, the central business district tends to move towards a high-class sector. Its old, large residences are taken over for office use, for which they give better returns (bid-rent theory).

There are also certain problems concerning the methods used in the work on the spatial structure of cities. For example, Burgess's delimitation of zones was rather subjective. Other workers distinguished different patterns in Chicago at the same time. Modern work uses more objective methods, in that the procedure is made explicit; and if it is repeated by different researchers, it should produce the same results. Such methods allow more meaningful comparisons between cities. Data concerning the characteristics of people and buildings are collected from the census for very many small areas over the city. Small areas with similar characteristics are then grouped together to form 'homogeneous' regions. In this approach the data provide the pattern, rather than the researcher imposing a zonal or concentric pattern onto the data. The interpretation of the results may, however, be dependent on the size of the data-collecting units, the variables chosen, and the delimitation of the city. The larger the data-collecting units, the more heterogeneous they are. Certain scales of spatial variation may thus be lost. The variables used in American and British studies are rather different since the American census provides more social, and the British census more housing, characteristics. The wider the limits that are set to define the city, the more zonal rather than sectoral the pattern becomes, because urban–rural differences begin to dominate. These methods certainly do not define 'natural areas'. The regions are not even homogeneous. Only certain characteristics of the region distinguish it from the surrounding ones. Other characteristics may vary a great deal within the region.

Finally, most of the work on the residential structure of cities is concerned with the demand, rather than the supply, side. Thus the distribution of types of people are described, but no attempt is made to suggest why there are variations in housing. The assumption of a private property market with unlimited supply clearly does not fit many cities. As well as council, or public, housing there are many additional complexities in the supply of housing. Recent work is examining the housing market by means of the operation of financial institutions, developers, builders, and planners. More established work on urban morphology takes on an added significance, since it includes descriptions of land-ownership patterns over time. The timing and size of land sales may well influence the type of development on it. Thus the study of the supply of land and housing stock is only beginning to complement the results of the work on residential structure.

Conclusion

Burgess's and Hoyt's work has undoubtedly stimulated much research on the internal structure of cities and the processes operating within them. Very little worth is now attributed to Burgess's and his colleagues' concept of 'natural areas', but ecological processes do have their place in modern thought. In many ways it was the Chicago sociologists of the 1920s who emphasized that people's local environment was increasingly becoming a social, man-made environment rather than a physical, more natural one. They occupy an important place in the history of the human ecology school of geography.

Their work has led to a study of urban structure that is deeper than the older established geographical work on urban morphology. Yet in many ways it has also been mainly descriptive. Modern work on residential structure has lacked theories that might explain the observed pattern and the way that it changes. Some research is now attempting to integrate the demand and supply sides by examining changes in the housing market as well as the location of people. The development of models of cities is also needed in planning so that the planner may observe the possible consequences on the future structure of the city of decisions that might be taken. This work is at a very early stage and uses ideas that will be discussed later (Chapter 8).

Research also continues at another level. Just as geographers are studying the decisions made by consumers and industrialists (Chapters 1 and 3), so they are also analysing those of migrants within the city. Questions are posed such as who moves; where they move to and from; and when, how often, and why they move. These are often related to the three basic factors which summarize the spatial variation in residential structure (socio-economic status, stage in family life-cycle, and ethnic status). Such studies have shown that although the distance of the journey to work has been counted as an important factor in many of the urban planning models, it plays quite a minor role in the choice of residence.

Burgess's and Hoyt's work provides a stimulating and useful introduction to the study of cities. It is too easy, though, for a student to overemphasize the simple geometric patterns of concentric rings and sectors, and to underestimate the importance of the processes producing them.

Bibliography

Berry, B.J.L., and Horton, F.E., *Geographic Perspectives on Urban Systems* (Prentice-Hall, 1970)
Burgess, E.W., and Park, R.E., (eds.), *The City* (University of Chicago Press, 1925)
Carter, H., *The Study of Urban Geography* (Arnold, 1972)
Everson, J.A., and FitzGerald, B.P., *Inside the City* (Longman, 1972)
Herbert, D., *Urban Geography: A Social Perspective* (David & Charles, 1972)
Hoyt, H., 'The Pattern of Movement of Residential Rental Neighbourhoods', pp. 499–510 in Mayer, H.M., and Kohn, C.F., *Readings in Urban Geography* (University of Chicago Press, 1959)
Johnson, J.H., *Urban Geography* (Pergamon, 1972)
Jones, E., *Towns and Cities* (Oxford University Press, 1966)
Robson, B.T., *Urban Analysis* (Cambridge University Press, 1969)
Robson, B.T., *Urban Social Areas* (Oxford University Press, 1975)

Essay questions

1. With reference to a town or city you have studied in some detail, outline and comment on the location and structure of:
   (a) the central business district,
   (b) residential areas, and
   (c) industrial areas. (Cambridge, 1975)
2. Consider the contention that in most large British cities the poorest people live close to the centre. (Oxford and Cambridge, 1974)
3. Why do land values increase toward the centre of cities? What effect does this have on
   (a) building heights and
   (b) land uses? (Oxford and Cambridge, 1975)
4. What factors govern the areal specialization of functions within cities? Illustrate your answer with reference to a specific city or cities you have studied. (Cambridge, 1976)

Section 2

Transport and movement

The basic models of the spatial structure of economic and social activities have been described in Section 1. They made simplifying assumptions about transport systems and costs so that the effects of distance on spatial structure could be demonstrated. In this section, the assumptions about transport are relaxed. The location of routes and costs of transport are specifically studied, and their effects on economic activity examined.

The basic models of Section 1, because of their assumptions, mostly involved a minimization of movement. In this section, the movement of goods, people, and ideas through space and time becomes the focus of study. The spatial impact of such movement on economic and social activities is also noted.

Chapter 6

Transport routes and networks

Introduction and link

Most of the preceding chapters assumed that ease of transport was equal in all directions. In this chapter that assumption is relaxed, the location and development of transport routes and networks are examined, and their impact on the location of economic activity is noted.

Geographers have paid relatively little attention to transport routes. Even then, most of their consideration has been given to the location of the termini, for example ports, than to the routes themselves. Traditionally, in the explanation of the position of the termini, the emphasis has been on the physical characteristics of sites and the size and economic nature of hinterlands.

In this chapter the location of the termini are often assumed to be known. It is assumed that there is sufficient need for them to be joined, for transport performs the role of linking supply and demand. The problem under discussion is the route by which they should be linked. Some of these routes can be seen on the surface, like roads and railways. Others, like sea and air routes, may be mapped but have no physical expression.

The ideas discussed emphasize the importance of economic factors in locating routes, with physical factors being expressed through builder costs. These economic factors involve the minimization of builder costs and user costs and the maximization of traffic. Economic factors along with political ones also dominate the discussion of the location and development of sets of routes, or networks. The description of these networks, using a branch of mathematics called topology, is an illustration of the application of science to geography.

There is no one dominant model or author in this chapter. Haggett, Lösch, and Bunge were interested in location theory as a whole, while Kansky and Hay were particularly concerned with transport. The latter two, along with Taaffe, Morrill, and Gould, have directed much of their interest towards developing countries and the evolution of their transport networks.

Main aim

The main aim is to describe and explain the location and development of transport routes and networks.

Fig. 6.1 *Three alternative routes between two points (x and y)*

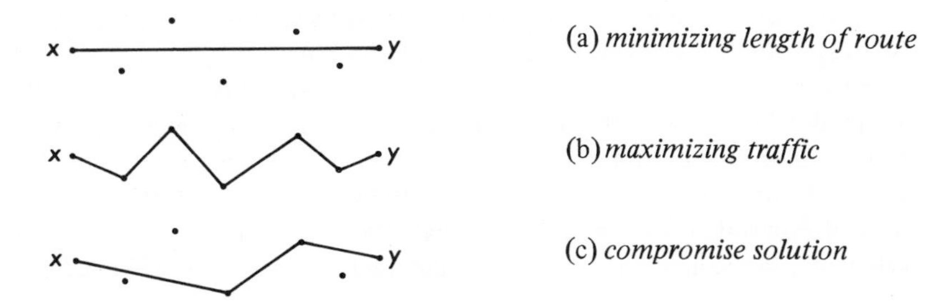

Principles and examples of single-route location

The building of the shortest straight-line (geodesic) route between origin and destination is rare. Even the Roman roads and the present-day motorway routes only approximate to this ideal. Haggett has used two terms to express the way actual routes deviate from the straight-line, shortest path solution: positive and negative deviations.

Positive deviations

A **positive deviation** is where a route is diverted to collect more traffic. This concept was looked at in an early work by Wellington. He was involved, in the latter part of the nineteenth century, in planning Mexico's railway system. He was especially interested in the effect of ignoring or connecting smaller centres lying along the general line of the route between Mexico City and Vera Cruz. He was aware of two goals which conflicted with one another. The first was the need to minimize the length of the railroad (Fig. 6.1a). The second was the need to maximize the amount of traffic (b). A compromise solution is shown in (c).

Fig. 6.2 *National Express bus route from Blackpool to London (showing positive deviations off motorways to gain traffic)*

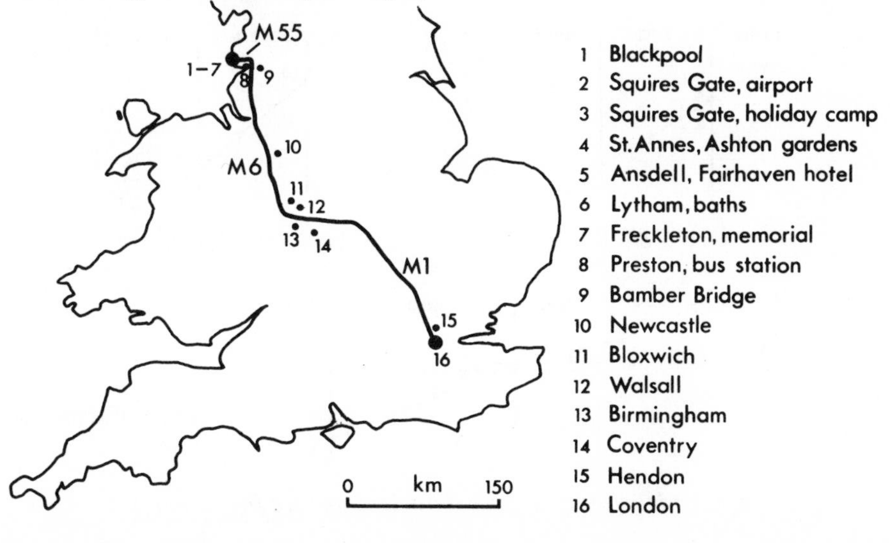

Present-day airline operations illustrate the principle of positive deviation, too. For example, the Manchester–Toronto flight often calls in at Prestwick, Scotland, in order to gain extra custom, although in the past a stop there was mainly to refuel. Railways in rural areas in Britain built in the nineteenth century were also frequently routed via even the smallest centres to gain their custom. In the early 1960s Beeching showed that this form of positive deviation could no longer pay for British railways and, as a result, a vast number of such lines have closed (Figs. 6.8a and 6.9). Another example is the long-distance bus services between the north-west of England and London. Many buses deviate from the M1 – M6 main route to call in at intermediate points to collect and discharge passengers (Fig. 6.2).

Negative deviations

Negative deviations involve the avoidance of certain features of the physical environment which act as obstacles because they would necessitate very high costs of construction. They can also be a response to 'high-cost' areas such as those of attractive landscape or good agricultural land. In the case of a natural feature, the deflecting effect is usually considered in terms of construction costs.

Lösch applied the laws of refraction to the study of route location. His problem was to select the cheapest route between two places. The chosen route would have had to cross two areas with different transport costs. Lösch suggested that the least-cost location could be determined by using the sine law (Fig. 6.3). A product at X has to be transported as cheaply as possible to Y. Where should the port be located, assuming every point along the coast is favourable for port construction? The direct route (a) crosses the coast at R. If it is assumed that the ocean freight rate (T_1) is

Fig. 6.3 *Transport routes and the law of refraction. Law applied in* (c)

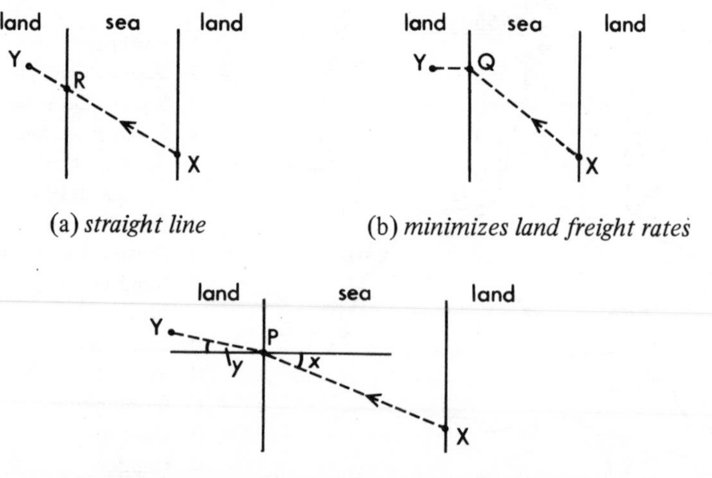

(a) *straight line*

(b) *minimizes land freight rates*

(c) *minimizes total costs (both land and sea freight rates)*

Fig. 6.4 *Route construction across a mountain range (plan view)*

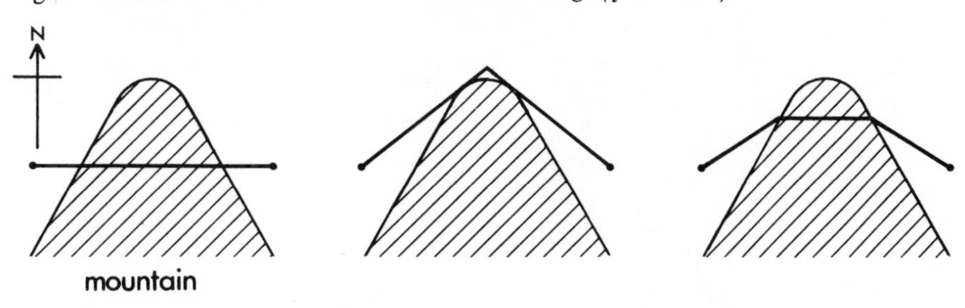

cheaper than the land freight rate (T_2), then according to Lösch, the least-cost location for the port will be where

$$T_1 \sin x - T_2 \sin y = 0$$

where x and y are the angles that the two transport routes make to a line perpendicular to the coastline. The best site in this case will be point P, as shown in (c).

Lösch applied the same refraction principle to the problem of a route crossing a mountain range (Fig. 6.4). Again the direct route is unlikely to be the cheapest because of the high cost of construction through the mountain range. The greater this cost, the higher the refraction, then the more likely it is that the least-cost route will be deflected northwards.

Lösch uses, as an example of such deflection, trade between the west and the east of the U.S.A. in the nineteenth century. This was deflected south via the Cape Horn route rather than the much more direct but costly overland route. A contemporaneous example is that of canal and railway construction from New York inland across the Appalachians. Because of the high cost of a direct route, some of the early routes chosen were deflected north to benefit from the 'line of least resistance' offered by the Hudson-Mohawk gap. Lösch suggests that this general principle is a useful addition to location theory.

Builder and user costs

Many modern studies of transport planning have carefully analysed **builder costs** and **user costs**. The former is the optimal route location as far as construction costs are concerned and the latter is the least cost for the user (Fig. 6.5). This relationship

Fig. 6.5 (a) *Minimizing builder costs*; (b) *minimizing user costs*

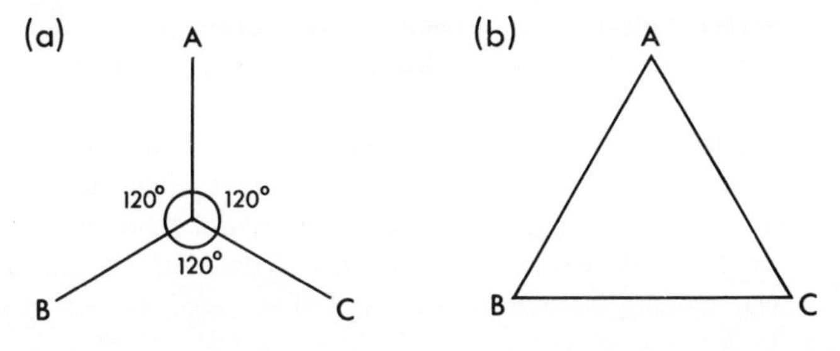

Fig. 6.6 *Three alternative routes for the Abingdon by-pass*

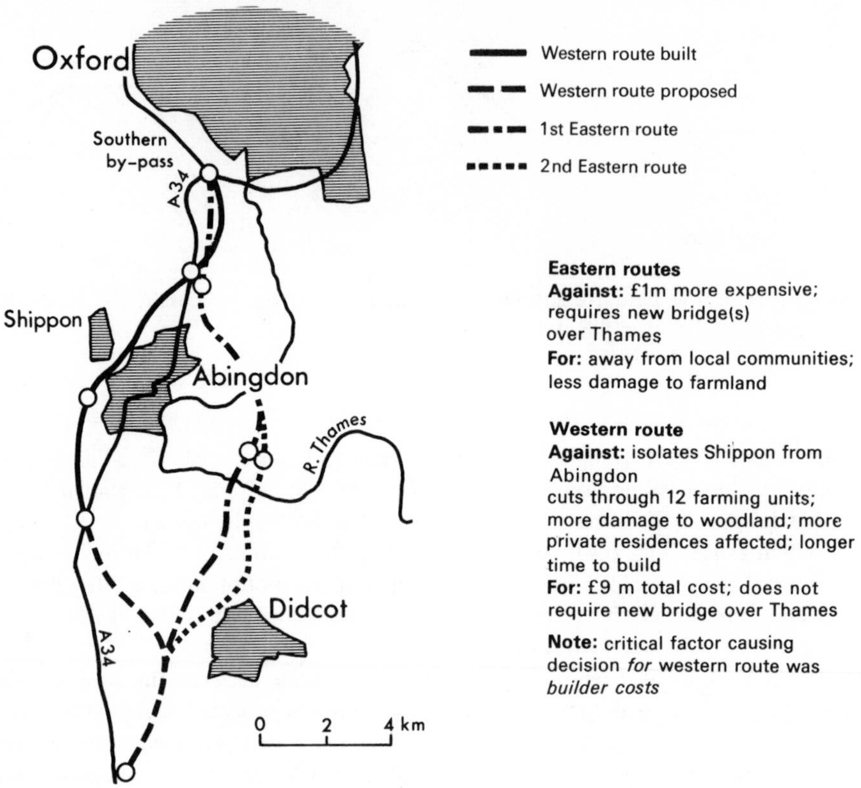

Oxford
Southern by-pass
A34
Shippon
Abingdon
R. Thames
Didcot
A34
0 2 4 km

Western route built
Western route proposed
1st Eastern route
2nd Eastern route

Eastern routes
Against: £1m more expensive; requires new bridge(s) over Thames
For: away from local communities; less damage to farmland

Western route
Against: isolates Shippon from Abingdon
cuts through 12 farming units; more damage to woodland; more private residences affected; longer time to build
For: £9 m total cost; does not require new bridge over Thames

Note: critical factor causing decision *for* western route was *builder costs*

between user costs and builder costs can determine the actual pattern of route building. Other factors, however, will determine the least-cost location route. These include the interest rates on the borrowed money and the likely economic life of the project. Even so, it has been suggested that the pattern of the railway network in north-eastern U.S.A. reflects the dominant user costs. This is because of the great volume of traffic generated by the closely spaced cities. On the other hand, the railway network of western U.S.A. is seen as being a response to the dominant builder costs. Here cities are few and far between, and traffic is light. The greater need was to find the cheapest route through a difficult physical environment.

A contemporary British example illustrating the dominant builder costs can be seen in the choice of the Abingdon by-pass route shown in Fig. 6.6.

On the other hand most of the development of motorways in Britain reflects the importance of user costs. Such roads tend to be direct and, in general, less influenced by the physical environment. The great volume of traffic generated by such inter-city routes will outweigh the large costs of motorway construction.

Another theme being stressed by transport planners when they are choosing a route is the need to minimize damage to the local environment, whether it be rural or urban. Much of the debate concerning the route of the M40 through the Chilterns, an Area of Outstanding Natural Beauty, was dominated by the environmental lobby. A similar pressure group, the 'Houses for People' lobby, greatly influenced the decision to abandon the London motorway box scheme, a system of three ring roads in and around the metropolis.

Builder, user, and environmental costs are also considered in the location of transport termini. Recently the implicit or explicit use of **cost-benefit analysis** in important route and terminal location decisions has occurred. Here, the likely costs are quantified and compared with the predicted and quantified benefits. Cublington, the site proposed for the third London airport was chosen on the basis of cost-benefit analysis, but eventually rejected on environmental grounds.

Principles and examples of route networks

Description of networks

It is very difficult to describe accurately in words the difference between two route networks or to determine for two points on a network their accessibility to all other points. However, very simple mathematical measures can be used which are precise, concise, and meaningful. These not only help in describing networks, they also facilitate the explanation of the pattern and development of actual networks by permitting easy comparison between the predictions of models and real networks.

A network is a set of routes which connect junctions and termini. An example of a rail network to the south-east of Manchester is shown in Fig. 6.7. In order to

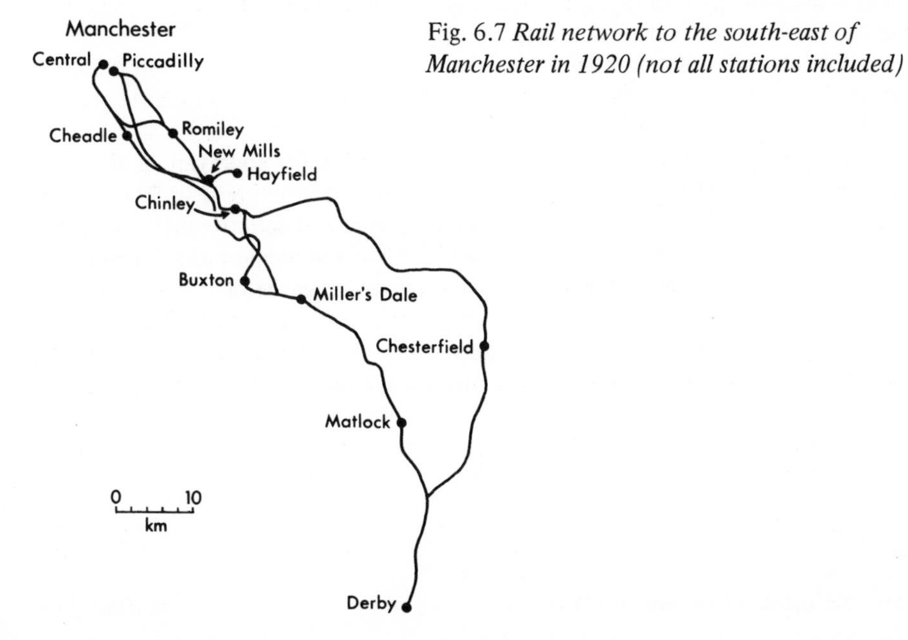

Fig. 6.7 *Rail network to the south-east of Manchester in 1920 (not all stations included)*

Fig. 6.8 (a) *Graph of 1920 rail network with König and Shimbel numbers*

Fig. 6.8 (b) *Alternative graph of 1920 rail network*

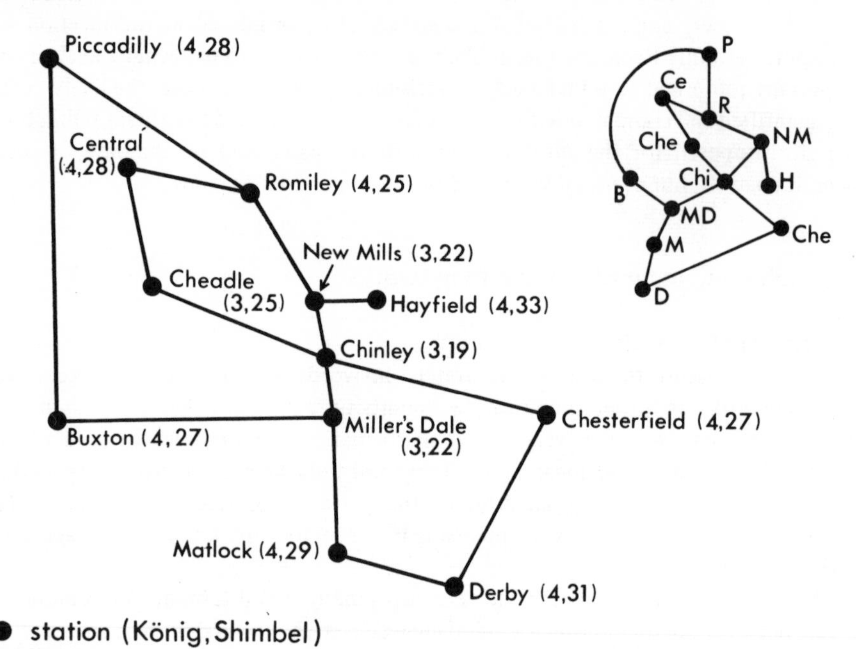

describe and compare such networks, they are reduced to a simple form (Fig. 6.8a) where the basic pattern of connections between junctions and routes is preserved, but route length and direction may be distorted. This simplified form is called a **topological map** or **graph.** The map of the London Underground system is a good example. Such graphs may take on alternative forms (Fig. 6.8b) because distance and direction are disregarded.

Such a graph consists of vertices and edges. **Vertices** (or **nodes**) are, in this case, stations. An **edge (link** or **arc)** is a direct route connecting two vertices. The number of vertices (v) and number of edges (e) may be used in descriptive measures of the graph. An additional definition is also used. This is the number of **sub-graphs** (s), or subsidiary, unconnected graphs. In the diagram there is only one (Fig. 6.9). However, if there were no edge between Romiley and New Mills there would be two sub-graphs, two unconnected graphs. Note that the shortest path between vertices on a graph is measured by the smallest number of edges, not the length of the edges.

Two basic measures are used in more refined descriptions. They are the **cyclomatic number** (u) which is

$$u = e - v + s$$

and the **diameter** (d) which is the maximum number of edges in the shortest path

Fig. 6.9 *Graph of 1975 rail network with König and Shimbel numbers*

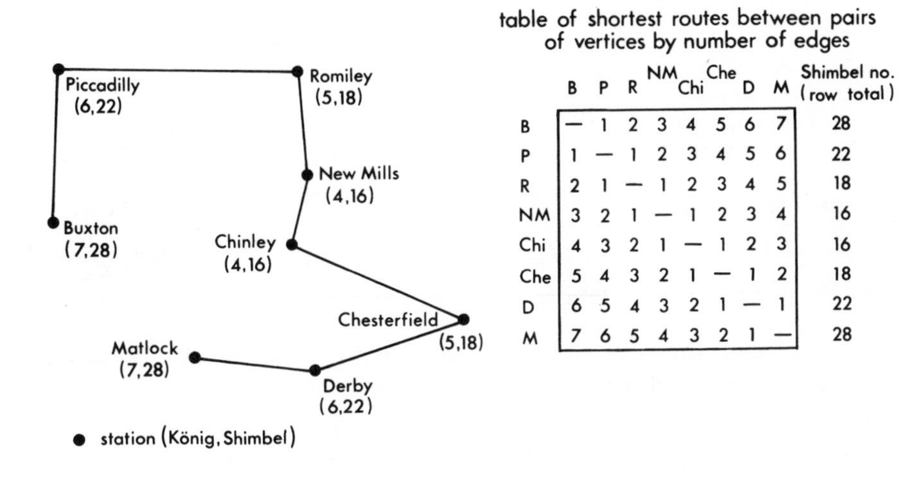

table of shortest routes between pairs of vertices by number of edges

	B	P	R	NM	Chi	Che	D	M	Shimbel no. (row total)
B	—	1	2	3	4	5	6	7	28
P	1	—	1	2	3	4	5	6	22
R	2	1	—	1	2	3	4	5	18
NM	3	2	1	—	1	2	3	4	16
Chi	4	3	2	1	—	1	2	3	16
Che	5	4	3	2	1	—	1	2	18
D	6	5	4	3	2	1	—	1	22
M	7	6	5	4	3	2	1	—	28

between each pair of vertices (maximum value (7) in the table of shortest routes between pairs of vertices in Fig. 6.9). For example, the diameter of the graph for 1920 (Fig. 6.8a) is 4. No two vertices are more than four edges apart by the shortest route. These and some of the following measures are used in comparison of the two networks, 1920 and 1975, which shows the decline of the railways in this area (Fig. 6.10).

The more refined measures include a number which describe the degree of connectivity of the network. The **beta index** is one of the simplest. Connectivity increases as β increases. In other words, for a given number of vertices the more edges there are that connect, then the greater the connectivity. The β value of maximum connectivity for a given network, however, increases as the number of vertices increases:

$$\beta = \frac{e}{v}$$

The **alpha index** is more useful for comparative purposes. It uses the cyclomatic number, which is the observed number of circuits within the graph, a circuit being a path starting and finishing at the same point and traversing by the shortest route some or all of the system. The alpha index compares the observed number of circuits (numerator) with the maximum possible number of circuits for a given number of vertices (denominator):

$$\alpha = \frac{u}{(2v - 5)}$$

Alpha varies between 0 and 1 (maximum connectivity). The 1920 network is obviously more connected than that of 1975 (Fig. 6.10).

Other measures include the geographical magnitude of the network which

Fig. 6.10 *Table of measures comparing 1920 and 1975 rail networks*

	1920	1975
number of edges (e)	14	7
number of vertices (v)	12	8
number of sub-graphs (s)	1	1
cyclomatic number (u)	3 (= 14 − 12 + 1)	0 (= 7 − 8 + 1)
diameter (d)	4	7
beta index (β)	1·2 ($\simeq \frac{14}{12}$)	0·875 ($= \frac{7}{8}$)
alpha index (α)	0·158 $\left(\simeq \frac{3}{2 \times 12 - 5}\right)$	0 $\left(= \frac{0}{2 \times 8 - 5}\right)$

incorporates route distances, specifically the total network length (M). The **average edge length**, η, is a simple measure:

$$\eta = \frac{M}{e}$$

The π **index** indicates the shape or compactness of the network:

$$\pi = \frac{M}{d}$$

In this case the actual length of the diameter (d) is used, rather than the number of edges. High values reflect a closely knit network.

Finally, there are some measures which describe the accessibility of individual vertices within a given network. The **König number** (Figs. 6.8a and 6.9) demonstrates the centrality of a vertex, giving the maximum number of edges from any given vertex by the shortest path to any other vertex in the network (maximum in each column, Fig. 6.9 table). Lower values indicate greater centrality. The centrality of Buxton is less than that of New Mills (Figs. 6.8a and 6.9). The **Shimbel index** expresses the total number of edges needed to connect any vertex with all other vertices in the network by the shortest path (Figs. 6.8a and 6.9; see table). New Mills and Chinley were the most accessible vertices in 1975 whereas Chinley was the most accessible in 1920. Lower values again indicate greater accessibility.

All these measures are useful in comparing networks over time and space. The connectivity of a country's transport network has also been employed to indicate its degree of economic development since the two variables are somewhat related. Another measure, the density of the network (the total network length divided by the country's area) has been similarly used. It is a useful exercise to consider what variables might influence the connectivity and density of a country's road or rail networks.

The location of route networks

After reviewing these different descriptions of networks, it is worth while considering their location. Bunge, for example, has suggested that there are six alternative solutions to the problem of building a route to connect five centres (Fig. 6.11). For

Fig. 6.11 *Six alternative solutions to connect five centres*

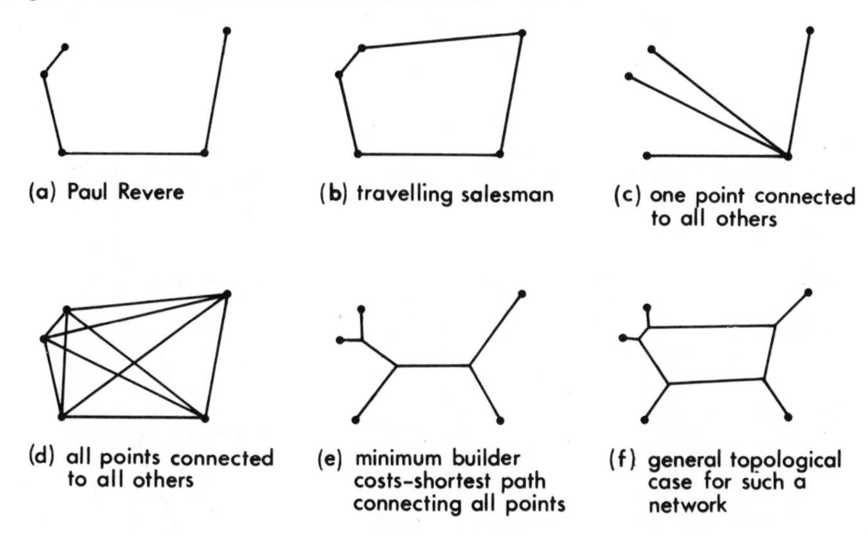

example, solution (a) is the 'Paul Revere' type of network where starting from one point, it is the shortest route passing through all the other points. Solution (b) is the shortest distance around the five points (the 'travelling salesman' solution). A good illustration as to how such principles could be applied is the problem of planning new road networks in rural areas in the Dutch polders (Fig. 6.12). In the two simple cases shown, the two distances to be minimized are: (a) of the farmer from the farmhouse to the fields, and (b) of the farm to public services (water supply, roads, electricity).

A more complex application of Bunge's theoretical ideas can be seen in the case of siting an oil terminal, an exercise in planning a distribution network. The 1950 supply and distribution scheme for certain oils from the refinery at Llandarcy in South Wales is shown in Fig. 6.13. These oils were shipped by general-purpose tankers to Avonmouth, and from there by rail to eleven small depots which, in turn, supplied individual consumers by road tanker. The cost of transporting these oils

Fig. 6.12 *Two alternative road networks in the Dutch polders*

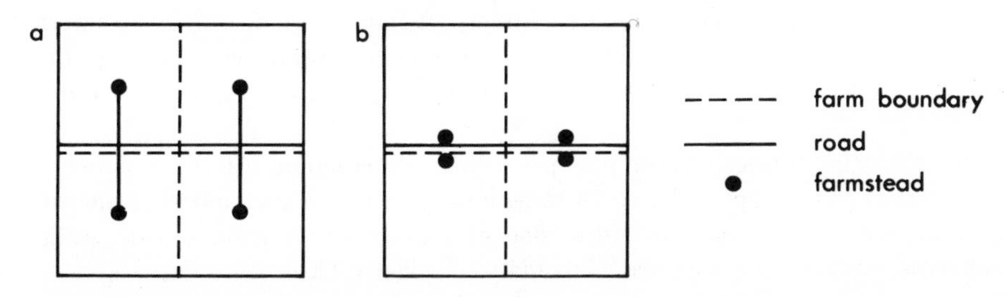

Fig. 6.13 *Oil distribution in part of south-west England*

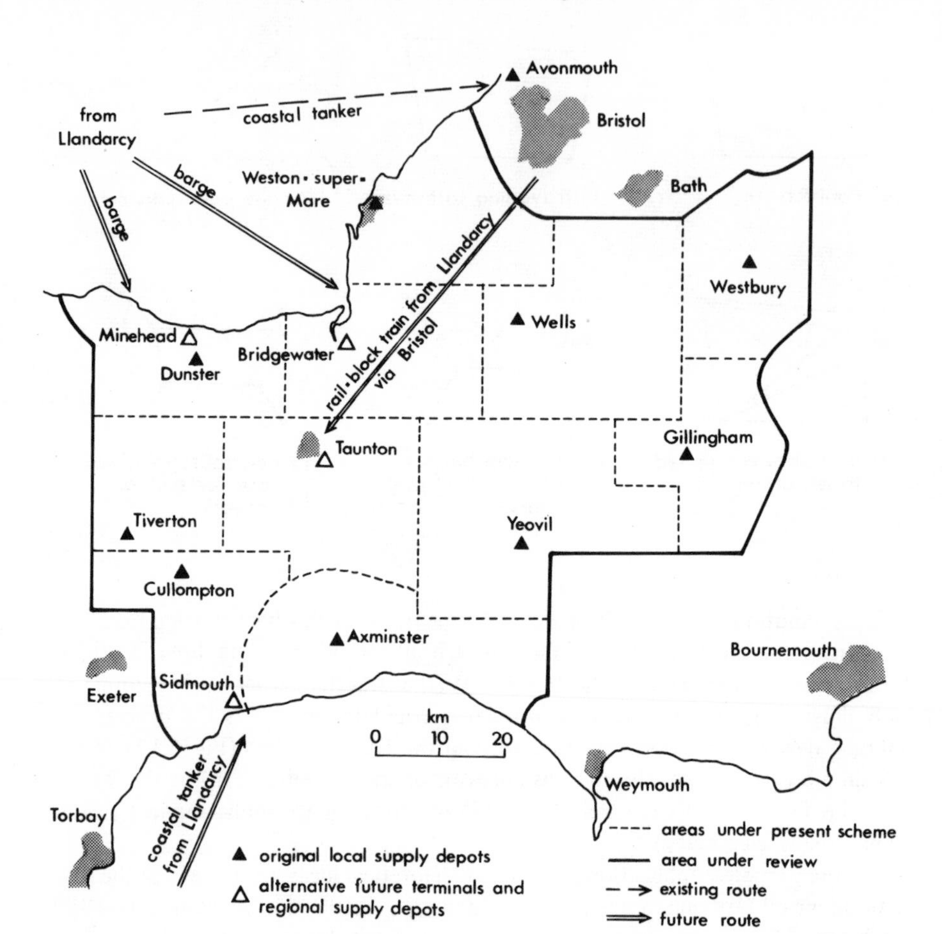

was determined and found to be too expensive. A new supply and distribution system was proposed and four possible locations for a new terminal in the area (Minehead, Bridgewater, Sidmouth, and Taunton) were assessed.

The costs of transporting oils to these alternative terminal sites were scrutinized, and the relative advantages of modes of transport (rail, barge, coastal tanker) were discussed. On the basis of the collected statistics, Bridgewater was chosen as the optimal choice. This was a real example of the attempted minimization of transport costs.

Finally, the political factor has had a great determining effect on network patterns. The two maps in Fig. 6.14 show how some routes are duplicated and run parallel with one another on either side of a boundary (aligning effect), while others approach but do not cross a boundary (blocking effect).

Fig. 6.14 (a) *Rail networks on the Spanish/Portuguese border;* (b) *rail networks on the eastern Russian/Chinese border*

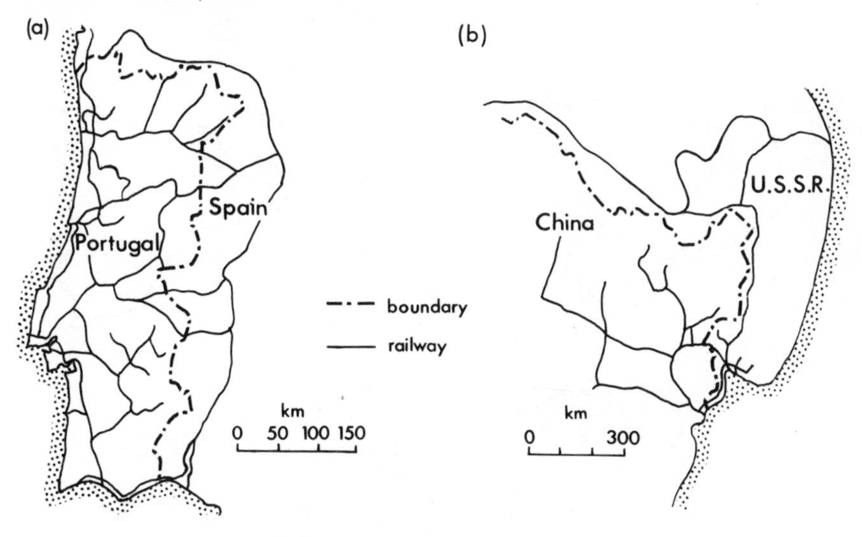

Principles and examples of network growth

Several attempts have been made to evolve a theory of network structure. Hay has subdivided such efforts into **cross-sectional approaches** to a network pattern where the network at a particular time is explained, and **evolutionary approaches** which involve the explanation of the development of the network through time. The former refers to variables (factors) relevant at the time, the latter to a number of changing variables.

Cross-sectional approach: Kansky's model

Kansky's research is the best example of the cross-sectional approach. His aim was to predict the form of the Sicilian railway network in 1908 (Fig. 6.15a; in its topological map form, Fig. 6.15b). The topology of this network was measured by the number of vertices (16–17) and edges, and the β (1·13) and η (28·2 km) indices. Thirty urban settlements were chosen. The likelihood of their being served by the network was related to the total estimated income of the settlement. Other rules were devised according to the size of the centres and their distance away from existing parts of the network. The outcome of Kansky's model is shown (Fig. 6.15c) in contrast to the actual network built (Figs. 6.15a and 6.15b).

Evolutionary approach: Taaffe, Morrill, and Gould model

The best-known example of the evolutionary approach is the suggested sequence of transport expansion in underdeveloped countries put forward by Taaffe, Morrill, and Gould. The sequence developed was based on empirical work undertaken in Nigeria and Ghana. The six phases of the development are shown in Fig. 6.16.

Fig. 6.15 *Kansky's simulation of the railway network of Sicily in 1908.* (a) *As built in 1908;* (b) *topological map of actual network* (a); (c) *simulated pattern (edges numbered according to order in which simulation occurred)*

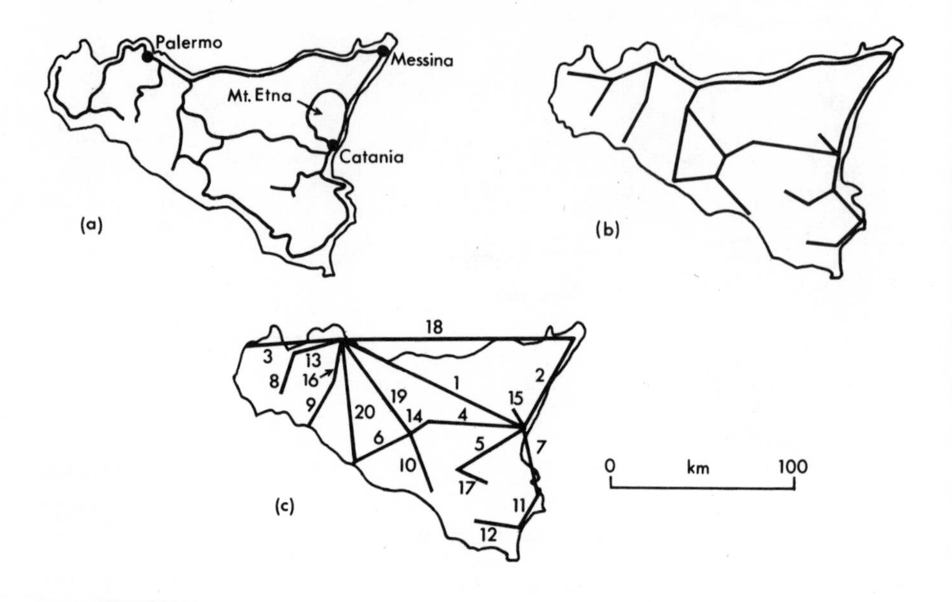

1. Stage A shows a scatter of small ports and trading posts along the sea coast. Only small indigenous fishing craft and irregularly scheduled trading vessels provide lateral intercommunications. Each port has an extremely limited hinterland.
2. Stage B shows that market areas have expanded for two ports (P_1 and P_2). Transport costs into the hinterland are reduced for these two ports. Port concentration begins (P_1 and P_2). Feeder routes begin to focus on the major ports and interior centres (I_1 and I_2).
3. Stage C. The major ports begin to enlarge their hinterlands at the expense of the smaller ports. Feeder development continues and small nodes develop along the main lines of penetration.
4. Stage D. Certain of the nodes (N_1 and N_2) capture the hinterlands of the smaller nodes on each side. Feeder lines continue to develop and some of the large feeders begin to link up.
5. Stage E. Lateral links occur until all the ports, interior centres, and main nodes are linked. There are the beginnings of the development of national trunk routes or 'main streets', again increasing the connectivity of the network.
6. Stage F. These main streets have reached their full development, and an urban hierarchy has emerged.

The reasons for links inland seem to have been threefold: to connect politically and militarily a coastal administrative centre with its inland centres, to exploit mineral resources, and to tap areas of potential agricultural production.

The problem with applying this sequence to other situations is, firstly, that it is

Fig. 6.16 *A model for the development of a transport network in a developing country*

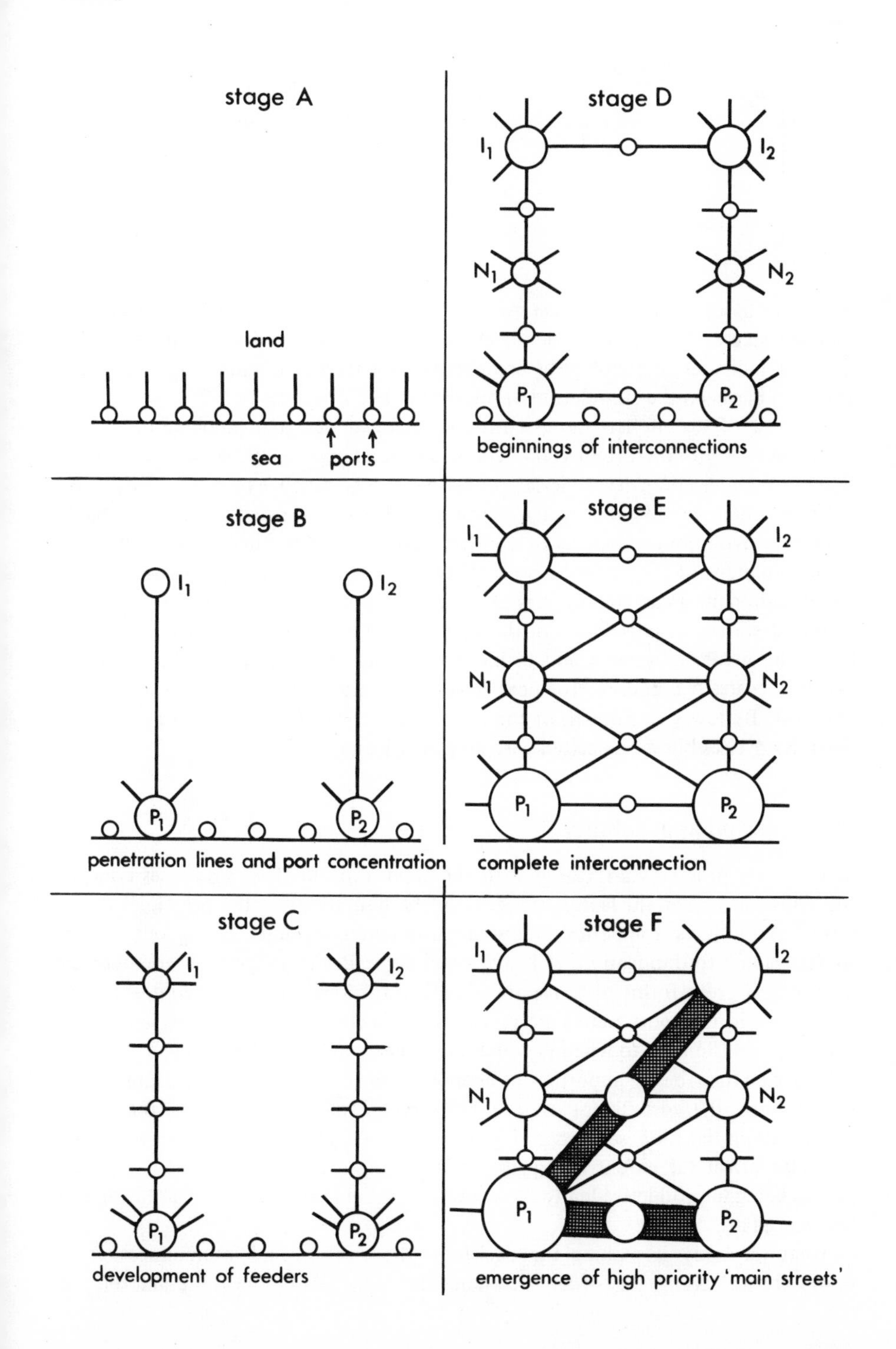

Fig. 6.17 *Route development through exploration*

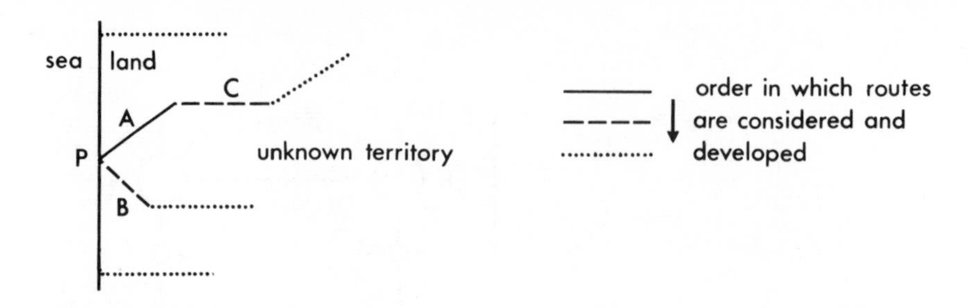

so closely based on the two West African states. Secondly, it is difficult to justify separate stages. Finally, there is no explanation of the precise way in which the network increases in topological complexity over time. The model's greatest contribution has been the stimulation of discussion, and research.

In most of the models discussed it has been assumed that both the origin and destination of proposed routes and networks were known. Gould suggests, however, that in colonial countries at least, routes were very much exploratory with destinations unknown and that really **search theory** is far more appropriate as a background to evolutionary models of such transport networks. The choice at all stages of development of the network is one between speculative route construction and consolidation in areas already served by an incomplete network. In Fig. 6.17 the colony is started at port P and in the first stage of transport development a choice has to be made between A and B. Based on a limited assessment of builder costs and user costs, A is chosen. The next stage of transport development is the possible choice of B, now well known, or the new alternative C. C may potentially lead to great discoveries but is associated with greater risk and cost.

Problems and applicability

Most of the problems associated with the application of these principles concern the omission of certain factors rather than the limitations of the principles themselves. As well as competition between different companies laying out similar routes leading to duplication, as in the canal and rail 'mania' periods, competition between different forms of transport will affect the location of their routes. Nowadays, though, transport routes are much more affected by governments, who often make the decisions as to whether routes are opened and closed. Social and strategic factors can then be as important as economic; for example, in the closure of rail branch lines, the curtailment of rural bus services, and the building of the Soviet railway along the Chinese border (Fig. 6.14b). Governments' attitude to transport may also affect the extent and quality of networks. The U.S.S.R.'s view of transport as being unproductive led to little investment being allocated to it in the earlier five-year plans.

Whatever body is making the decisions, the location and interconnection of routes are just two facets of any decision. The capacities of the route and termini are particularly important. It is the point along the route with the least capacity that affects the flow. This is often related to the capacity of the vehicle, for example size of ship and length of train. The ability of ports and stations to accommodate larger vessels and trains and to unload and load at speed greatly affects the amount of traffic attracted to the route. For example, the depth of harbour, the modern handling facilities, and the reliable and efficient dock labour have contributed much to making Rotterdam/Europoort the largest port in the world by tonnage handled.

These termini and access points obviously play a key role in a network, yet there is disagreement in the literature on network description as to what constitutes a vertex or node. Some researchers only use termini and junctions, omitting ordinary stations, for example on rail networks. Since these are access points to the network, and important geographical locations, it makes more sense to include them, as in Figs. 6.7 and 6.8a. The description of networks is limited by the non-comparability of certain indices. The applicability of the measures described in this chapter is also limited to planar, rather than non-planar, graphs (that is to networks in one plane, rather than to those, like air-routes, where the fact that two routes cross does not imply an interconnection).

The simulation procedures using these measures also have limitations (Chapter 9), although they are useful devices to aid understanding. One problem is that even if the simulated pattern fits reality, it does not necessarily mean that the rules of the simulation are the same as the processes that generated the pattern in the real world.

The effect of transport routes on the location of economic activity requires some comment. The existence of a route is usually both a response to a demand and an encouragement of further use. It is only usually so, because the existence of a route does not necessarily mean that it will be used or that it will create use. The provision of transport is a passive factor. It is necessary but not sufficient for the development of economic activity.

Certain activities are transport-oriented since their custom is derived mainly from the traffic using the route on which they are located. The business of these activities may be reduced by the location of a new route, a by-pass or motorway, to which most of the traffic is diverted. The new routes, however, then attract new traffic-oriented activities.

For industry in general, transport improvements have been extremely important. The building of the canals (so extending cheap sea transport inland) and the railways increased the accessibility both of certain points of access along the routes and of the termini, especially those from which routes radiated. Transport improvements permitted the extension of the hinterland and market of these points for the collection of raw materials and the distribution of finished products. They allowed production at a point (**punctiform** production) with the economies of increased scale of production. The possibility of **external economies** (Chapters 3 and 12) via industrial linkages and sharing of services led to the agglomeration of industry and the growth of large cities. The continual improvement of communications between these large cities through the superimposition of different networks – rail, road, and motorway – enabled further growth derived from their greater accessibility, especially to the national market. Because improvements are usually made first where the traffic most demands them, the routes between the large cities were the first to benefit from innovations. The resulting greater relative accessibility encouraged even further growth and even more traffic. The transport improvements have thus permitted concentrations of economic activities, especially those central to the national market.

The large cities were also first to receive transport innovations affecting movement within the cities, for example the tram (Fig. 9.12). Buses, underground railway systems, electrified railways, and cars permitted the suburbanization of people, allowing many to live away from their work. The articulated lorry/truck enabled factories to move away from the docks and railways, out to the cheaper land along the arterial roads of the city. The new route systems thus allowed the expansion of the city. New communication links, such as telephone and telex, have permitted further decentralization of the production side of firms. They have enabled a spatial division of labour to occur, with the decision-making branch, the head office, staying in the city centre close to the ideas of complementary and competitive institutions, while the production branch, the factory, is able to locate outside the city where cheaper land, buildings, and suitable labour are available. On the city-region scale, improvements in communications have thus permitted decentralization, particularly to the more accessible sites, resulting in concentrated dispersion. For example in London's case there are several New and Expanded Towns within a radius of 80 km.

Conclusion

Many important and interesting principles are demonstrated by this rather neglected part of geography. The descriptive measures of networks are useful for comparative purposes but as yet have not had any profound effect on research. But it is fair to say that research on routes and networks is still at an early stage.

The effects of route location on the distribution of economic activity are significant, but not of overriding importance, as is sometimes argued. The presence of transport routes is a necessary, but not a sufficient, condition for economic development. The relationship between transport and economic activity is an interdependent one, because the distribution of economic activity also influences the location of transport routes. Such interdependent relationships are common in human geography, and account for much of its complexity.

Bibliography

Bunge, W., *Theoretical Geography*, Lund Studies in Geography, Series C, no. 1, 2nd edition (Gleerup, 1966)

Haggett, P., and Chorley, R.J., *Network Analysis in Geography* (Arnold, 1969)

Hay, A., *Transport for the Space Economy* (Macmillan, 1973)

Lösch, A., *The Economics of Location* (Yale University Press, 1954)

Taaffe, E.J., Morrill, R.L., and Gould, P.R., 'Transport Expansion in Underdeveloped Countries', *Geographical Review*, vol. 53 (1963)

Essay questions

1. What factors may affect the choice of routes for and the density of networks of one of the following:
   (a) canals,
   (b) railways,
   (c) motorways? (Cambridge, 1971)
2. What geographical considerations are likely to affect the choice of an itinerary (route, performance sites, and lengths of stay) of a large travelling organization such as a circus? (Oxford and Cambridge, 1974)
3. Although the shortest distance between an origin and a destination is the straight line between them, in practice people rarely follow such a path. Use a variety of examples to explain why. (Oxford and Cambridge, 1973)
4. 'The connectivity of the transport network is the best evidence of a country's degree of development.' How far do you agree? (Manchester University)

Chapter 7

Transport costs and modes

Introduction and link

The preceding chapter analysed the location and growth of transport routes. This short chapter examines the costs of using the different means of transport that follow these routes. They vary according to the type of traffic being transported, be it passenger or freight. The assumption of earlier chapters that there is only one means or **mode** of transport is thus relaxed. The modes include foot, road, rail, sea, and air. The competition between modes and the effect this has on the location of economic activity are then studied. There are no main models in this chapter, rather a series of empirically based ideas.

Main aim

The main aim is to show the factors affecting the cost and choice of modes of transport.

Principles and examples

Types of cost

There are a number of types of cost for any transport system. The relative importance of these varies between modes and to some extent for a given mode in different areas, because of the terrain, for example. There are **costs of construction** of routes and termini and **running costs** which include the costs of maintenance and movement. The construction costs of an oil pipeline are very high, while the running costs are relatively low. For an oil tanker, construction costs are relatively low, but running costs, which include time in ports, are high. Thus, if demand and supply are great and lasting, building a pipeline may be cheaper in the long run, especially if the area is secure and the product to be transferred is standard and unvarying.

Running costs include two major types: fixed and variable costs. **Fixed costs** refer to those incurred regardless of the length of the journey. They include maintenance of the network and vehicles, interest on borrowed capital, and depreciation costs. They also include handling charges at termini, which again do not depend on the length of the haul. The latter are called **terminal costs** (Fig. 7.1). **Variable costs** refer to the costs of movement which obviously vary with the distance travelled.

Fig. 7.1 *The effect of distance on total transport costs*

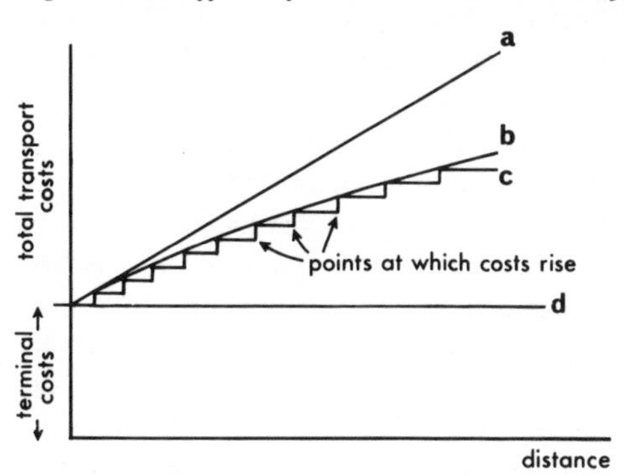

Although movement costs are higher for road than rail, over shorter distances road transport is more economical because terminal costs are so much lower than those of rail (Fig. 7.2).

Cost variation with distance

The simple assumption that transport costs vary proportionally with distance rarely holds. The inclusion of terminal costs (Fig. 7.1, line a) means that average transport costs per kilometre decrease as the length of haul increases. Economies in the variable costs over longer hauls lead to further reductions in average cost per kilometre with increasing distance (Fig. 7.1 line b). In reality, it is difficult to administer continuously varying rates, so stepped tariffs are often used (Fig. 7.1 line c). Sometimes it is even more convenient for transport costs not to vary with distance within a given area (Fig. 7.1, line d). The postage costs of letters within Great Britain and the U.S.A. are an example.

The varying proportions of types of cost and the varying rates of increase with distance for different modes are summarized on the idealized graph (Fig. 7.2).

Fig. 7.2 *Transport costs of three transport modes*

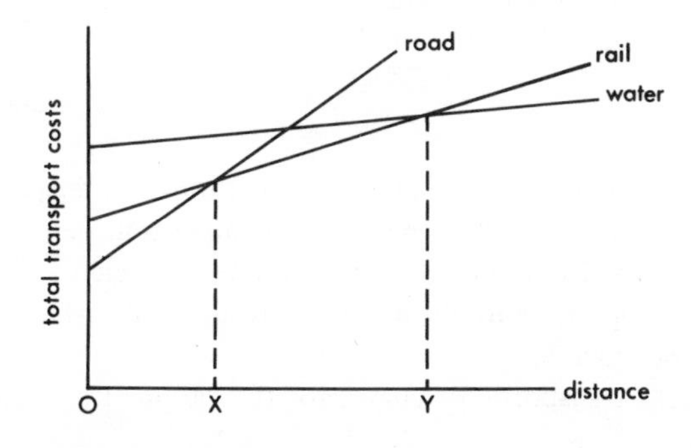

Factors affecting freight rates

A whole variety of other influences affect the costs of transport and thereby the rates charged. This applies often to both passenger and freight rates. Economies of scale of transport often have the effect of reducing costs per kilometre on more heavily used routes. Where vehicles are always returning empty from a given place, it will pay the transport authority to offer cheaper backhaul rates in order to fill the vehicles and gain additional revenue. Such backhaul rates may influence the location of economic activity. For example, western Superior iron ore has been transported to the Pittsburgh iron and steel complex for many years. This allows the backhaul of coal from Pittsburgh via the Great Lakes to Duluth which has stimulated the development of an iron and steel industry there using the ore. Ports such as Cleveland, *en route* between the ore and the coal supply areas, have also been able to base steel works on the material flows. This is partly a result of their **break of bulk location**, that is where freight changes mode, say from ship to rail.

The characteristics of the commodity to be moved may affect freight rates; for example its value, perishability, ease of loading, danger, and bulkiness. Higher freight rates would be expected for more valuable, more perishable, awkward, dangerous, and bulky items; for example finished cars are more valuable, fragile, bulky, and awkward to transport than the component parts. This partly explains why the assembly of American cars has been decentralized from the Detroit region, which still manufactures most of the component parts.

What the traffic will bear is another principle that influences transport charges. This implies that a tonne of gold can more readily withstand a higher transport cost than a tonne of iron ore. For the gold, transport costs will clearly be a small part of the total costs, and it can therefore sustain a higher freight rate. This often means that finished products, in general, pay higher freight rates than component parts or raw materials.

Related to this principle is one of charging more to customers with an inelastic demand than to customers with an elastic demand. Demand is said to be elastic (inelastic) if a slight rise or fall in transport costs produces a considerable change (no appreciable change) in the demand for the use of the transport system. The elasticity of demand is likely to be greater for longer hauls since the cost of movement is a larger part of the total transport cost in such instances. Therefore, the rates set for long hauls may be relatively lower than those for short hauls. With the combined influence of all these factors, a very complex set of tariff schedules could result. To avoid this, commodities are usually assigned to one of a limited number of classes with a single set of rates applying to each class.

Competition between modes

Where two modes of transport or two agencies of the same form of transport compete over the same route, there is likely to be strong competition in rates offered. Rail and air fares between London and Glasgow are one example of this (Fig. 7.3). Profit levels on such competitive routes are likely to be small, whereas in monopoly situations they can be much larger.

As a result of the very different transport-cost curves for the various transport

Fig. 7.3 *Market share by mode of London to Glasgow passenger traffic*

mode	number of passengers (1968)	fare (£) (1969)	time (hours) (1969)
bus	300 000	2·80	12·00
rail	500 000	5·20	7·00
air	700 000	9·65	1·00
car	200 000	4·95 (estimated)	9·90
	1 700 000		

modes, each mode tends to offer price advantages over different lengths of haul (Fig. 7.2). Road haulage offers clear advantages between O and X, rail between X and Y, and water beyond Y. Competition between the modes is likely to be greatest around the distances X and Y.

Competition between modes affects the freight rates that can be charged. There are numerous examples: rail rates were reduced once the St. Lawrence Seaway was opened, canal rates fell when railways were built in Britain, and railway companies in Britain were often involved in cut-throat price wars during the late nineteenth century. The competition between the modes of transport has been severe in

Fig. 7.4 *Goods transport in Great Britain*

mode	1955		1965		1972	
	million tons	percentage	million tons	percentage	million tons	percentage
road	997	75·1	1565	83·3	1698	86·1
rail	274	20·9	229	12·1	175	8·7
coastal shipping	39	3·0	53	2·8	47	2·4
inland waterways	10	0·8	8	0·4	5	0·3
pipeline	2	0·2	26	1·4	51	2·5
total	1322	100	1881	100	1976	100
	thousand million ton/miles	percentage	thousand million ton/miles	percentage	thousand million ton/miles	percentage
road	23·0	40·1	42·1	57·2	51·4	63·8
rail	21·4	37·3	15·4	20·9	14·2	17·6
coastal shipping	12·7	22·1	15·3	20·8	13·0	16·1
inland waterways	0·2	0·3	0·1	0·1	0·1	0·1
pipeline	0·1	0·2	0·8	1·1	1·9	2·4
total	57·4	100	73·7	100	80·6	100

Source: Basic Road Statistics, 1973, quoting from Annual Abstract of Statistics and (1972) Department of Environment estimates

Fig. 7.5 *Passenger transport in Great Britain*

mode	1955 thousand million passenger/ miles	1955 percentage	1965 thousand million passenger/ miles	1965 percentage	1972 thousand million passenger/ miles	1972 percentage
air (including N. Ireland and Channel Is.)	0·2	0·2	1·0	0·5	1·3	0·5
rail	23·8	18·6	21·8	10·5	21·1	7·6
road						
public service vehicles	49·8	38·9	39·2	19·0	34·2	12·3
private vehicles	54·3	42·4	144·7	70·0	222·2	79·6
total	128·1	100	206·7	100	278·8	100

Source: Passenger Transport in Great Britain, Table I, and (1972) Annual Abstract of Statistics, 1973

Britain since 1945. Road transport has emerged as the leading mode for both freight and passengers (Figs. 7.4 and 7.5).

The individual customer is invariably faced with a **modal split** decision. A simple example of a passenger modal split problem is that of commuting from Reading to central London (Fig. 7.6). The alternatives are going door to door by car or travelling by rail with secondary modes (foot/car/bus/underground railway)

Fig. 7.6 *Passenger modal split: Reading to central London commuting (1976)*

mode	cost (£) (one way)	travel (hours)	door-to-door time (hours)	convenience	comfort
car	1·10	1 – 1¼	1 – 1¼ (40 miles)	1. no need to wait for connections 2. not affected in general by weather 3. problem of parking 4. door to door	1. room without overcrowding 2. mental/physical discomfort of having to drive in rush hour
rail (Reading General)	1·38 Tube 0·20 Bus 0·15 1·73	35 mins	1¼	1. refreshments available 2. able to work, read, sleep, socialize 3. may have to wait for connections	1. can be over-crowded; may have to stand 2. if 1st class, less crowded and more comfortable

Fig. 7.7 *The break of bulk/transshipment point and its effect on location*

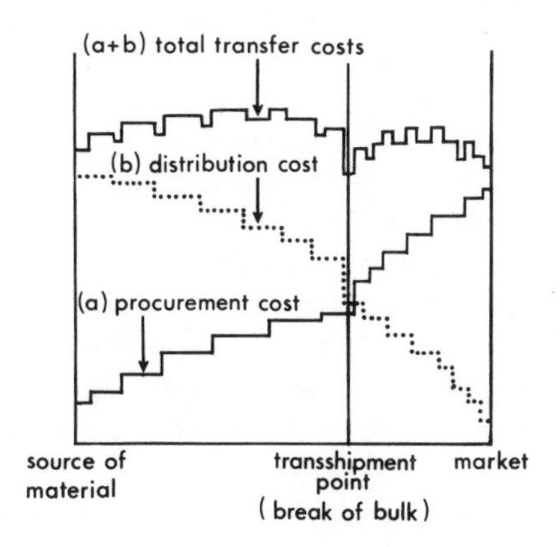

being used to and from the stations. As there is little difference between average travel times, the choice must be based upon such factors as cost, comfort, and convenience.

The effect of transfer between modes on location: break of bulk point

When either raw materials or finished product have to be transshipped from one mode to another *en route* from the raw material source or the centre of the market, it sometimes lowers total transport costs if manufacturing or processing occurs at the transshipment or break of bulk point (Fig. 7.7). This is particularly the case when the freight rates of material and product are similar. Flour milling is a classic example.

Problems and applicability

As in the preceding chapter, the problems are not with the logic or applicability of the principles, rather that many factors are omitted within them. The principles are mainly economic. Yet with increasing government involvement in transport, social costs are also considered and subsidies granted so that the user does not bear the full economic cost.

Competition between modes is not only over certain distances and along certain very busy routes. By offering specialist facilities, for example, some modes can obtain a near monopoly on the transport of certain goods; for instance, the automatic handling by large railway trucks which carry most of the coal to power-stations by bulk transport.

As competition between modes has varied through time there are also historical factors to consider. The typical stages are innovation and growth of networks, then relative dominance over other modes, followed by relative, and often absolute, decline. Road transport seems to be the dominant mode at present on a national scale. For each mode, innovations increase the speed of travel and the volume that may be transported, leading to economies of scale, so that over time transport costs have relatively declined. Competition, though, is not only on cost, but also on speed, convenience, and often reliability. Air freight, for example, as well as being suitable for high-value, low-weight goods, can also be used for urgent deliveries when 'time is money'. Competition within modes may also be important in reducing costs, and may lead to greater competition between modes. For instance, the emergence of a new organization in air freight has led to economies of scale and reduced costs, making air freight more competitive with shipping. Other air freight companies act as feeders, sending consignments to the large company which can then deliver them in bulk to their destination. This process of **consolidation** permits lower rates, which encourage traffic. In these circumstances the goal of the transport company, to maximize traffic, is not in conflict with the aim of manufacturers, to minimize transport costs.

The modes can be complementary as well as competitive. On some routes a number of modes are used. Change from one mode to another at the break of bulk point, though, is costly. The main idea of containers is to minimize that cost, making modes even more complementary.

The principles of transport costs and modes have numerous effects on the location of economic activity. The decline in average costs per kilometre with distance would permit the extension of the margins of cultivation (Chapter 2). The stepped freight rates would mean that there was no longer an optimum point for the location of a factory, rather an optimum area. With successive innovations, the decline in transport costs relative to other costs has permitted many changes in location. In the simplified von Thünen model (Chapter 2), cultivation can occur at greater distances from the market, and the rings of agricultural production may be potentially much wider. Demand must increase, though, before more land will be used, otherwise supply will exceed demand, the market will fall, and the extent of cultivation will be reduced. The decline in the relative importance of transport costs for many industries has widened the choice of profitable alternative locations. It has enabled a larger area to be used for the supply of raw materials, a larger market to be served, and thus an increased scale of production to be achieved. Accessibility, especially to the market, is still highly valued, less because of lower total transport costs and more because of convenience, time, and ease of after-sales service.

The relative lowering of costs and reduction in travel time (**space-time convergence**) between places has not been uniform. The reduction in time has been greatest on the routes between very large cities. Intermodal competition and economies of scale of movement have also tended to lower the real costs of movement between these places faster than between smaller ones. The larger cities thus retain and increase their advantages of accessibility for the location of economic activity.

Conclusion

Although transport has been a rather neglected subject in traditional geography, the role of transport costs in economic geography has for long been very important. In more recent times, the effect of such costs on the location of economic activities has perhaps been overestimated. The relative decline in transport costs and the nature of much of modern industry, with its emphasis on the value added in processing rather than the use of large quantities of raw materials, have meant that transport costs constitute a smaller proportion of total costs than in the past. However, convenience, and reliability are important, although difficult to quantify. With the increased costs of oil and of energy supplies in general since 1973, the impact of transport costs as such may become much more important again.

Bibliography

Hay, A., *Transport for the Space Economy* (Macmillan, 1973)
Hoover, E.M., *The Location of Economic Activity* (McGraw-Hill, 1948)

Essay questions

1. What have been the geographical effects of technological change in ocean-going transport? (Cambridge, 1974)
2. How do transport costs affect the location of industry? (Cambridge, 1975)
3. 'Not only is there likely to be an irreducible handling cost which sets a minimum to shorthaul rates but, over and above that, the ton/mile rate generally declines with increasing length of haul.' (Hoover)

   What are the implications of this statement for the location of manufacturing industry? (Manchester University)

Chapter 8

Movement in space: the gravity model

Introduction and link

The two preceding chapters examined transport systems and their costs. This chapter studies the movement of people, goods, and ideas between places within a transport system for a given period of time. Such movement over space is called **spatial interaction**. Geographers have long been interested in the similarities and differences between regions. Only more recently have they been concerned with interaction between regions, which itself affects and is affected by the character of the regions. In this chapter, yet another kind of scientific approach to geography is demonstrated. Researchers have borrowed a theory from physics, Newton's universal law of gravitation, and attempted to apply it to movement in geographical space. Early workers were particularly concerned with the migration of people between pairs of towns. Later authors have used this **gravity model** or modifications of it to examine other forms of interaction such as trade flows and journeys to work and shop. The scale of movement to which the model applies is important. It predicts the movement of large groups of people, not individual people. It is this scale of movement which will affect the character of towns and regions.

Main aim

The main aim of researchers using the gravity model is to predict the amount of movement between places in a given period of time.

Basic principles and model

First, it is useful to remember Newton's famous law: 'Any two bodies attract one another with a force that is proportional to the product of their masses and inversely proportional to the square of the distance between them.' If F is the force, M_1 and M_2 the masses of the two bodies, D their distance apart, and G a 'universal constant of nature' called the gravitational constant, this law can be expressed as

$$F = G\,\frac{M_1 M_2}{D^2}$$

Note that as the distance D between the bodies increases, D^2 increases and the force F between them decreases (inverse or negative relationship). If the masses M_1

and/or M_2 increase, so does the force F (direct or positive relationship). Such a law is applied to the gravitational force between interstellar bodies.

A number of social scientists during the late nineteenth and early twentieth century applied the ideas of the model to the movement of people. Ravenstein considered that the extent of migration between one place and another varied directly with the number of people available to move and inversely with the distance they would have to move. The analogy was made explicit by Warntz, a Harvard geographer, during the 1940s. His aim was to predict the amount of interaction, I_{ij}, between two towns, i and j, over a given time period. Migration could be one type of interaction. The two towns replaced the two bodies. Their **populations** P_i and P_j represented their **masses**.

$$I_{ij} = G \frac{P_i P_j}{D_{ij}^2}$$

In social science G is a constant of proportionality which ensures that the extent of interaction predicted approximates the actual movement. It will be related to the average number of moves per capita.

This is the **simple gravity model** used in social science. Obviously the theory behind Newton's law does not apply to people, but the model reasonably suggests two basic relationships:

1. as the size of one or both towns increases so does the movement between them, and
2. the further apart are the towns the less the movement between them.

This indicates that distance has a frictional effect on movement: the **friction of distance**.

The model is more precise than the second of the two relationships. It says movement is inversely related to the square of the distance (Fig. 8.1). This part of

Fig. 8.1 *The relationship between movement and distance, with varying distance exponents showing different distance decay functions*

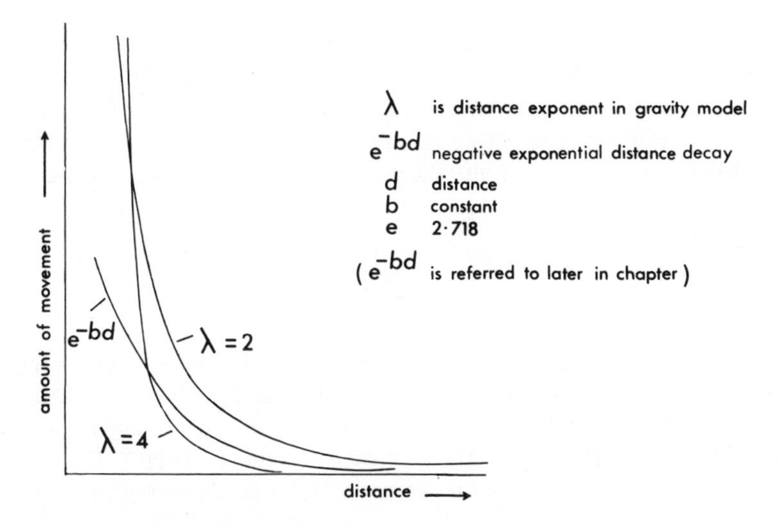

the model was rapidly modified. An inverse relationship was usually observed, but not always with a **distance exponent** of 2 (D_{ij}^2). The precise value of the exponent could depend upon such things as the terrain, the transport technology available which affects mobility, and indeed the type of movement predicted, for example migration, journey to work, journey to shop. The exponent used became the one that best fitted the particular interaction. Fig. 8.1 shows how the exponent affects the relationship between movement and distance. Where the exponent is high (4), there is a rapid decrease in movement with increased distance. The gradient of the curve is steep. Movement decreases more slowly with distance as the exponent value decreases. When it is zero, there is no frictional effect of distance ($D^0 = 1$). The curve describing the decline in movement with distance is called the **distance decay function**. It varies with the value of λ, which is the best-fitting distance exponent for any particular situation. The modified model then becomes

$$I_{ij} = G \frac{P_i P_j}{D_{ij}^{\lambda}}$$

For a given type of movement the appropriate distance decay function can vary for different areas and for the same area over time. For example, the frictional effect of distance on movement to work is much less in the U.S.A. than in West Africa, requiring a low and high exponent respectively. A comparison of journey to work patterns in Britain through time would require a much higher exponent for 1800 than 1976.

Example

The simple example shown in Figs. 8.2 and 8.3 concerns the volume of movement of industry, rather than of people, to some of the peripheral regions (j) of the United Kingdom from the South East (i) between 1945 and 1965. The movement (I_{ij}) is measured in terms of the number of jobs created (Fig. 8.2, observed values column 5). A simplified gravity model is used to predict the movement from the South East region to peripheral regions. Only the movement in one direction is observed, unlike the normal gravity model in which two-way movement between the masses is estimated. Because of this, only one mass, M_j, that of the destination, is used. A measure of the attractiveness of the peripheral regions (j) to mobile industry is needed to represent this mass. It is thought that industry is attracted by labour availability, so the number, not the percentage, unemployed in the regions at the mid-point of the period is taken as the mass term (Fig. 8.2, column 1). The model is then simply

$$I_{ij} = G \frac{M_j}{D_{ij}^{\lambda}}$$

where D_{ij} is the straight-line distance between the cores of the regions (column 2). The best-fitting distance exponent, λ, is estimated as 2 (column 3). With this exponent, the observed and predicted values most closely fit a straight line when plotted on the graph (Fig. 8.3). The estimated G value is 53 000. This ensures that the predicted movement is of the same scale as the actual movement (Fig. 8.2,

Fig. 8.2 *Simplified gravity model applied to industrial movement from the South East region (including the Greater London Council) to the peripheral regions, 1945–65*

	basic data		simplified model			modified model	
	M_j average total unemployed workforce in 1954	D_{ij} distance miles	$\frac{M_j}{D_{ij}^2}$	predicted movement of jobs $I_{ij} = \frac{GM_j}{D_{ij}^2}$	actual movement of jobs	weights: market potential w_j	$\frac{Gw_jM_j}{D_{ij}^2}$ $(G=50)$
Northern Ireland	33 000	320	0·32226	17 079	16 900	800	12 890
Scotland	59 500	360	0·45910	24 332	24 500	1000	22 955
Northern	28 300	250	0·45280	23 998	35 800	1100	24 904
Wales	22 900	140	1·16836	61 923	43 200	1100	64 259
Merseyside	18 900	180	0·58333	30 916	36 000	1300	37 916
Devon and Cornwall	8 600	190	0·23822	12 625	10 600	900	10 720
	(col. 1)	(col. 2)	(col. 3)	(col. 4)	(col. 5)	(col. 6)	(col. 7)

Source: modified from two tables in Keeble, D.E., 'Employment Mobility in Britain,' pp. 24-68 in Chisholm, M., and Manners, G., (eds.), *Spatial Policy Problems of the British Economy* (Cambridge University Press, 1971)

Fig. 8.3 *Actual and predicted movements from the South East region to the peripheral regions (see Fig. 8.2)*

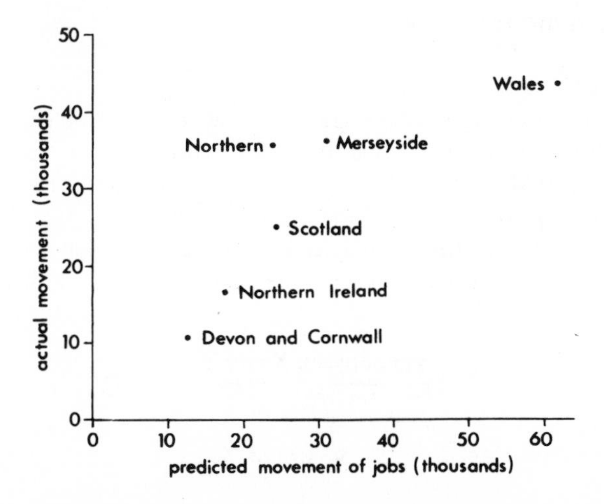

columns 4 and 5). The need for a scaling value G is shown by comparing column 3 (without G) with column 4 (with G).

Although the predictions of the gravity model are better than those of distance alone or labour availability alone, they are not a very close fit. The movements to Wales and the Northern region are highly overpredicted and underpredicted, respectively (Figs. 8.2 and 8.3). In an attempt to improve the fit, a set of weights was added to the mass terms. Industry is attracted not only by labour availability. Access to a large market is also an important factor. A measure of the **market potential** of the regions is employed to weight the masses (Chapter 3).

The measure of market potential is similar to the gravity model.

$$P_i = \sum_{j=1}^{n} \frac{K_j}{D_{ij}}$$

where P_i is the market potential of place i, K_j is the market of place j (population size), D_{ij} is the distance from i to j, and Σ is the summation of K_j/D_{ij} for all n places. It measures the accessibility of a place to the national market.

In the example the average market potential figures (Fig. 8.2, column 6) refer to accessibility to the national market for manufactured goods and to major export outlets. The measure obviously includes the opportunities of regional sales. The results of the amended model (column 7) show that although the prediction is improved for Merseyside and for Devon and Cornwall, there is little gained generally by the use of this particular set of weights.

The example demonstrates the simple and more complex uses of the gravity model. In this particular case, there are numerous limitations to the model, one being the use of only one year's statistics to represent labour availability over a twenty-year period. Note that this is a simplified use of the gravity model, in that it predicts only one-way movement and therefore employs only one mass term.

Extensions and modifications

The Reilly model

Reilly applied the principles of the gravity model to the problem of delimiting market areas (Chapter 1). He stated that two centres attract trade from intermediate places approximately in direct proportion to the sizes of the centres and in inverse proportion to the square of the distances from these two centres to the intermediate place. From these principles he derived a 'breaking-point' equation, where the trade area boundary between two towns X and Y is, in kilometres from Y, equal to:

$$\frac{\text{km between X and Y}}{1 + \sqrt{\dfrac{\text{size of X}}{\text{size of Y}}}}$$

For example, the boundary between Leicester (X) and Oadby (Y) should be 2·32 km from Oadby, since the distance (XY) is 5·1 km and the sizes, which in an intra-urban situation (within a city) may be represented by the number of types of functions (goods and services), are 94 and 66 respectively. The actual market areas are shown in Fig. 8.8. With present-day mobility, market areas are overlapping rather than discrete, especially in intra-urban situations, as can be seen in Fig. 8.8. Reilly's model is more useful where mobility is still poor, or distances between towns great. Even then, it is unreliable, because human movement is not always inversely proportional to the square of the distance. If any other distance exponent fitted the movement (say 3), the square-root term in the denominator of the breaking-point equation would have to be changed (cube-root).

Modification to the simple gravity model

The gravity model assumes that the populations of the two towns, although possibly different in size, are the same in character. Yet, for example, people in town *i* may be richer and perhaps have a greater propensity to move than those in town *j*. By applying weights (w_i) and (w_j) to P_i and P_j where (w_i) is greater than (w_j), the difference between the two populations may be taken into account. (Market potential is used as a weight in Fig. 8.2.)

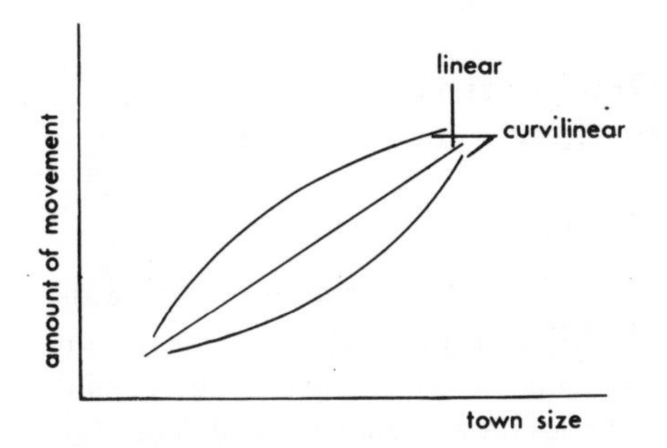

Fig. 8.4 *Possible relationships between movement and town size*

The model also assumes a simple **linear relationship** between town size and movement (Fig. 8.4). Yet movement may increase proportionally more (or less) as the population grows, that is, **curvilinearly** (Fig. 8.4). To represent this, exponents *a* and *b* may be added to the populations. The more **complex gravity model** is now

$$I_{ij} = G\frac{(w_i)P_i^a(w_j)P_j^b}{D_{ij}{}^{\lambda}}$$

The weights and exponents *a, b*, and λ are all estimated for a given situation.

Interaction between more than two places

The extension of the model to movement between more than two towns or regions ensures that the researcher poses three questions which are basic to any form of spatial interaction. It also reveals many of the problems associated with the use of gravity models.

Fig. 8.5 *Matrix showing trip generation, movement, and destination*

origins \ destinations	X	Y	Z	total originating
X	-	20	30	50
Y	30	-	10	40
Z	25	35	-	60
total arriving	55	55	40	150 (total number of moves)

Fig. 8.6 *Matrix of shopping trips: movement and destination*

origins (residential zones) \ destinations (shopping centres)	1	2	3	4	total number of customers in each zone
A	20	30	20	10	80
B	10	20	30	10	70
C	10	10	20	20	60
total number of customers for each centre	40	60	70	40	210 (total number of customers in town)

The matrix (Fig. 8.5) shows the migration between three towns X, Y, and Z. The three basic questions are:

1. How many will move from each town? (**Trip generation.**)
2. How many of those originating from, say X, will move to Y and how many to Z? (**Movement.**)
3. How many are destined for each town? (**Destination.**)

The matrix of origins and destinations shows an example of movement where the right-hand column displays the total number originating in each town, the bottom row the total number arriving at each town, and the remaining cells the number moving from one town to another. The number of moves generated will depend on the economic and social imbalances between the towns, that is, the attraction of the destinations relative to that of the origins; the economic and social climate of the time affecting movement, for example, availability of mortgages; and the cost of overcoming the distance between the towns. The distribution of moves from one town to the other two will depend on their relative attraction or mass (measured as job opportunities rather than population) and their distance.

In this case of migration the model has to estimate origins, movement, and destinations. The modified model is more simply explained with a shopping example, where the number of customers (origins) is usually known. A town is divided into three residential zones, A, B, and C, for each of which the number of households is known. The prediction needed is the number of households from each zone using each shopping centre (movement). From this the total number of households using each shopping centre (destinations) can be estimated. The matrix (Fig. 8.6) shows an example of actual movement. Of the 80 households in zone A, 20 use centre 1. The model developed by Huff aims to predict the cell values which represent movement.

The Huff model

The likelihood or **probability** (p_{A1}) of households in zone A using centre 1 is positively related to its mass or size (S_1) and inversely related to the distance it is away (D_{A1}), giving

$$\frac{S_1}{D_{A1}^{\lambda}}$$

But the probability of using centre 1 also depends upon the size and distance away of the other centres, giving

$$\sum_{j=1}^{4} \frac{S_j}{D_{ij}^{\lambda}}$$

The model becomes

$$P_{A1} = \frac{\dfrac{S_1}{D_{A1}^{\lambda}}}{\displaystyle\sum_{j=1}^{4} \frac{S_j}{D_{ij}^{\lambda}}} \quad \begin{matrix} \} \text{ numerator} \\ \\ \} \text{ denominator} \end{matrix}$$

$$\text{probability of zone A shopping at centre 1} = \frac{\text{attraction of centre 1}}{\text{total attraction of all centres}}$$

where zones are i and centres j. The numerator is the usual gravity formula. The denominator is the summation of the attraction ($\frac{\text{size}}{\text{distance}}$) of all four centres. The probability is then the degree of attraction of one centre over all centres. Huff used the amount of floor selling space and travel time to measure the size and distance variables. The distance exponent λ varies with the type of good. For example, it is higher for groceries than clothing because, in general, people travel shorter distances to grocery shops than to clothing stores. The best-fit exponent is found when the predicted and observed flows of shoppers are most highly correlated.

To obtain the number of households from zone A visiting centre 1, (T_{A1}), the probability p_{A1} is multiplied by the total number of households in zone A. The probabilities of households in the other zones shopping at centre 1 may similarly be calculated. To find the total number of customers using centre 1, the sub-totals T_{A1}, T_{B1}, and T_{C1} are added together. If the characteristics of the people in the residential zones are known, it is possible from national figures to estimate the average weekly household expenditure, e_A, e_B, and e_C on a particular set of goods for each zone. The total sales of that set of goods in centre 1 may be estimated as ($e_A\, T_{A1} + e_B\, T_{B1} + e_C\, T_{C1}$). This model has been used in such a way to predict sales for a new shopping centre.

A number of characteristics of Huff's model are important. It applies to a specified number of zones and centres, so the model must be 'closed'. A boundary enclosing zones and centres is demarcated where travel to shop across the line is at a minimum. This answers one of the problems of the simple gravity model where some interaction is predicted between towns, however far apart.

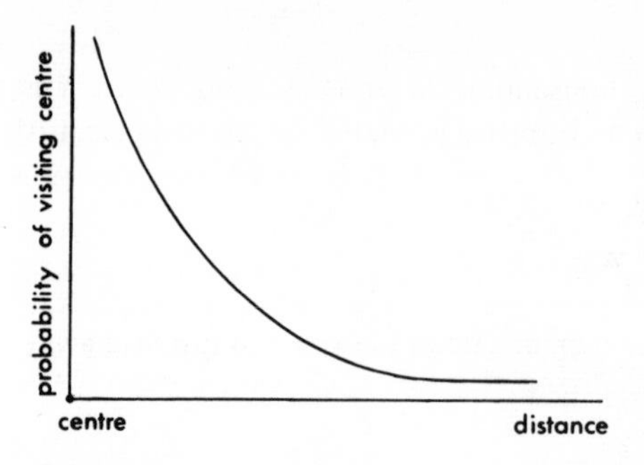

Fig. 8.7 *Probability of visiting a shopping centre with distance away from it*

Unlike the assumptions of central place theory (Chapter 1), all households do not visit their nearest centre. The probability of visiting a particular centre declines, though, as the distance of the zone from the centre increases (Fig. 8.7). So there is still a frictional effect of distance. In this model the frictional effect of distance is compensated for, to some degree, by the 'mass' of the centre.

As can be seen from Fig. 8.8, because not all people use their nearest centre, market areas are overlapping rather than discrete (separate) as in central place theory and Reilly's model. The diagram displays lines of equal probability of visiting a centre. In other words, 90 per cent of the households at C and 90 per cent of those elsewhere along the 0·9 line will visit Leicester's town centre. The closer spacing of probability lines around Oadby than Leicester demonstrates that the probability of visiting Oadby declines more rapidly with distance. Leicester has a greater mass than Oadby which enables it to attract households from longer distances. At D in the diagram households have a probability of 0·6 of going to Oadby, and 0·1 of visiting Leicester. The probability of using other centres is 0·3 because the probabilities at any one point must always add up to 1·0.

Fig. 8.8 *The probabilities of shopping at Oadby and Leicester: overlapping market areas*

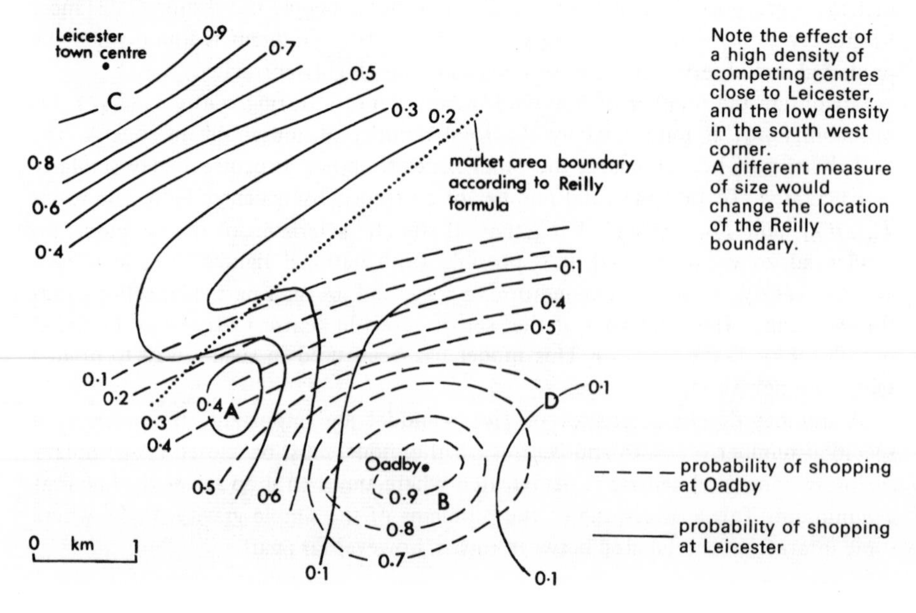

Journey to work

In the journey-to-work case, even more information is usually known. The origins are again zones where known numbers of employees reside. The destinations are work areas where known numbers are employed. The model then has to predict the movement (cell values), that is, how many employees from a particular zone travel to a particular work area. Such estimates are very useful in planning the transport system of a city. **Labour fields** may be established for particular work areas in a similar way to shopping centre market areas.

Disaggregation

As in all applications of gravity models, the movement can be disaggregated, that is, the total or aggregate movement can be divided into a particular set of constituent parts. In the journey-to-work case, it might be according to the mode of transport used, for example, public and private transport. Such a **modal split** model is more complex, since more information is needed, like car-ownership in the zones. Yet the predictions are more useful in planning transport systems. A similar modal split could be used for shopping (Fig. 8.9).

Disaggregation may also be by type of good and household in shopping, or type of house and migrant household in migration. Although the results of disaggregated models are more helpful, for example, in the migration case for predicting the future demand for particular house types or, less directly, the future demand for school places in a residential zone, they are typically less reliable, since the gravity model seems to fit movement less perfectly the more it is disaggregated.

Commodity flows: transferability, complementarity, and intervening opportunities

Finally, in studying commodity flows, some further factors affecting interaction will emerge. Ullman in the 1940s suggested that trade is affected by three conditions: transferability, complementarity, and intervening opportunities. **Transferability** relates to the ease with which a good can be transferred from place to place. The

Fig. 8.9 *Modal split for shopping in Oadby and Leicester*

mode from area A	Leicester	Oadby	mode from area B	Leicester	Oadby
walk	0	7	walk	0	60
bus	22	5	bus	3	0
car	18	28	car	7	20
total	40	40	total	10	80

A and B are located on Fig. 8.8.
No direct bus from A to Oadby.
Poorer bus service from B than from A to Leicester.
Both A and B are higher income areas; many will use cars for even short distances, especially when parking is easily available as at Oadby rather than Leicester.

distance factor of the gravity model obviously needs to be, and can be easily modified to reflect such factors as transport costs and handling charges, if it is to be applied to commodity flows.

No matter how cheap it is to move a product from one place to another, there must be a supply in one area and a demand in another for the product if trade is to take place. Such a condition is called **complementarity**. The two areas are complementary since one can supply what the other needs. To some extent the gravity model can incorporate this concept in its mass term, since for commodity flows the trade generated at the origins is measured by their supply of the product and the mass of the destinations by their demand for the product.

The simple gravity model does not, however, include the concept of **intervening opportunities**. It was first stated by Stouffer, a sociologist, when studying migration. He suggested that the amount of mobility between say, two towns A and B, depends less on distance and more on the number of intervening opportunities, that is, the number of towns within a circle centred on A with radius AB. In trade terms, two countries, W and X, may be the same distance apart as two others, Y and Z, and both pairs complementary, yet Y and Z may do little trade together compared with W and X, since Y has many closer complementary countries to it than Z, while X is W's nearest complementary nation. The Huff model to some extent incorporates the notion, because the relative distance of all alternatives is considered.

Problems and applicability

Some of the problems and applications have already been mentioned in the discussion of modifications. The problems involve the choice of appropriate measures of mass and distance, the fitting of the correct distance decay function, and the interpretation of the exponents. Despite these problems the model can be and is applied by planning and business organizations.

Experimentation, sometimes with weights and exponents, often provides the best measures of mass and distance for particular interaction types. For example, number of job opportunities is far better than population size for fitting migratory flows. Average travel time is better than straight-line distance for shopping movement within the city, and yet is more difficult to measure. Sometimes the mass and distance measures should reflect perceived, rather than real, values because it is these that affect people's behaviour. The shanty town is a geographical entity partially reflecting the difference between the perceived and the actual job opportunities that attract migrants. Care has to be taken that the chosen measure does not provide a circular argument in the logic of the model. Sometimes total sales is used for the mass of a shopping centre when the aim is to predict just that. It is not surprising that such models fit observed movement!

In this discussion, the fitting of the distance decay function has depended upon the value of distance exponent, λ. It is possible that the decline in movement with distance does not follow this form. In Fig. 8.1 a third curve shows a rather different relationship. Here movement is related in a negative exponential manner to distance just as population density is to distance from the city centre (Chapter 5). There are many different forms the relationship may take. The wrong choice of distance

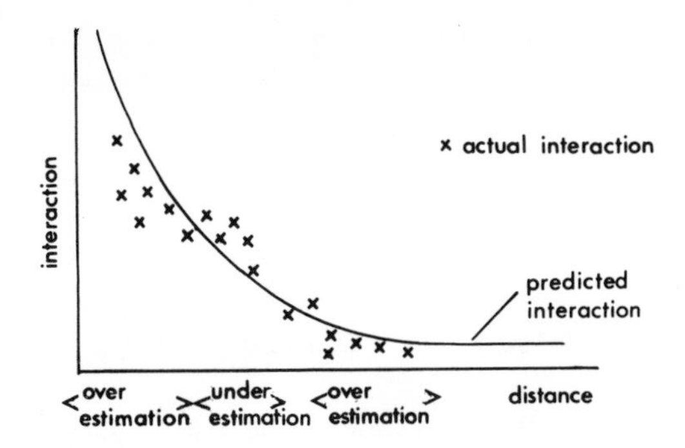

Fig. 8.10 *Predicted and actual interaction related to distance*

decay function has often resulted in an overestimation of interaction within a short distance (Fig. 8.10). The diagram shows a typical situation where the wrong function has been chosen. Plotting of the **residuals**, the difference between predicted and actual interaction, helps to spot this problem. With the correct function there would be a narrow band of residuals which are distributed in approximately equal numbers on either side of the predicted line, all the way along it.

Once the correct function is fitted, the interpretation of its constant(s), λ in the simple model, is not easy. It varies with so many factors, for example, the trip purpose, the mode of travel, the perception of distance, cost or travel time, and the measure of mass. In the Huff model, it is also affected by the relative positions of origins and destinations, and by the boundary of the study area. This makes comparisons between towns of, say, their shopping or commuting behaviour, very difficult because the different spatial structure of the towns is reflected in the exponents, along with any differences in behaviour.

Despite all these problems, the models have been applied to various situations from the location of shopping centres and their market areas to commodity flows in England and Wales. They have also been used to forecast future flows. This is of very dubious value since in many cases the exponent applying at the present has been used to predict the future, while increased mobility from improved transport has been included in the model, thus necessitating a change in the exponent. Future research may give some guidance as to how these exponents are likely to change over time.

The model was also used by the Roskill Commission in the cost-benefit analysis of the third London airport. Although the model was misused in this highly criticized report, it can be a useful tool for very short-term forecasting and examining the effect of alternative future policies on the present situation.

Conclusion

The gravity model in one of its forms fits many types of spatial interaction, particularly aggregated, rather than disaggregated, flows. Thus it is a good way of describing movement. Unfortunately, it is not a very good explanatory model because there is little theoretical basis for it, particularly the simple model, and because the distance exponent is difficult to interpret. However, it is a useful way of examining the movement of people, goods, and ideas, because it incorporates the frictional effect of distance.

Bibliography

Berry, B.J.L., *Geography of Market Centres and Retail Distribution* (Prentice-Hall, 1967)

Huff, D.L., 'A Probabilistic Analysis of Shopping Centre Trade Areas,' *Land Economics*, vol. 39, pp. 81–90 (1963)

Keeble, D.E., 'Employment Mobility in Britain', pp. 24–68 in Chisholm, M., and Manners, G., (eds.), *Spatial Policy Problems of the British Economy* (Cambridge University Press, 1971)

Olsson, G., *Distance and Human Interaction: A Review and Bibliography* (Regional Science Research Institute, Philadelphia, 1965)

Essay questions

1. Suppose that you were given data concerning the origin and destination of all goods deliveries made recently during a 7-day period in your home region. Suggest a project in which this information could be used and explain in detail how you would go about it. (Oxford and Cambridge, 1975)
2. Show how changes in methods of transport have affected retail trading patterns in urban areas. (Oxford and Cambridge, 1973)
3. 'Although in principle gravity formulae appear to offer simple and effective guides to predicting movement between areas, in practice they meet a number of difficulties.' (Haggett) Discuss. (University College, London)
4. The table and diagram opposite show the number of telephone calls between six neighbouring towns, the distance apart of the towns, and an 'interaction' index derived from the formula:

   Population of place i multiplied by the population of place j, divided by the distance apart of places i and j, which can be more simply written

$$\frac{P_i P_j}{D_{ij}}$$

   What geographical relationships do these data reveal? (Oxford and Cambridge, 1973)

to town		A			B			C		
population		30			80			60		
from town	population (in thousands)	telephone calls	distance apart	interaction index	telephone calls	distance apart	interaction index	telephone calls	distance apart	interaction index
A	30	–	–	–	193	42	57	95	45	40
B	80	142	42	57	–	–	–	1325	8	600
C	60	103	45	40	1560	8	600	–	–	–
D	30	49	59	16	271	19	126	470	14	129
E	50	60	71	21	410	29	138	195	28	107
F	40	38	73	16	240	40	80	110	45	53

to town		D			E			F		
population		30			50			40		
from town	population (in thousands)	telephone calls	distance apart	interaction index	telephone calls	distance apart	interaction index	telephone calls	distance apart	interaction index
A	30	75	59	16	54	71	21	162	73	16
B	80	340	19	126	350	29	138	190	40	80
C	60	295	14	129	310	28	107	135	45	53
D	30	–	–	–	160	16	94	35	43	28
E	50	230	16	94	–	–	–	203	33	61
F	40	72	43	28	160	33	61	–	–	–

Source: adapted from Abler, R., Adams, J.S., and Gould, P., *Spatial Organization* (Prentice-Hall, 1971)

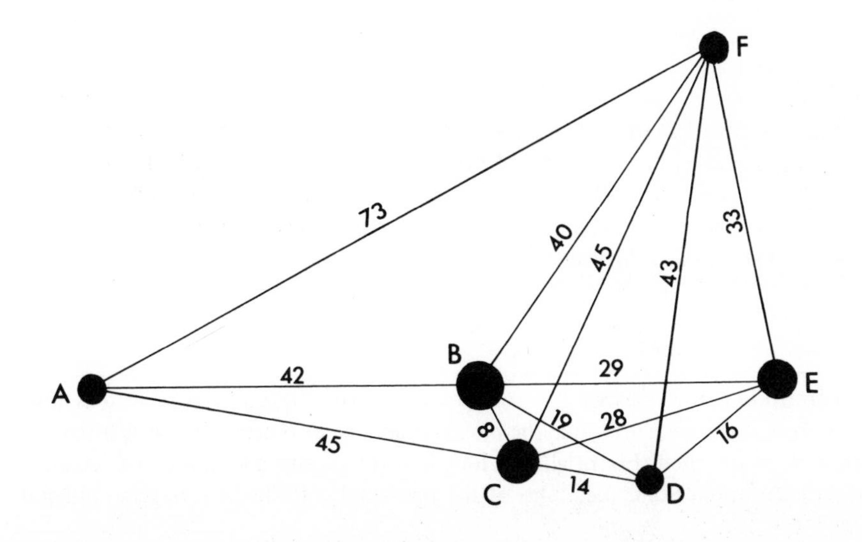

Chapter 9

Movement in space over time: diffusion

Introduction and link

The preceding chapter studied movement between places within a given time period. This chapter examines the movement of new ideas and people within an area over a number of time periods. Time and change are key factors. The chapter is concerned with the nature of changes in distributions over time, rather than distributions at any given time, the main interest of Section 1.

Although some works by historical geographers have studied spatial change through time, few have combined the depth of research and originality of content that is displayed in *Innovation Diffusion as a Spatial Process* by Torsten Hägerstrand. Hägerstrand, a Swedish geographer, published this work in 1953. It was translated in 1967. As well as describing the spatial stages in the spread of a number of new ideas and techniques, Hägerstrand constructed a series of Monte Carlo simulation models of the spread. In **simulation** procedures the researcher sets up a model of a real situation, and by experimenting on the model, gains a better understanding of the situation and a closer approximation to it in the output of the model. The **Monte Carlo technique** of simulation incorporates a chance element. The working of the model is akin to the spinning of a roulette wheel. Hägerstrand was the first social scientist to put such models to extensive use. He was also one of the first geographers to introduce the random element, or chance, into the study of geography. Both the aim and methods of his work were thus relatively new to geography.

Main aim

The main aim is to examine the nature of the process of spatial change. How does an idea (innovation) once introduced become widespread in an area? By examining maps of the distribution of an accepted idea at successive time periods, the main objective of 'gaining an understanding of **distributional changes** between close points in time' can be achieved.

Basic definitions and principles

An **innovation** is the successful introduction of ideas or artifacts, perceived as new, into a given social system. It may be based on an idea or prototype that is invented, borrowed, or imitated. Essentially, as long as it is recognized as new in a given area, it is an innovation. Some examples of the innovations studied by Hägerstrand and later authors are T.B. control in cattle, grazing-improvement subsidies, building societies, and television stations and sets. Population migration is rather different, but the introduction of a new person into an area is analogous to that of an idea, and may be treated in the same way as an innovation.

Diffusion is the process whereby the innovation is gradually adopted by more and more people through time and space. It can best be represented by a series of maps of an area at successive points of time, displaying those people who have adopted the innovation. The first map would show the initial innovator(s), the **leaders**, the second would add the first set of **adopters**, the third a further set, and so on until all the eventual adopters are shown (Figs. 9.1a–9.1d).

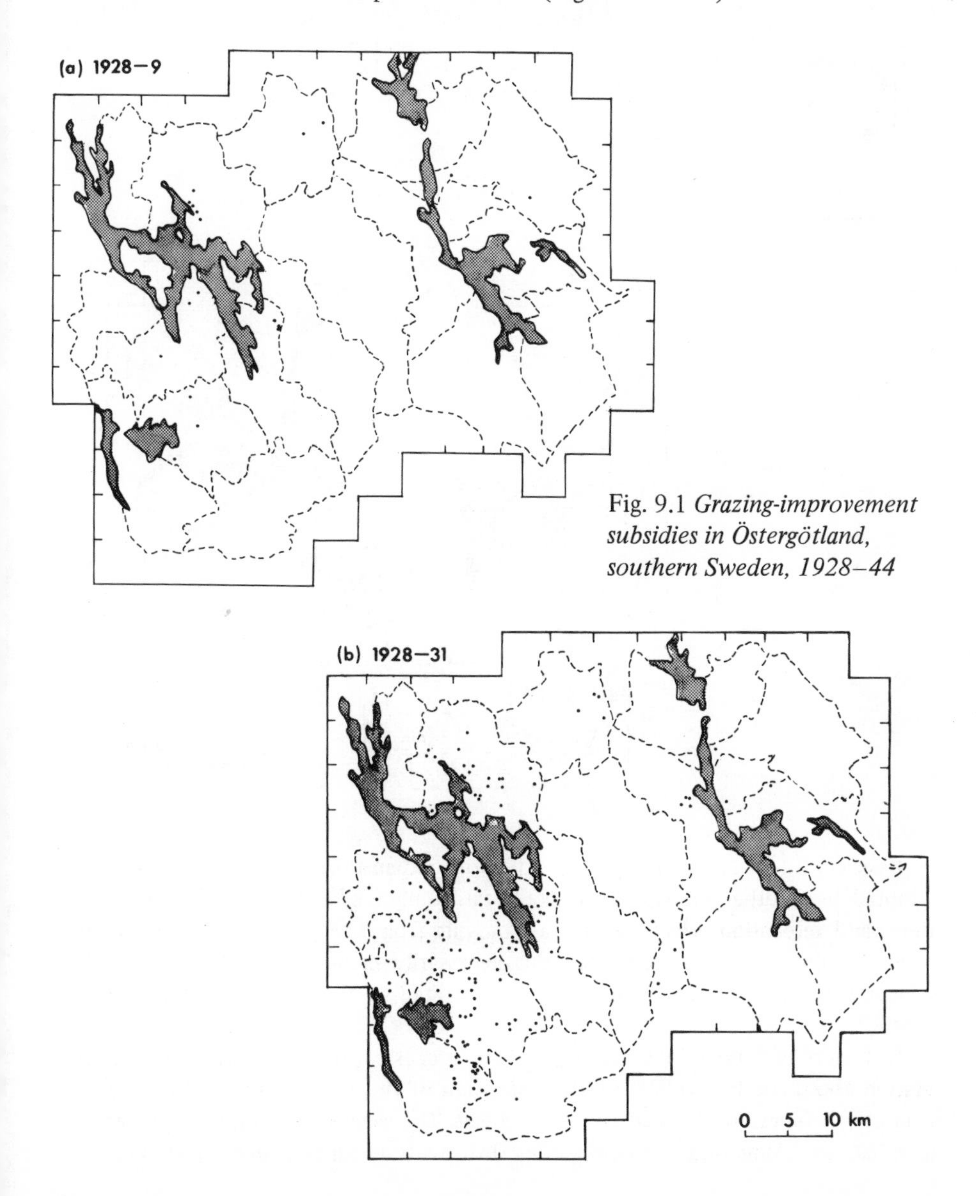

Fig. 9.1 *Grazing-improvement subsidies in Östergötland, southern Sweden, 1928–44*

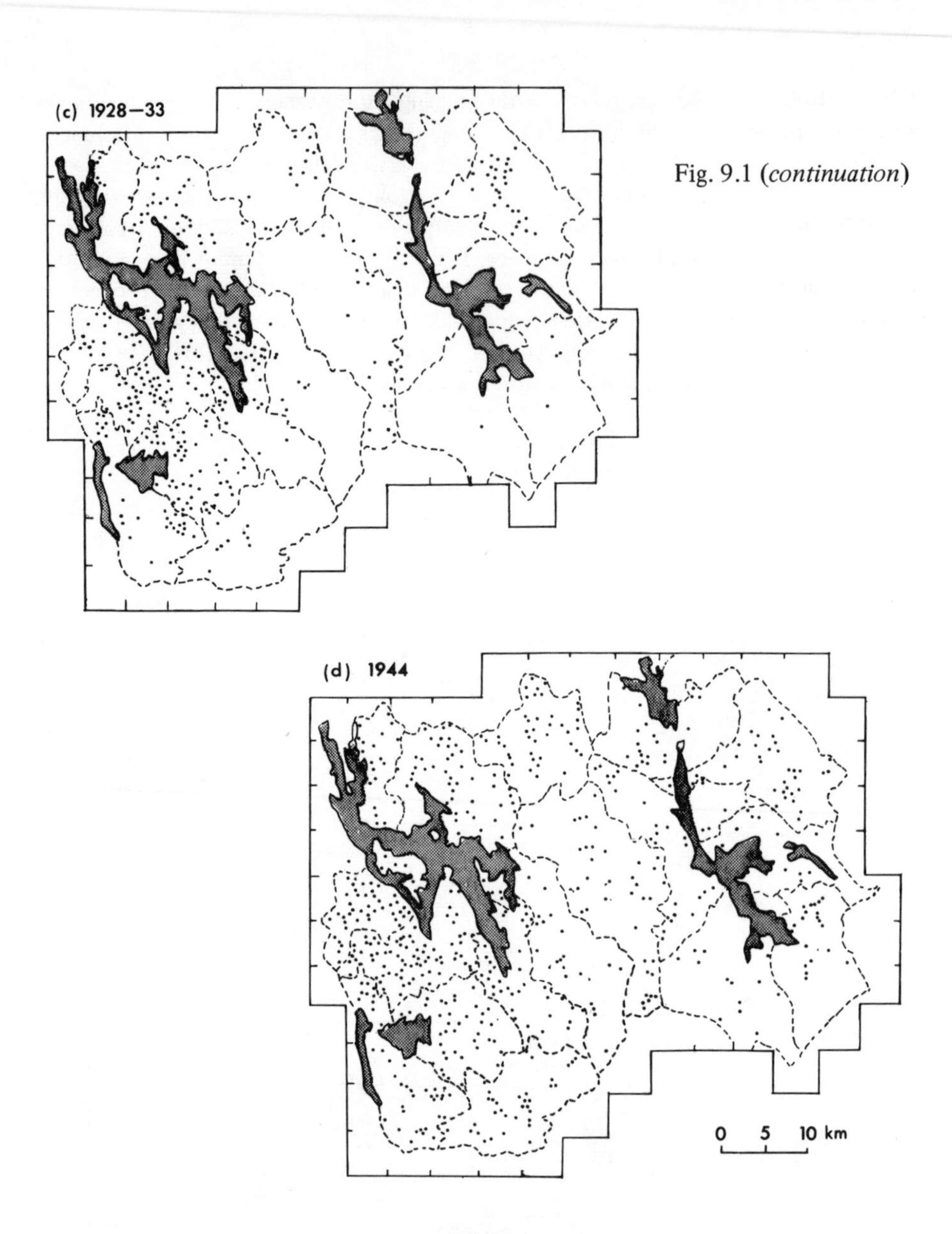

Fig. 9.1 (*continuation*)

Basically there are two types of diffusion: **expansion**, where the innovation is adopted by another individual, so the total number of adopters is growing over time; and **relocation**, where people are moving from one place to another, so the total population of adopters does not necessarily increase. Hägerstrand's model concerns the former. The latter will be illustrated by the spread of a city's black ghetto.

Diffusion of innovations consists of two processes: the **dissemination of information** about the innovation and the **adoption** of the innovation. The first process is largely a function of social communication. The second is a complex process of learning, accepting, and decision-making. Information can be communicated in two

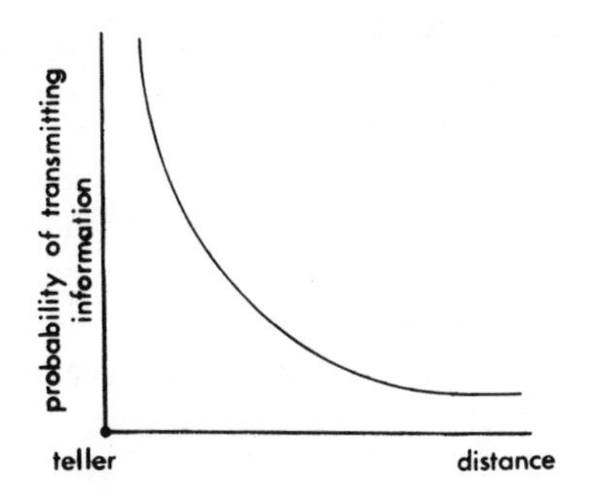

Fig. 9.2 *Probability of transmitting information in relation to distance*

ways: public, for example published material and mass media; or private, for example letter or word of mouth. The latter often seems to be more important from the viewpoint of adoption, even when information disseminated by the mass media is received. Thus the geographical character of interpersonal communication is an important factor in the diffusion of innovations.

The spatial extent of the contacts that a person has made in a given period is called a person's **information field**. By analysing short-distance migration and telephone calls, Hägerstrand depicted indirectly the structure of private information fields. He concluded that, on average, the density of contacts included in a person's private information field must decrease rapidly with increasing distance. Thus the probability of information being transmitted from an adopter to a potential adopter declines with distance (Fig. 9.2). The generalization of these fields for a group of similar people is called the **mean information field**. The process whereby future adoption is more likely to occur around existing adopters is called the **neighbourhood effect**. It is a key geographical process in diffusion.

Characteristically, the degree of acceptance of innovations over time follows a logistic function (S-shaped curve, Fig. 9.3) with three stages of adoption:

1. at first very slowly,
2. increases rapidly, and then
3. tails off as most of the population has accepted the innovation (towards saturation).

Fig. 9.3 *Adoption of innovations over time*

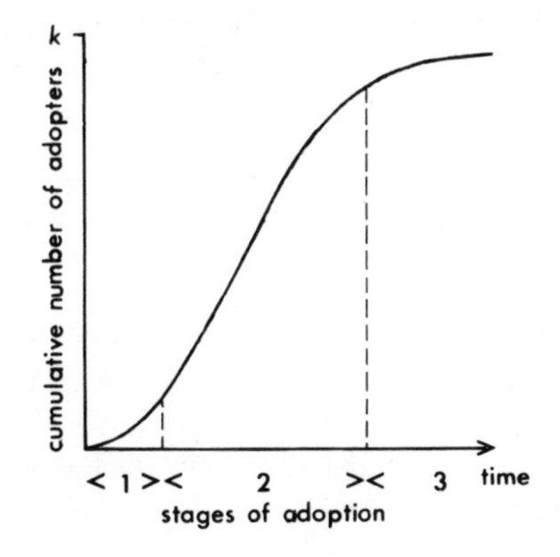

logistic function $p = \frac{k}{1 + ae^{-bt}}$

p proportion of adoptions at time t

k eventual maximum number of adopters

a constant

e 2·718

b rate of adoption

The rate of adoption depends upon the speed of information dissemination, and the degree of resistance in the population to the innovation.

The final principle, then, is that of resistance in the population to innovation, or the **barrier effect** as it is known. Although people might be informed of an innovation, they may not adopt it immediately for various economic, psychological, and social reasons. For example, they may not have the requisite capital. They may be averse to taking risks. They may not trust the judgement of their informant. Eventually adoption may occur, for example, when enough capital has been accumulated, or where the information has been received from a more reliable source. The degree of resistance in a population affects the speed, and indirectly the geographical pattern, of the diffusion. In relocation situations where people, rather than ideas, are diffusing, barriers can be physical or social features: for example the Appalachians served as a barrier to the movement west of settlers in the U.S.A., and poor whites who cannot afford to move act as a barrier to the in-migration of blacks within cities.

Author's assumptions, model, and example

Hägerstrand employed the Monte Carlo simulation technique in a probabilistic model. He was not interested in which particular individuals adopt, but in the general patterns of diffusion over time. Given certain conditions in his model, chance determines which individual accepts the innovation. Chance then replaces a set of factors which are not taken into account. The random or chance element is introduced by means of published 'random number tables'. In these, all the digits from 0 to 9 are in an unsystematic order. Each digit has an equal chance of being selected anywhere in the table. A sequence of such numbers was used in the three models that Hägerstrand proposed; in the first model to select the adopter, and in the second and third to select the relative location of the next person to receive the information from an existing adopter. Maps were drawn of the simulated diffusion at regular time intervals and compared with maps of actual change. Each successive model incorporated amendments to bring about a closer approximation to observed reality. He made comparisons with a number of observed innovation diffusions in Östergötland, a province in southern Sweden between Lake Vätter and the Baltic. The maps (Figs. 9.1a–9.1d) show one of his examples, the diffusion of grazing-improvement subsidies granted by the Swedish government from 1928 onwards.

In his theoretical models Hägerstrand made the familiar initial assumptions:

1. an even population density on a uniform plain, and
2. the information about the innovation was received in the same form by everyone. People were either informed or not.

In his **model I,** all 2430 people were informed at once by public communication, and adoptions occurred independently of one another in a random order of precedence. Information receipt meant immediate adoption. Each person was given a number and assigned to a cell in the model area. Cell 1 contained individuals 0–29; cell 2, 30–59; etc. (Fig. 9.4 right). The order in which the innovation was accepted

Fig. 9.4 *Model I: diffusion pattern after 50 adoptions*

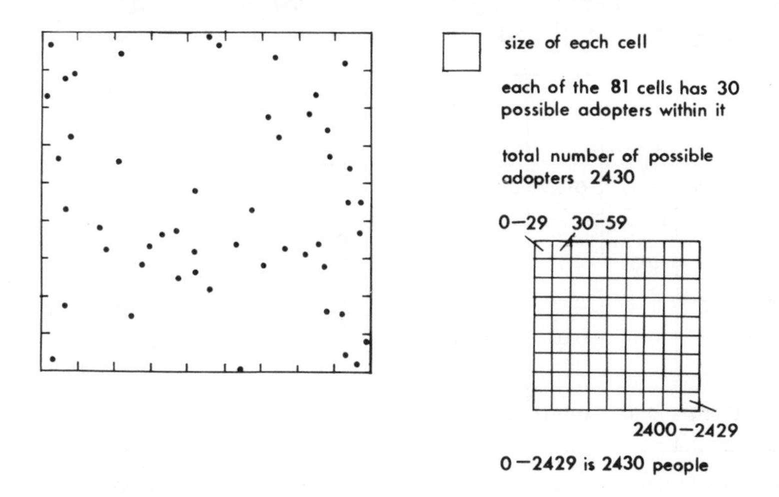

was determined by numbers drawn from random number tables. When the person's number was selected, an adoption was recorded in the appropriate cell. Fig. 9.4 shows the model area after 50 adoptions. The process produced a random or haphazard distribution of acceptance. Note that even with this purely chance-based process, there appear to be regional groupings which a geographer might fallaciously attempt to interpret, for example the south-central area.

In **model II** Hägerstrand tried to achieve the clustered pattern that occurred in reality, especially during the middle stage of adoption (stage 2, Fig. 9.3). Information was spread via private channels, and communications took place at constant intervals of time. Initially only one person was informed of the innovation. He was located at the centre of the study area. The neighbourhood effect, the principle that the probability of information transmission declines with distance, was introduced to govern the spread of information. So in this model adoptions did not occur independently of one another over time. A mean information field derived from empirical observation was made into a matrix of probabilities (Fig. 9.5a) which was centred over an existing adopter or 'teller'. The probability of the teller informing other people in his cell was, in this example, 0·3 (3 chances in 10). In the cells more distant from him, the probability of being informed declined, reflecting the neighbourhood effect. Digits from 0–999 were distributed in the matrix according to these probabilities (Fig. 9.5b). By drawing from random number tables, the cell location of the next adopter was found. If 700 was drawn, the adopter was situated in the cell to the east of the teller (Fig. 9.5b). Once having located the cell, drawing from another set of random numbers 0–29 identified which particular person of the 30 in the cell would adopt. In the next time period (generation) the mean information field was re-centred over the new adopter, and the next adopter similarly found via the mean information field. In each time period, the mean information field was centred over each teller in turn, and the new adoptions recorded on the model area map (Fig. 9.6, after 60 adoptions).

It must be noted that there were two different cell systems. One was the model

Fig. 9.5 *Mean information field*
The sum total of numbers in a cell divided by the total number of digits equals the cell probability, for example $\frac{300}{1000}$ = 0·3 (note 0–999 is 1000 numbers)

0·001	0·002	0·02	0·002	0·001
0·002	0·05	0·1	0·05	0·002
0·02	0·1	0·3	0·1	0·02
0·002	0·05	0·1	0·05	0·002
0·001	0·002	0·02	0·002	0·001

(a) *matrix of probabilities*

0	1 – 2	3 – 22	23 – 24	25
26 – 27	28 – 77	78 – 177	178 – 227	228 – 229
230 – 249	250 – 349	350 – 649	650 – 749	750 – 769
770 – 771	772 – 821	822 – 921	922 – 971	972 – 973
974	975 – 976	977 – 996	997 – 998	999

(b) *matrix of associated random numbers*

area with 30 people in each cell. The other was the mean information field matrix which shifted about in relation to the former, as it was centred over each model area cell containing a teller. Occasionally a teller would, by random numbers, inform himself of the innovation. In this meaningless situation, another person in his cell was randomly selected. More often a teller would inform an existing adopter. This could have happened in reality. It slowed down the dissemination of the information. Finally, since different sets of random numbers yield different results, the outcomes of the process were somewhat different every time the model was run. However, since the differences in the general pattern were slight, Hägerstrand regarded each run as representative of reality.

Although the results of model II were more realistic than those of model I, improvements could have been made by relaxing one assumption. In **model III**, it was not assumed that people accept an innovation upon initial contact with it. The principle of resistance to innovation or barriers was introduced. Five classes of

Fig. 9.6 *Model II: diffusion pattern after 6 generations giving 60 adoptions*

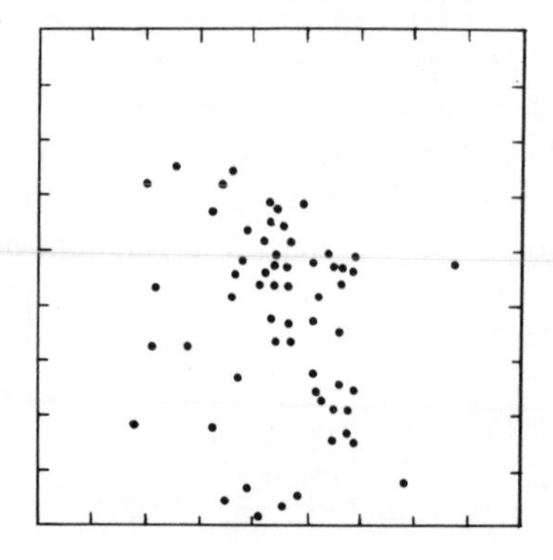

Fig. 9.7 *Model III: diffusion pattern after 52 generations giving 56 adoptions*

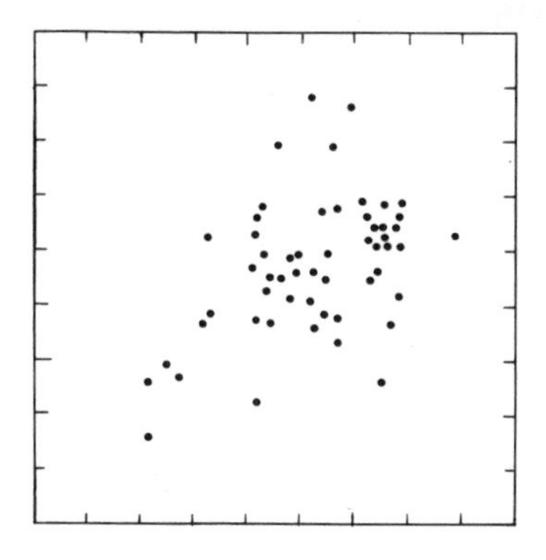

people were defined, with different degrees of resistance. Most people exhibited moderate resistance, while fewer displayed low or high resistance. The same frequency distribution of resistance was attributed to each cell from low to high, namely (for classes I–V respectively), 2, 7, 12, 7, 2 for a cell of 30 people. To represent resistance, a number of contacts needed to be made before acceptance. A person in class V, high resistance, needed five contacts before adoption occurred, while a person in class I adopted immediately. The introduction of this barrier effect accurately reproduced for the first time the slow ascent of stage 1 on the growth curve (Fig. 9.3). There were only 8 acceptances after 39 time intervals or generations. It also yielded a greater spatial concentration of acceptance (Fig. 9.7), similar to that empirically observed for grazing subsidies (Fig. 9.1). The similarity would never have been great because of the model's assumption of an even population distribution. However, by gradual amendment of his models, Hägerstrand was able to simulate a number of the basic characteristics of the empirically observed spatial and temporal distributions. He certainly demonstrated the importance of the neighbourhood and barrier effects.

Further principles

Hägerstrand later suggested another important geographical constituent of diffusion which had not been obvious from his scale of study. He observed that innovations were often adopted first in the capital city, then in the large towns, and eventually the smaller ones. The diffusion seemed to be down the hierarchy of cities (Chapter 1). Observations supported what the gravity model (Chapter 8) predicted: interaction is greater between larger cities. **Hierarchical diffusion** has become as important a geographical concept as the neighbourhood effect.

It has since been proposed that for many innovations the two effects are combined. Initial adoption occurs in the largest city. In the next time period the innovation moves down the hierarchy to the second tier, and by the neighbourhood effect to smaller towns located next to the largest city. For example, from London it might be adopted in Birmingham and Manchester by hierarchical diffusion, and in

Croydon and Hendon by neighbourhood effect. In the next period, acceptance further down the hierarchy would be accompanied by the operation of the neighbourhood effect around all the existing adopters.

Finally, the form of diffusion may be affected by the type of innovation. **Entrepreneurial innovations**, when adopted by a person, business, or institution, have direct consequences for people other than the adopter. **Household innovations** have an immediate impact on the adopting unit only. An example of an entrepreneurial innovation is a television station, while a television set is a household innovation. Entrepreneurial innovations are more likely to diffuse hierarchically, while household ones spread via the neighbourhood effect.

Examples

Relocation example

One of the most influential pieces of work on the movement of people over time has been Morrill's study of the expansion of the black **ghetto**. He outlined the characteristics of such areas in cities, concluding that 'inferiority in almost every conceivable material respect is the mark of the ghetto.' Three more factors may lead to the spread of the ghetto: the growth of the ghetto population, the expansion of the neighbouring central business district, and central city transport developments. He studied the nature of this expansion and observed the process of 'panic selling' by whites. He also observed that the proportion of white house-buyers climbed from less than 4 per cent adjacent to the ghetto itself to 100 per cent, only five to seven blocks away. Thus the role of proximity to a ghetto affects the nature of the house-buying. The real estate agent also encourages whites to sell on the edge of the ghetto and, if unscrupulous, can encourage 'panic selling' at deflated prices. Morrill therefore envisaged the spread of the black ghetto as a spatial diffusion process whereby the black is the active agent, and the white an agent of resistance or inertia. It appears that usually a black would have to try more than once to acquire a sale, or conversely the owner would have to be approached by more than one buyer.

Having observed this process, Morrill constructed a probabilistic simulation model, similar to that used by Hägerstrand, but where a migrant's move was analogous to an innovation adoption. It was probabilistic, that is, it involved chance, because he could predict only the expansion as a whole, and not the location of individual moves, for which he had insufficient knowledge. He emphasized that he did not expect his simulated patterns to match reality exactly. His main aim was to determine whether the predicted expansion was of the right extent and intensity.

The model itself assumed a natural increase of the black population of 5 per cent every two years; each would-be migrant behaved according to a migration probability field (mean information field) superimposed over his block. The probabilities reflected the decreasing likelihood of knowing about opportunities at greater and greater distances from home; thus there was a greater probability that a prospective migrant would have moved to adjacent blocks than to more distant ones. The

Fig. 9.8 *The simulated and actual expansion of Seattle's ghetto, 1950–60*

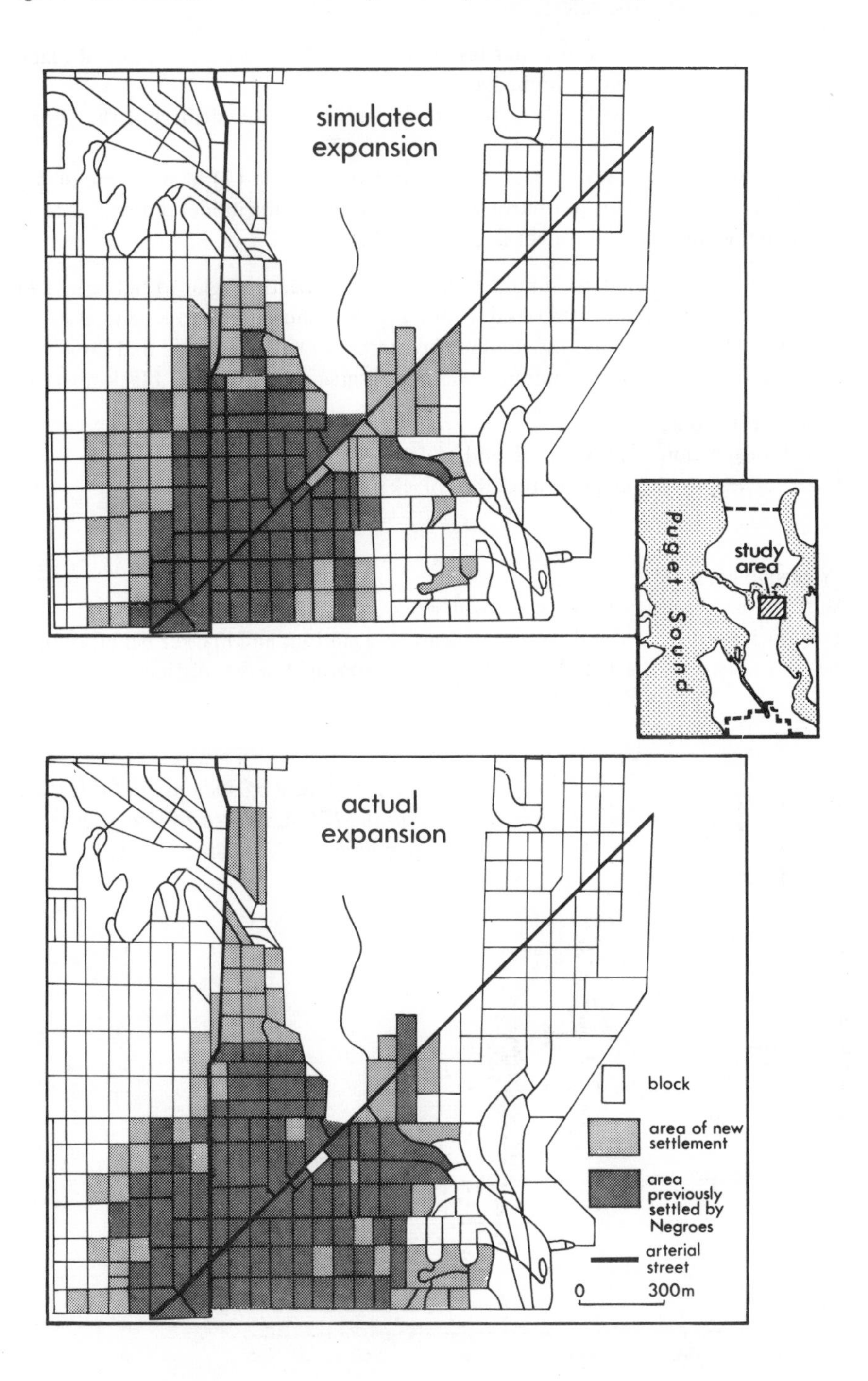

actual movements of a migrant were determined by drawing random numbers and according to three basic rules:

1. If the selected random number lay on a block which already contained blacks, then the move was made immediately.
2. If the block had no blacks within it, then no move was made but the contact was registered.
3. If another contact was made for the same block as in (2) in the same or next two-year period, then the move was made. Finally, the model put a limit to the number of families that might live in a block.

The model was used to simulate the growth of Seattle's ghetto between 1940 and 1950, and between 1950 and 1960. Fig. 9.8 shows the close general correspondence of the actual and the predicted patterns. Morrill concluded that three main factors were crucial in determining whether an area would receive black migrants:

1. proximity to ghetto,
2. high proportion of non-whites, and
3. acceptance by the neighbourhood of black entry.

Expansion example

Another piece of significant empirical work in the field of diffusion came from Berry in his study of the diffusion of television stations and market penetration by the TV industry in the U.S.A., 1940–68. Berry spotlighted two distinct, but related,

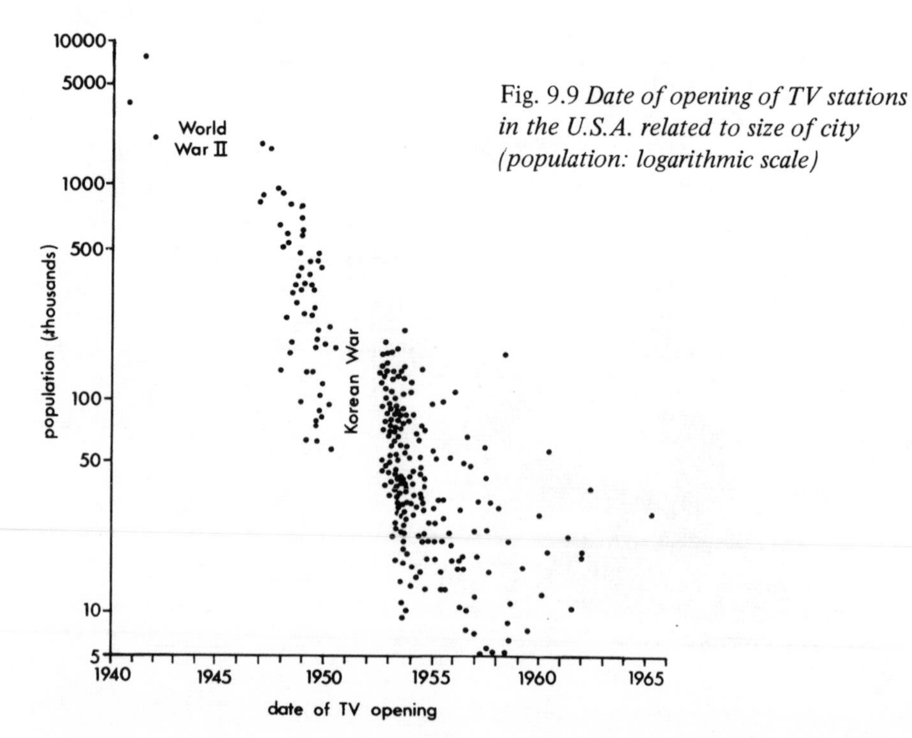

Fig. 9.9 *Date of opening of TV stations in the U.S.A. related to size of city (population: logarithmic scale)*

Fig. 9.10 *Percentage of households having TV sets, 1953*

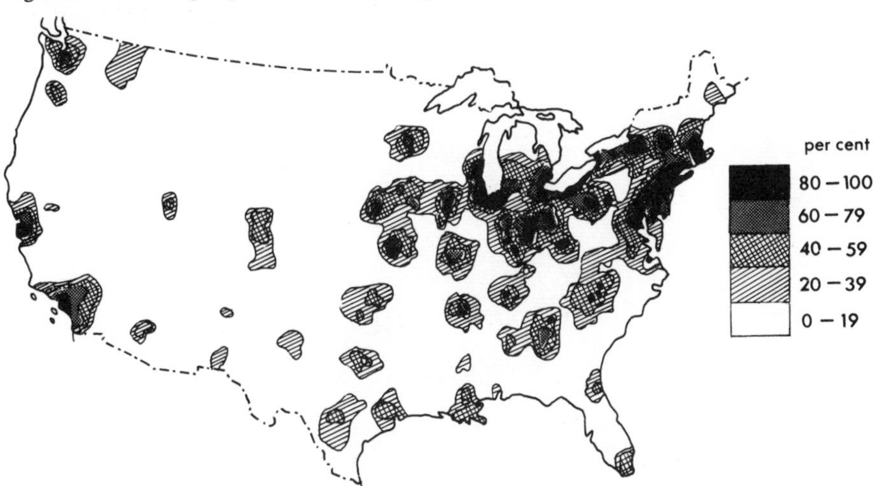

processes at work: entrepreneurial and household innovations. The opening of TV stations (entrepreneurial) since 1940 clearly indicated the Hägerstrand theory of hierarchical diffusion. The smaller the city, the later was the opening of its TV station, as the graph in Fig. 9.9 shows. The relationship between size of city and date of TV stations opening might well have been more perfect without the interrupting effect of the Korean war.

Similarly, from 1953 onwards Berry observed that the process of household adoption of sets declined with distance from the city with a TV station, and was greater in expanding high-income areas. It was retarded in communities of low income and of lower age levels (Figs. 9.10 and 9.11). Thus innovations are adopted more rapidly by larger cities (hierarchical diffusion), and the innovation spreads

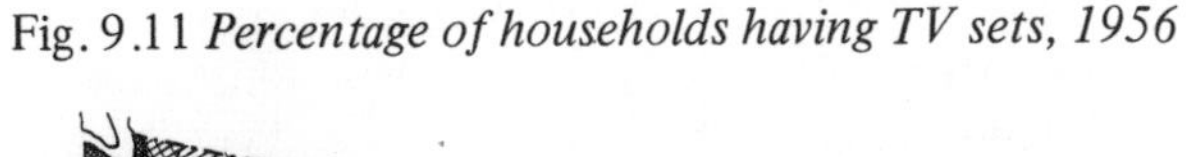
Fig. 9.11 *Percentage of households having TV sets, 1956*

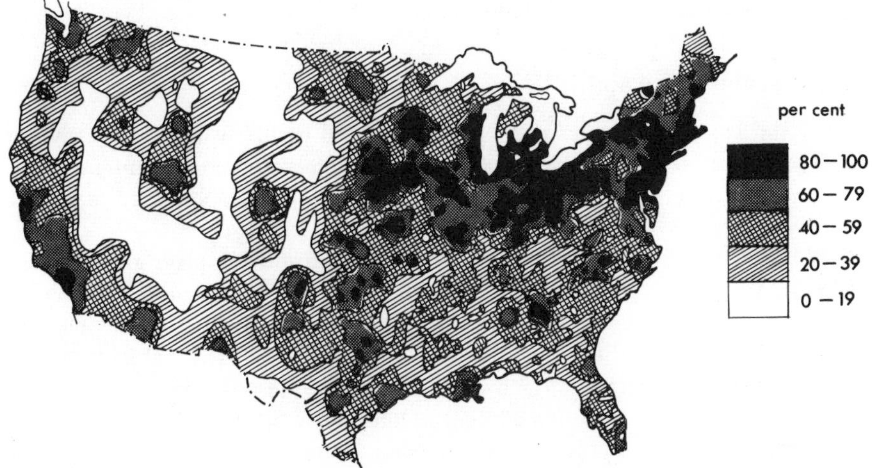

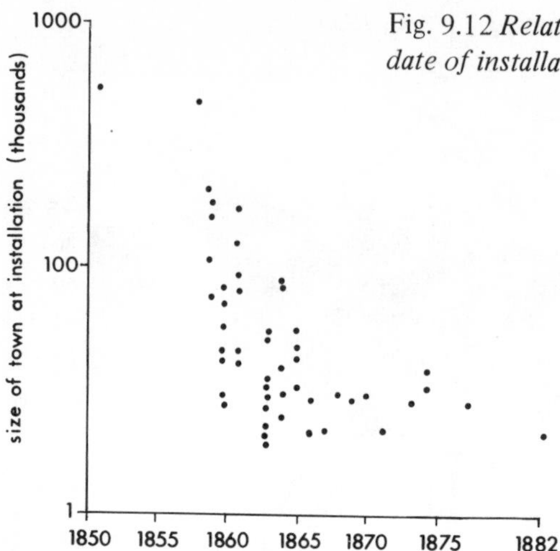

Fig. 9.12 *Relationship between city size and date of installation of street railways in the U.S.A.*

most readily to consumers living close to such adopting centres (neighbourhood effect). Hierarchical diffusion extends down to a critical city size, and then entrepreneurial innovation ceases. Household innovations also reach saturation level near adopting centres. The remaining unserved households are in those areas peripheral to the adopting hierarchy. From these findings, Berry suggested that diffusion theory can be a firm basis for a government's use of the growth centre idea, especially the likely impact of growth centres in peripheral declining zones (Chapter 12).

Similar processes have also been observed in the diffusion of building societies in Great Britain, whereby first the largest towns within a region adopted a building society, and subsequently adoption spread to other and smaller places within the region. The spread of telephone exchanges in the last quarter of the nineteenth century, as well as the spread of gasworks in the early nineteenth century, have diffused in a similar fashion. Finally, the timing of the installation of street railways in American towns shows a neat, but not perfect, relationship between population size and date of installation (Fig. 9.12).

Problems and applicability

Hägerstrand recognized many of the problems raised by his analysis. They involve the dependence on information transmission, and the simulation technique. More problems have emerged from the work of others, who have applied his ideas and methods less well.

For Hägerstrand, the receipt and acceptance of information plays a key role in diffusion, yet different interpretations of the information are ignored. Different individuals may perceive the same information in different ways. For example, the publicity campaigns on the recent innovation of the use of seat belts in cars are evaluated in quite different ways by different people, resulting in some adopters (seat-belt wearers) and some non-adopters. Other processes have been suggested as more significant than information transmission. Some postulate a **demonstration**

effect, where once an innovator has shown that an innovation works, others will adopt it. Agricultural pilot schemes in developing countries hope to use this effect, which, like information transmission, seems to reflect a decline in adoption with distance. Hägerstrand's agricultural innovations could be explained in this way.

Other forms of innovations, entrepreneurial ones, are more likely to reflect the minimization of risk, imitation, or profitability. The manufacture of a new product or adoption of a new process is less risky in a metropolis where there is a large labour pool and market potential, as well as a greater receptivity to change. Once successful, further adoption of the innovation is less risky, and production may follow in smaller cities by imitation. The role of contact and of communication is, in all these cases, less important.

Monte Carlo simulation was used because the problem was not suited to analytical methods. The method was criticized because many costly computer runs of the model are needed for the outputs to converge on a mean outcome which can be compared with reality. However, faster, more sophisticated computers and new mathematical methods are reducing the time and cost of diffusion research.

Some of the applications of the approach are demonstrated in the examples. Other diffusions that have been studied vary from innovations like the planned shopping centre to the spread of cholera in nineteenth-century U.S.A. In some cases little is learned from the simulation, since the information to be predicted is often used to establish the mean information field, for example the distance of immigrant moves to predict the spread of an immigrant ghetto. Hägerstrand, however, correctly measured the information field independently of the innovation. There has also been a tendency to apply the model to anything that is new, even though it might be a complex set of processes, like the factory system. In such cases information transmission is unlikely to be a key factor, since the message communicated would be so complex.

The effect of introducing time into the static models of Section 1 is immense. The neighbourhood effect and resistance to adoption suggest that optimum production will not occur in a given area because the necessary knowledge has not yet been diffused to it. Wolpert found that the difference between optimum and actual agricultural production in Sweden was particularly great far from the centre of innovation. It reflected the difference between 'optimiser' and 'satisficer' man, the latter having limited information (Chapter 3).

Although entrepreneurial innovations spread down the hierarchy of towns, they also act to change the hierarchy. Large cities obtain new processes first, often out of necessity because of their greater problems. Their much greater growth is permitted by innovations to the internal and external transport systems, for example underground trains and motorways. The neighbourhood effect around the large cities also means that nearby small centres receive an innovation much sooner than isolated centres of equal size, thus permitting their faster growth, and producing a change in the hierarchy.

Possibly as an indirect outcome of the neighbourhood effect, industry often locates near research institutes, which are frequently the source of innovations. Since these institutes typically cluster in or around areas of high amenities, particularly very large cities, this reinforces the growth of the cities.

Conclusion

Hägerstrand's excellent work is of major importance. As well as stimulating much research on innovations and diffusions, it has also directed attention to social communication networks and private information fields. There are many indirect insights which are worth noting. Geographers often attempt to explain a distribution (for example, vegetation type) at a given point in time by the distribution of other variables (for example, amount of rainfall and average temperature). Yet the similarity of the spatial distributions of two variables at one point in time does not necessarily indicate a functional or causal relationship. Hägerstrand demonstrated that a lot can be learned from the nature of the change in the distributions themselves. He also indicated the problems of drawing conclusions about the past from present distributions. For example, the point of maximum density of adoptions now is not necessarily the point of the initial innovation: secondary clusters often appear. He introduced the idea of chance into geographical studies. He suggested that many ingredients of individual human behaviour are causally so complex that their aggregate spatial expression is usually randomly determined within certain constraints, even though the decisions behind each individual's behaviour are not randomly motivated. This significant proposal underlies much recent research. Finally, his approach has also permitted the human geographer, in building simulation models, to gain insights through experimentation.

Bibliography

English, P.W., and Mayfield, R.C., *Man, Space, and Environment*, Section 4, 'Spatial Diffusion', (Oxford University Press, 1972)

Hägerstrand, T., *Innovation Diffusion as a Spatial Process*, translated by A. Pred (University of Chicago Press, 1967)

Hansen, N.M., *Growth Centres in Regional Economic Development* includes Berry, B.J.L., 'Hierarchical Diffusion', pp. 108–38 (Collier-Macmillan, 1972)

Morrill, R.L., 'The Negro Ghetto: Problems and Alternatives', *Geographical Review*, vol. 55 (1965)

Robson, B.T., *Urban Growth: An Approach* (Methuen, 1973)

Essay questions

1. Discuss the changing distributions of population within large modern cities. (See also Chapter 5.) (University College, London)
2. 'The key to development is innovation'. Examine the spatial implications of this statement. (Manchester University)
3. How significant are the additions which have been made to the theory of spatial diffusion since Hägerstrand's work in *Innovation Diffusion as a Spatial Process*? (Cambridge University)

Section 3

Growth and development

In Section 1 an even population distribution was assumed over a uniform plain on which resources were at first ubiquitous and later, under modified assumptions, localized. The models produced an uneven population distribution with a hierarchy of city sizes and variation in the density and type of population living within the cities. The discussion of transport systems and movement in Section 2 indicated that these would affect the characteristics of the cities and regions. In Section 1 time was not an important element in the models of spatial relationships. They were static rather than dynamic. Time was more important in Section 2 where the growth of networks and the diffusion of ideas and people were discussed. In this section time is a variable basic to all the models, since they involve growth and development. The section studies factors affecting the rate of growth of population, the relative growth of different types of economic activity, and the growth and spatial distribution of real income within a country.

The complexities of the topics examined in this section mean that only a few of the main theories and ideas can be presented. Consequently readers are recommended to refer to the bibliography at the end of each chapter for suggestions for further reading.

Chapter 10

Population change: Malthus's model

Introduction and link

The interest of geographers in the relationship between population and resources has long been established. It is reflected in the **ecological approach** to geography which centres on the relationship between man and his environment. At the beginning of Section 1 population was assumed to be evenly distributed and resources to occur ubiquitously. These assumptions are now completely relaxed so that the relationship between population and resources may be studied over both time and space.

Although geography has in the past paid much attention to population and resources, it has often considered their distributions somewhat independently, and rarely viewed their relationship over time. In this chapter, the main components of population change are defined and the factors affecting them discussed. In particular, some theories on the relationship between population and resources are outlined. Two of them regard the resources available at a given time as a 'ceiling' to population growth, while another sees population growth as a stimulus to the development of new techniques which will use resources more efficiently, thus permitting further population growth. Finally, a descriptive model of population growth is examined which is based on western experience in the past few centuries.

Such fundamental subjects as population and resources are not the concern of just the geographer. They are the focus of study in many other disciplines, including demography and economics. It is not surprising, then, to find that the basic ideas described below do not belong to geographers. The main theory discussed is that proposed by Thomas Robert Malthus in 1798 in his *Essay on the Principle of Population*, the first of seven editions. During his life (1766–1834) his employment ranged from curate to professor of history and political economy. Malthus's views are often misrepresented; their clear statement presents a basis for the discussion of a complex relationship. The more recent (1965) views of Ester Boserup, an agricultural economist, are presented to demonstrate an alternative view. A current sophisticated model, commissioned by the Club of Rome, is also described. The Club of Rome is an informal group of thirty individuals from ten countries which was formed in 1968 to discuss the present and future predicament of man. It commissioned an international team to undertake phase one of the 'predicament of mankind' study, and their initial findings were published in 1972 as *The Limits to Growth*.

Main aim

The models aim to describe changes in the size of an area's population, particularly in relation to the resources it has available at a given level of technology.

Principles

Before considering the models, it is necessary to introduce certain key demographic terms. **Crude birth-rate**, for instance, the most common index of fertility, is the ratio of the number of live births in a period of time, usually one year, to the total population, often at the mid-point of the year. It is expressed as the number of births per 1000 population. The measure is crude because it does not relate the events, in this case births, to the specific group of people who produce them. One measure that does is the **fertility-rate** (or child/woman ratio which relates the number of children under five to the number of women of reproductive age (usually 15–44).

The **crude death-rate** is the number of deaths per 1000 inhabitants, and it may be calculated for the population at the mid-point of the year or at the beginning of the year. A particularly important influence on the crude death-rate is the **infant mortality-rate** defined as:

$$\frac{\text{deaths at age 1 year or under}}{\text{live births}} \times 1000$$

Natural increase is usually determined by subtracting the crude death-rate from the crude birth-rate. To illustrate how the crude birth- and death-rates interact and affect natural increase and total population, the case of Taiwan in the twentieth century may be observed (Fig. 10.1).

Population growth in particular can be seen to be affected by two sets of factors. In Fig. 10.2, on the left, a **positive feedback loop** is demonstrated, showing that an increase (decrease) in births per year leads to an increase (decrease) in the number of parents, which in time increases (decreases) the number of births. A positive

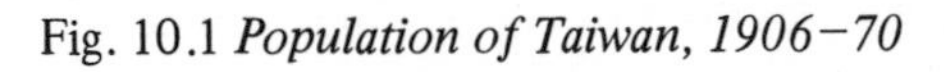
Fig. 10.1 *Population of Taiwan, 1906–70*

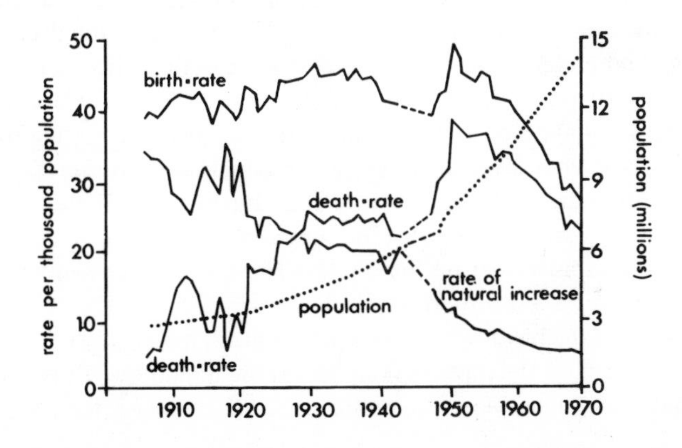

Fig. 10.2 *Positive and negative feedback loops*

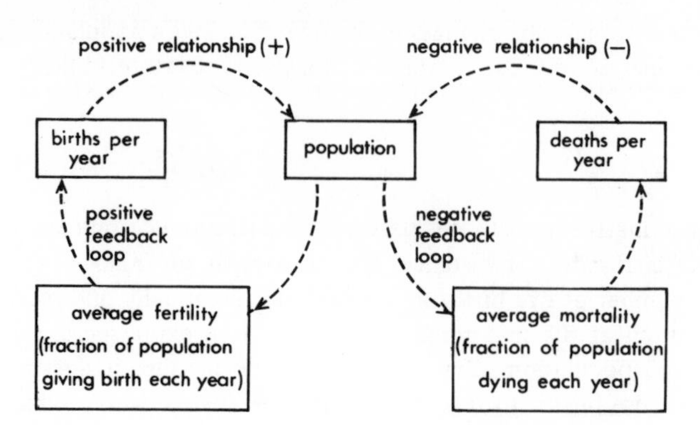

feedback loop then helps to accentuate change in either direction, leading to increased or decreased population. The **negative feedback loop**, on the other hand, regulates the population growth and holds the system in a more stable state. The initial change is somewhat counteracted: with a growth of population and a standard mortality-rate more deaths per year will result, thus reducing the initial increase in population. Both feedback loops act on populations with the thermostatic effect of negative feedback helping to control what in some circumstances can be the runaway growth of population.

Having defined the main terms of demography, the critical influences on the birth-rate and death-rate can now be assessed. A multitude of factors appear to affect the birth-rate. Race is one of these factors. In general, the highest fertility-rates are associated with mestizos (a mixture of white South Americans and Indians) and mulattoes (a mixture of whites and negros). Next in order come Asiatics, blacks, and then whites. Some religious communities tend to have high birth-rates, partly because they are generally opposed to contraception, for instance Catholics. Traditional customs, such as the age at and nature of marriage, also have an effect. Polygyny (one man with several wives) for instance, is sometimes associated with lower birth-rates than monogamy. Diet, climate, and health also influence birth-rates.

The other major group of factors which affect the birth-rate are those connected with economic and social development. In advanced countries, education is a major influence on the size of families, women have a larger role in the decisions related to family size, and children are looked after more carefully. Economic crises, such as the world depression of the 1930s, tend to lower birth-rates. Place of residence, whether town or countryside, is also important, the latter having the much higher birth-rates. Governments also can either encourage (Germany before the Second World War) or discourage (India today) a high birth-rate, and this has become a significant contemporary influence. The development of birth control has, of course, had the greatest effect on birth-rates. These and other factors combine to make the interpretation of birth-rates complex.

The evolution of the birth-rates in various countries has been studied and certain general trends observed. The most striking fact is the diminution of the birth-rate in developed countries. Some areas, such as Britain and Scandinavia, have had a declining birth-rate for a long time. Elsewhere, birth-rates have declined very rapidly (Japan because of government policy) or very gradually (traditional and developing parts of the Mediterranean and Eastern Europe). Rapid short-term rises in the birth-rate have occurred in opposition to the general trend, for example in the late 1940s and early 1950s in the U.S.A., France, and the United Kingdom.

As with the birth-rate, many factors influence the death-rate, such as sanitation, medical care, general living standards, and the age composition of the population. Three groups of countries may be distinguished at the present time according to their death-rates.

1. The first group (such as the U.K. and the U.S.A.) has had low death-rates for a long time and the rate diminishes only very slowly indeed.
2. The second group (such as Sri Lanka, the U.S.S.R., and Japan) has experienced in recent times a dramatic reduction in death-rates.
3. The third group includes much of the tropical world where death-rates remain high.

In particular countries, three stages in the evolution of the death-rate have been observed:

1. Death-rates are high for both rich and poor.
2. Medical advances enable the rich to have a much lower death-rate than the poor. This tends to coincide with the industrial revolution when the inequality between rich and poor is most marked.
3. Inequality between classes becomes much less as social legislation is introduced and death-rates in general are low.

The most important influence on the fall of the death-rate has been the drastic reduction in infant and adolescent mortality.

Malthus's theory

Malthus's theory is based on two principles:

1. In the absence of any checks, human populations could potentially grow at a **geometric rate**. They could double every twenty-five years.
2. Production from the land, even under the most favourable circumstances, could at best increase at an **arithmetic rate**.

Thus population could increase as the numbers 1, 2, 4, 8, 16 (geometric) while the means of subsistence increase as the numbers 1, 2, 3, 4, 5 (arithmetic). If the time intervals are twenty-five years, in a century the ratio of population to food production would be 16 to 5. Lack of food, then, is argued to be the principal ultimate check to population growth.

These principles state the potential, not actual growth, of population and production. In later editions of his essay, to justify principle (1), Malthus observed the growth of population (1790–1820) in North America, where there seemed at that time to be few checks on growth. Allowing for immigration, he estimated that the population was doubling every twenty-five years. This demonstrated the 'prodigious power of increase', that was being held in check in other countries.

Principle (2) reflects Malthus's view of land as the ultimate source of all material wealth. The means of subsistence could not increase as fast as potential population growth, because of 'scarcity of land' and 'the decreasing proportion of produce which must necessarily be obtained from the continual additions of capital applied to land already in cultivation' (diminishing returns, Chapter 2). Thus, 'the power of population is indefinitely greater than the power in the earth, to provide a subsistence for man.'

The limit to the amount of food produced created a 'ceiling' to the population growth in a given country. Malthus suggested preventive and positive checks as the two main ways by which population would be curbed once this ceiling had been reached.

As a rational being, man can consider the effects of his potential fertility and curb his natural instinct, the so-called 'passion between the sexes'. Thus **preventive checks** include abstinence from marriage or delay in the time of marriage. These reduce the fertility-rate. For example, Malthus and others noted a strong negative correlation between wheat prices and marriage-rates. Thus, as the demand for food began to exceed the supply, prices rose, and as a consequence the poor, in particular, postponed getting married (Fig. 10.3).

Positive checks, such as lack of food and clothing, diseases, war, and infanticide, directly affect mortality. The positive checks which arise from the laws of nature he called 'misery' and those which are brought about by man he called 'vice', leading often to misery.

Fig. 10.3 shows an example of two negative feedback loops whereby checks keep the population numbers oscillating around the means of subsistence. Malthus thus indicates that there is a total population beyond which further increase inevitably

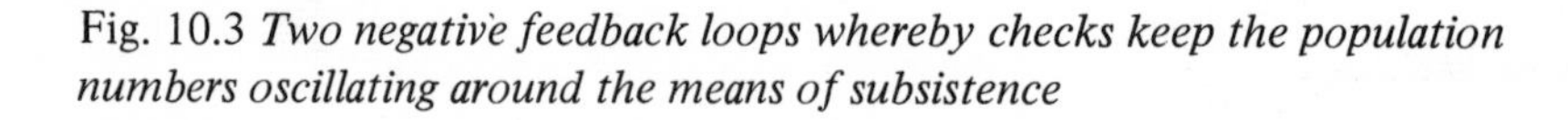

Fig. 10.3 *Two negative feedback loops whereby checks keep the population numbers oscillating around the means of subsistence*

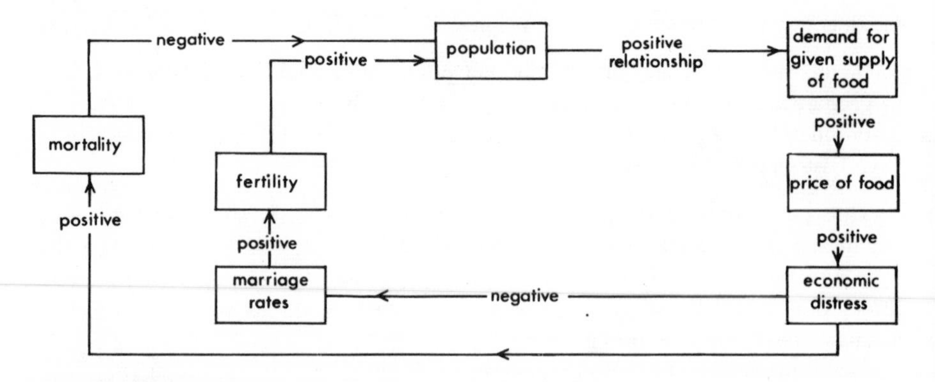

a positive relationship is when an increase (decrease) in one variable is associated with an increase (decrease) in the other
a negative relationship is when an increase (decrease) in one variable is associated with a decrease (increase) in the other

depresses living standards, and therefore an **optimum population** related to resources and level of technology must exist. At that time he regarded North America's population as well below that limit, so that its population was growing rapidly with few checks. Other countries seemed closer to the limit, and positive and preventive checks, perhaps with varying emphases, were operating.

Other writers have discussed the concept of an optimum population in more detail, and have indicated **overpopulated** and **underpopulated** areas (greater than and less than the optimum). However, the optimum population of a given area is extremely difficult to identify. It may be related to economic criteria so that it becomes the number which allows the maximum real income per capita for a given level of technology. It may also be viewed in terms of social welfare and military power. Certainly it may vary over time for a given area as technology improves and social attitudes change.

Other models

Boserup's theory

The essence of Boserup's ideas may be stated briefly. Whereas Malthus thought that food supply limited population size, Boserup suggested that in a pre-industrial society an increase in population stimulated a change in agricultural techniques so that more food could be produced. Her ideas may be summarized by the old saying 'necessity is the mother of invention'. Population growth has thus enabled agricultural development to occur.

She examined different land-use systems which were classified according to their intensity of production. This was measured by the frequency of cropping. At one extreme was the forest fallow associated with shifting cultivation. At its least intensive any one piece of land would be used less than once every hundred years. At the other extreme were multiple-cropping systems which yielded more than one harvest a year. She suggested that there was a close connection between the agricultural techniques used and the type of land-use system. For example, the axe and digging stick were associated with forest fallow, the hoe with bush fallow, and the plough with short fallow where fields were left uncultivated for two or more years.

She considered that any increase in the intensity of production by the adoption of new techniques was unlikely, unless population increased. If population increased beyond a certain point and no extra land were available, in order to maintain the same level of consumption per capita the length of fallow would have to be shortened, leading to a decline in soil fertility and output per man hour. In these circumstances of population growth, the new techniques would be advantageous, and therefore adopted. Thus population growth led to agricultural development and the growth of the food supply.

Boserup's thesis was based on the idea that people knew of the techniques required by a more intensive system. When the population grew, they then became willing to adopt them. If knowledge of the techniques was not available, then she recognized that the agricultural system would regulate the population size in a given area. She may be criticized for describing agricultural systems simply in terms of intensity of production, because different types of system occur at a given intensity. However, her basic thesis that population growth necessitates agricultural development, is a useful contrast to that of Malthus.

A similarly contrasting view to Malthus was held by Durkheim, a French sociologist. He contended that an increase in population density leads to a greater division of labour which allows greater productivity to be attained. Indeed, he even suggested that population pressure is necessary in order that an increasing division of labour occurs.

The Limits to Growth model

The *Limits to Growth* study examined the five basic factors that determine and therefore ultimately limit growth on this planet: population, agricultural production, natural resources, industrial production, and pollution. Many of these factors were observed to grow at an **exponential rate**. A quantity exhibits exponential growth when it increases by a constant percentage of the whole in a constant time period. The authors neatly illustrate exponential growth by considering the growth of a patch of lilies in a pond. The patch doubles in area every day. When the pond is half covered by lilies, the gardener has, in fact, only one day left to clear them before the pond is totally covered. This illustration emphasizes the apparent suddenness with which the exponential growth of a phenomenon approaches a fixed limit. It also demonstrates the very short period of time within which corrective action can be taken. If the predicted growth of world population (Fig. 10.4) is correct, it suggests an alarmingly short space of time for such preventive action to be implemented.

Having explored the nature of exponential growth especially in world population and industrial output, the team examined the various **limits** to such growth. These they classified into two types:

1. physical necessities that support all physiological and industrial activity, for instance food, raw materials, and fossil and nuclear fuels, and
2. (much more difficult to quantify), social necessities such as peace, social stability, and education.

The components of a world model were discussed, and then the model was run to see the effects on the five basic factors mentioned earlier. The first and standard run of the model was based on the assumption that in future no great changes in human values nor in the functioning of the global system as it has operated for a hundred years would occur. This is illustrated in Fig. 10.4.

In essence, collapse of the system occurs well before 2100 because of a resource crisis. As the team expressed it, 'We can thus say with some confidence that, under the assumption of no major change in the present system, population and industrial growth will certainly stop within the next century, at the latest.'

The model was then compared with the standard run by incorporating other assumptions, for instance a more optimistic estimate of the global stock of resources. Also various stabilizing policies were introduced to the model with the aim of achieving the **state of global equilibrium**.

Fig. 10.4 *The world model proposed by the* Limits to Growth *team*
The 'standard' world model run assumes no major change in the physical, economic, or social relationships that have historically governed the development of the world system. All variables plotted here follow historical values from 1900 to 1970. Food, industrial output, and population grow exponentially until the rapidly diminishing resource base forces a slowdown in industrial growth. Because of natural delays in the system, both population and pollution continue to increase for some time after the peak of industrialization. Population growth is finally halted by a rise in the death-rate due to decreased food and medical services.

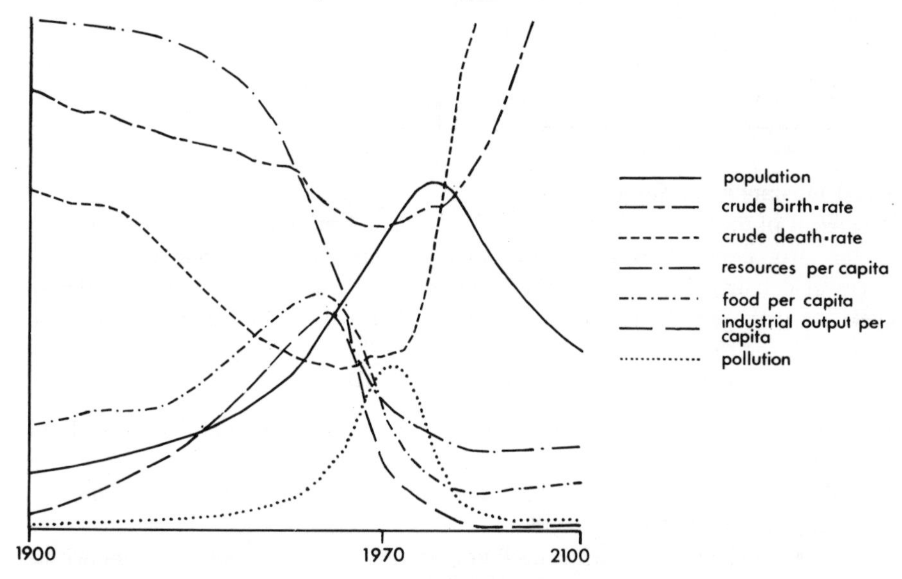

The conclusions reached by the group as a result of this work were:

1. 'If the present growth trends in world population, industrialization, pollution, food production, and resource depletion continue unchanged, the limits to growth on this planet will be reached sometime within the next one hundred years. The most probable result will be a rather sudden and uncontrollable decline in both population and industrial capacity.'
2. 'It is possible to alter these growth trends and to establish a condition of ecological and economic stability that is sustainable far into the future. The state of global equilibrium could be designed so that the basic material needs of each person on earth are satisfied and each person has an equal opportunity to realize his individual human potential.'
3. 'If the world's people decide to strive for this second outcome rather than the first, the sooner they begin working to attain it, the greater will be their chances of success.'

They stress that in order to survive, the world must undergo a period of great transition from growth to global equilibrium.

Much of this – including the title, of course – is remarkably reminiscent of Malthus's predictions of doom.

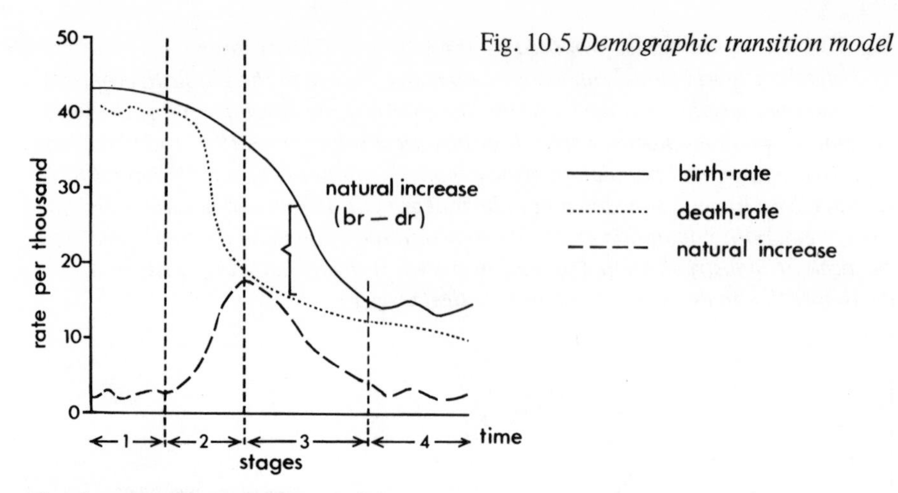

Fig. 10.5 *Demographic transition model*

The demographic transition model

As a result of the historical study of birth-rates and death-rates and the relationships of the two, populations of specific countries seem to have undergone distinct stages in demographic growth. These stages are usually known as the **population cycle** or **demographic transition**. Essentially this model is based on European experience and therein lies its weakness.

The stages are best related to the diagram (Fig. 10.5):

1. High stationary stage, with high fertility and mortality, and only slow growth or a stationary population.
2. Early expanding stage, with high fertility and declining mortality causing a rapidly increasing rate of growth.
3. Late expanding stage, with declining fertility and mortality and increasing population.
4. Low stationary stage, with low fertility and mortality causing a fairly stationary population.

These stages are well illustrated by the experience of England and Wales (Fig. 10.6). Some writers have even suggested that there is a declining fifth stage, as a result of fertility falling below mortality.

Different parts of the world can be observed at different stages.

Stage 1. These inevitably tend to be the less developed countries and therefore data are less forthcoming and reliable. Parts of tropical Africa and some parts of south-east Asia still approximate to this primitive stage.

Stage 2. This includes almost all the countries of Africa, the Middle East, and eastern Asia, as well as some moderately developed Latin American countries, for example Paraguay and Argentina. Some would argue that between one-half and two-thirds of the world's population is in this category.

Stage 3. The U.S.S.R. is a good example of this, where the birth-rate is a moderate figure but the death-rate is now quite low.

Stage 4. This includes most Western European countries where for quite a considerable time both birth-rates and death-rates have been low.

Fig. 10.6 *Birth-rates and death-rates for England and Wales, 1721–1971*

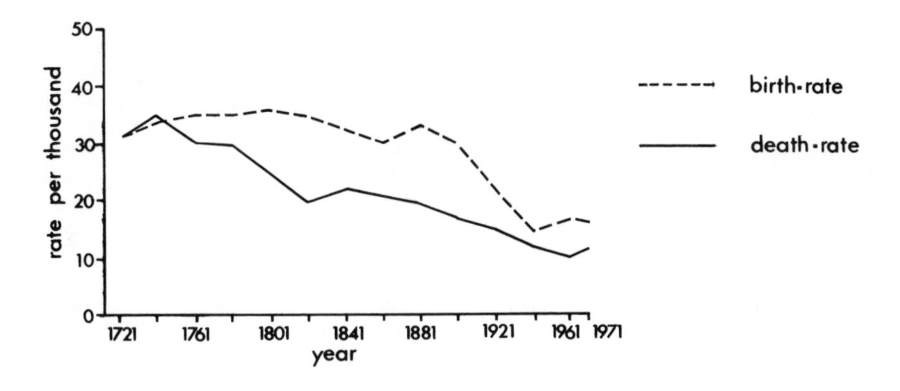

Fig. 10.7 *Typical population pyramids and three actual population structures*

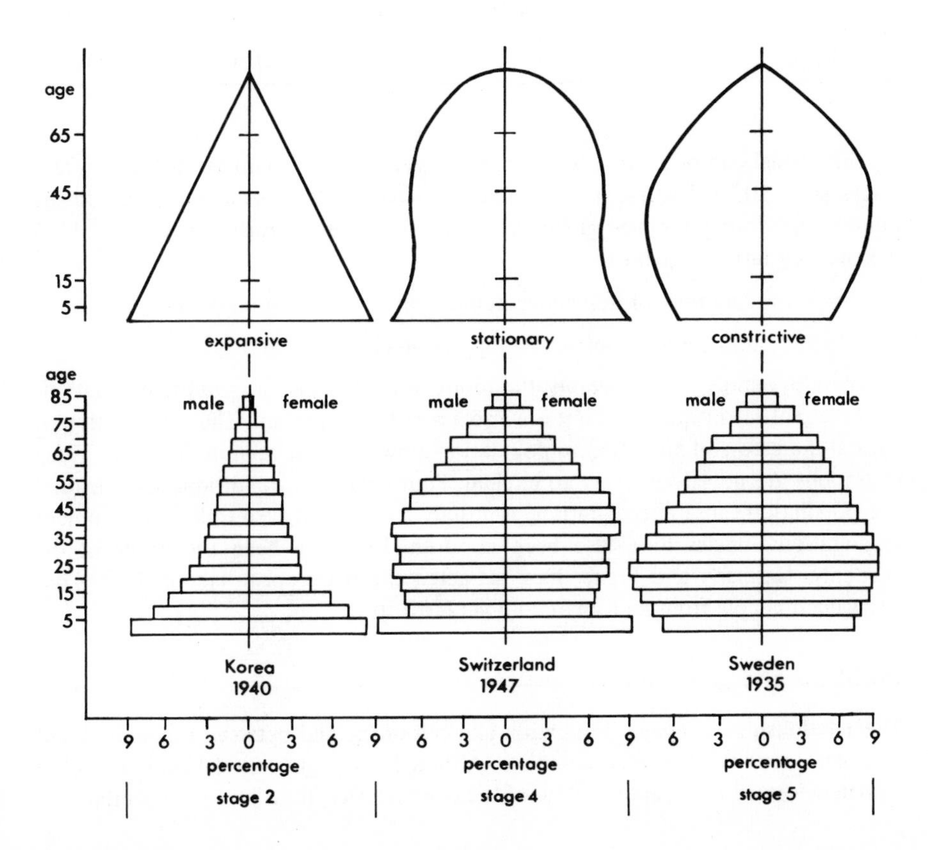

Fig. 10.8 *Natural increase and migration for selected countries (1950–70)*

country	increase in population (thousands)			ratio of net migration to total increase (percentage)
	total	from natural increase	from net migration	
Western Europe	26 176	17 428	8748	33·4
Austria	488	591	–103	–21·1
France	9407	6149	3258	34·6
Germany, Federal Republic	10 732	5952	4780	44·5
Netherlands	2863	2913	–50	–1·7
Northern Europe	8389	9087	–698	–8·3
Irish Republic	–14	544	–588	
Sweden	1026	729	297	28·9
United Kingdom	5373	5554	–181	–3·4
Southern Europe	14 742	20 761	–6019	–40·8
Portugal	1156	3108	–1952	–168·9
North America	61 457	52 759	8698	14·2
Canada	7689	5887	1802	23·4
United States	53 768	46 872	6896	12·8
Oceania	5247	3390	1857	35·4
Australia	4295	2583	1712	39·9

This model can be related to the age/sex pyramids of countries at the different stages (Fig. 10.7). The expansive pyramid of stage 2 shows a large increase in the number of young people, giving a higher **dependency ratio** than stage 1. A dependency ratio is equal to:

$$\frac{\text{number of non-active population (0–14, 65 and over)}}{\text{number of active population (15–64 years)}}$$

These pyramids are not simply the result of natural increases in the populations of the countries in question, but are also a result of migration. The contribution of natural increase and migration to population growth can be seen in Fig. 10.8. These migrations are not always easy to explain. Poor economic conditions such as rural overpopulation cause out-migration, as in Italy and Ireland even today. Government immigration policies have also been important, as have been the needs of the economy. Germany and France have attracted cheap European labour. France has also gained people from its former colonial territories.

Problems and applicability

The relationships between population and resources, and between population and economic activity, are very complex. Although Malthus's model and the other models reviewed here capture some of the complexities, they have their limitations.

It is probably worth retaining Malthus's first principle about the potentially geometric growth of population, while remembering that the potential is rarely actually observed. His preventive and positive checks do affect population growth; but since he wrote, modern birth-control techniques, to which he would have objected, have been widely introduced. These should now be included among his preventive checks.

He may be criticized for his suggestion that as the standard of living increased (decreased) so the birth-rate would increase (decrease). He himself indicated elsewhere the argument against this positive relationship. He suggested that the poor should be educated, so that they would adopt the attitudes of the richer social groups who had smaller families. Thus within a given population, increased well-being might lead to lower birth-rates. Although this may be viewed as a contradiction in his writing, it shows that he recognized the importance of the effect of social attitudes as well as standard of living on birth-rates.

Further criticism may be directed at his second principle about the arithmetic rate of growth of production. The industrial revolution, during his lifetime, led to a rapid rate of growth of production which was much greater than the arithmetic rate and exceeded the rate of growth of population. Malthus's ceiling (means of subsistence) was always ahead of, and moving further away from, the population, because of the rapid rate of technological development.

As well as increasing the rate of economic growth in general, industrial development has had a direct effect on agricultural production which Malthus did not fully appreciate. There are two main ways by which farmers can increase production: **intensification** and **extensification**. To **intensify** a farmer increases the amount of capital and labour applied to a given area of land. To **extensify** he brings more land into production. Industry helped both. It provided better equipment, machinery, and later inorganic fertilizers and pesticides, which permitted increased production per unit of land and per man. This increase in output per capita allowed more labour to leave the land for industry. Industry also provided the machinery and equipment which permitted the development of new lands, for example the extensive cereal production on the prairies. Other land was brought into production by reclamation or irrigation. Finally, the provision of tractors allowed food crops to be substituted for the fodder crops which had been needed for the horses which the tractors replaced. In all these ways food production increased rapidly, so that the expanding populations of Europe and North America could be fed. Improved transport and storage techniques also allowed a more varied diet, and incidentally permitted the emergence of specialist agricultural areas which served distant markets (the prairies wheat belt served Western Europe).

While these developments cast doubt on Malthus's second principle, the rates of growth and sizes of populations of the developing countries, and the rates of exhaustion of resources have created sufficient alarm to stimulate such research as the *Limits to Growth*, which is reminiscent of Malthusian theory. It, too, has some major limitations. It is a world model which does not distinguish between what is happening in different parts of the world. In fact, it ignores the spatial distributions of population, resources, agricultural and industrial production, and pollution. People and resources, for example, do not always coincide in space. Their relative distributions, as well as their relative magnitudes, are part of the world's problem. Although the model emphasizes exponential growth, it does not include the rate of discovery of new resources or of new uses of resources, which have probably grown at such a rate recently. It neglects the substitution of resources for one another as one becomes less abundant and more expensive. Only slight modifications of its assumptions and equations lead to the model predicting a more encouraging future. Other, more realistic models are being produced.

However, the rates of population growth of densely peopled developing countries are a problem because they often hinder the process of development, sometimes even exceeding the rates of increase in production. The demographic transition model seems inapplicable to many of these countries, because the introduction of medical techniques has drastically reduced the death-rate, especially infant mortality, without any accompanying changes in social customs and attitudes, such as age of marriage and attitude to birth control, which are necessary for the birth-rate to be reduced. It is this interaction between countries, in this case the introduction of medical technology from advanced to developing countries, which the Limits to Growth model ignores. Such interaction between countries also makes the models based on past observations of questionable predictive value. For example, the introduction of technology from a country in stage 4 of the demographic transition model to one in stage 1 or 2 will probably itself affect the evolution of the country and deflect it from the predicted stages.

Despite the limitations of the models, many useful ideas emerge from the chapter. The models indicate various forms of population growth. It may be unlimited. Positive feedback loops may predominate. Exponential or geometric growth may result. It may be checked by a resource or technological ceiling, about which fluctuations occur, and negative feedback loops are then predominant. Alternatively, growth may be logistic (Chapter 9, Fig. 9.3) whereby, after a technological or resource barrier has been broken through, growth is at first slow (Fig. 9.3, stage 1), then rapid (stage 2), and finally reduced as a new barrier is encountered (stage 3). It is interesting to note that the early part of the rapid stage may be mistaken for exponential growth.

Associated with the idea of ceilings is the concept of an optimum population. Like an optimum location for a factory, it is very difficult to define and measure because there may be various optima associated with various goals and because the level of technology and resources available are constantly changing. However, the related ideas of overpopulation and underpopulation are useful summary descriptions of countries at given points in time.

The practical application of these and related models is in population forecasting, but the complexities of the subject and the scarce and often unreliable data make it a hazardous business. For example, the fluctuations in birth-rates, which are smoothed out in many of the models, but which occur in reality, cause gross errors in predictions.

Conclusion

The models yield some, but not complete, understanding of the factors of population change. The complex relationship between economic and social factors within a country and the interaction of countries makes it extremely difficult to construct a model to fit all places at all times. The rapid rate of growth of the world's population and the recent coincidence of bad harvests in many of the world's main food-producing areas have stimulated much research into all aspects of the subject. Perhaps a similar substitution may be found, as occurred during and since the industrial revolution: inorganic raw materials were used instead of organic ones, for example coal for charcoal, and nylon for wool and cotton. The substitution of inorganic for organic food may help solve a major problem, the scarcity of new agricultural land.

Bibliography

Boserup, E., *The Conditions of Agricultural Growth* (Allen & Unwin, 1965)
Cipolla, C.M., *The Economic History of World Population* (Penguin, 1972)
Clarke, J.I., *Population Geography* (Pergamon, 1972)
Glass, D.V., (ed.), *Introduction to Malthus* (Watts, 1953)
Meadows, D.H., *et al., The Limits to Growth* (Pan, 1972)
Petersen, W., *Population* (Collier Macmillan, 1975)
Wrigley, E.A., *Population and History* (Weidenfeld & Nicolson, 1969)

Essay questions

1. *Either*: 'The growth of population in an area is a product of the rate of natural increase and net gain or loss by migration.' Comment on this statement.
   Or: 'The pressure of population on resources is a matter of increasing concern.' Discuss this statement. (Cambridge, 1975)
2. 'There is no single world population problem, rather a series of distinctive national or regional problems.' Discuss this opinion. (Oxford and Cambridge, 1973)
3. How far do you think the population problem is one of growth rates and how far one of maldistribution? (Oxford and Cambridge, 1975)
4. To what extent have the theories of Thomas Malthus and the concept of the Demographic Transition aided or obscured the understanding of world population development? (Manchester University)

Chapter 11

Economic growth: the sector and development-stage models

Introduction and link

The preceding chapter studied population growth and the interrelationships of population and resources. This chapter examines the aspect of development that concerns the way in which populations have changed their use of resources, discovered new uses for them, and exploited their own human skills. It considers the emergence of manufacturing, service, and research sectors from an agricultural base. The accompanying changes in spatial relationships are noted, particularly the process of **urbanization**. The spatial aspect of development is taken up in detail in the final chapter.

The **economic-sector theory** is derived from the empirical observations made independently by Clark and Fisher, two British economists. It has been linked to the location theories of Lösch and Hoover to form a **theory of development stages**. A similar model of economic growth has been proposed by Rostow, an economic historian. Along with the demographic transition model (Chapter 10), these theories demonstrate the application of evolutionary models to regions and nations, and to their associated problems.

Main aim

The aim of the sector theory is to trace and explain the varying proportions of people employed in the major types of economic activity through time, while the development-stage model establishes a 'normal' sequence of stages through which areas experience economic growth. Both are applied to individual regions within nations as well as to the nations as a whole.

The models

Sector model

To appreciate this model it is necessary to define three terms:

1. **Primary employment** includes agriculture, forestry, hunting, fishing, and extractive industries like mining and quarrying.
2. **Secondary employment** includes manufacturing, the production of electric power and gas, and construction.
3. **Tertiary employment** includes commerce, transport, communications, and services of all kinds.

Fig. 11.1 *Graphical description of the sector model*

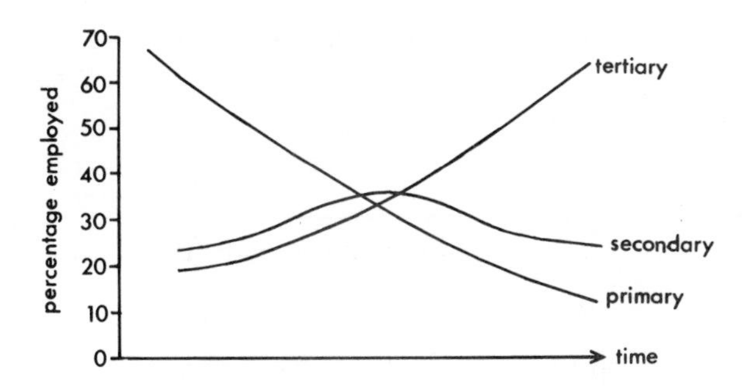

Clark and Fisher observed that a rise in real income per capita in a country is generally accompanied by a decline in the proportion of the labour force employed in agriculture, and by a rise, first in the proportion working in secondary activities, and then in the proportion working in tertiary activities. As the proportion working in the tertiary sector rises, that in the secondary sector declines. The shift in the relative importance of the different sectors is illustrated in Fig. 11.1.

The two main reasons for this shift are different income elasticities of demand (Chapter 7) for the products of the different sectors, and differential rates of change in labour productivity. The demand for food is fairly inelastic (as income increases, demand increases very little). It does not increase as rapidly as real income per capita, so people have excess money to spend on other goods. At the same time, farm output per man can be increased because of gains in productivity through the use of improved techniques, machines, and fertilizers. Because diminishing returns set in rapidly with agriculture, farm labour is released for other activities. Thus, the demand for consumer goods and the labour to supply them is then available; the secondary sector expands. A further rise in income per capita, although accompanied by an increase in demands for manufactured goods (which are more elastic than for food), still allows some surplus income to be spent on services. Output per man gradually increases in manufacturing, too, by means of division of labour, specialization, and mechanization, so total output can be maintained whilst releasing labour to provide the services demanded.

The ideas of the model have been illustrated with regard to household demand, but similar arguments hold for industrial demand. More efficient production and use of raw materials means less raw material is used per unit product. More profit is then available to buy or develop needed services, such as finance, insurance, marketing, and advertising, in order to improve the efficiency of the commercial side of the organization. Gradually, as the organization becomes more efficient in its office departments, owing to automation, and its profits increase, it has money to spend on research and development of new products and processes to expand the organization still further. These latter activities have been called the **quaternary sector**. They are typical of the twentieth-century establishment of institutions which develop and sell specialized knowledge. It has been called the 'knowledge

Fig. 11.2 *Percentage annual growth rates in Great Britain: employment and labour productivity*

	employment		labour productivity	
	1924–37	1951–64	1924–37	1951–64
manufacturing	1·1	0·6	2·2	2·6
services and distribution	2·2	1·0	–0·5	1·4

Source: George, K.D., *Industrial Organization* (Allen & Unwin, 1971), p.22

Fig. 11.3 *Changes in employment structure in Great Britain*

employment by sector		index 1966 (1959=100)	change 1959–66 (thousands)	total June 1966 (thousands)
primary	agriculture, mining, and quarrying	70·8	–436	1058
secondary	manufacturing	106·3	+536	9055
tertiary	financial, professional and scientific services	128·6	+717	3222
tertiary	government services	107·3	+94	1383

Source: George, K.D., *op. cit.*, p.24

revolution', and is typified by the emergence of 'the expert', consultancies, and research establishments.

Some statistics for Great Britain (Fig. 11.2) show how one stage of the model works. Labour productivity is increasing much faster in manufacturing than in services, thus releasing some labour. The faster increase in employment in services than in manufacturing demonstrates that it is the tertiary sector that is taking on the released labour. In fact, service activities took on so much labour before 1937, with few accompanying improvements in efficiency, that labour productivity actually declined.

Fig. 11.3 shows a more recent change in the employment structure, when primary employment was in absolute decline, and employment in some services was growing very rapidly. Some of that growth reflects the quaternary, as well as the tertiary, sector. An important part of the growth of tertiary activity in the twentieth century is employment in government services. Its growth has been so rapid that it now exceeds the total employment in the declining primary sector.

Development-stage model

The sector theory links neatly with the model of development stages. It suggests that the development of most regions will proceed in the following way:

1. A stage of **self-sufficient subsistence economy**. This ranges from primitive hunting, collecting, and fishing to sedentary cultivation where the basic forms

of settlement are farms and villages. Improved techniques lead to the production of surpluses, permitting stage 2.

2. Growth through **specialized production in primary activities** and **interregional trade** which can be expected to accompany transport improvements. At this time small market towns emerge.
3. The introduction of **secondary industries**, particularly for the processing of primary products. Most industries are at first small-scale and local. If the products are exported or imported, somewhat larger-scale industries may develop in the ports.
4. A shift from a concentration on processing of farm and forest products and the simpler branches of textile, leather, and clothing industries as well as on mining and mineral reduction, to more **diversified industrialization** based on internal **industrial linkages** and rising incomes. The industries are linked, since the raw materials of some are the products of others. For example the product of the steel mills is the raw material for manufacturing railway engines. During this stage, industrial activity is concentrated much more into towns. The increasing linkages within groups of industries also lead to clusters of towns associated with particular industries, for example the Lancashire textile towns and the Ruhr, eventually leading to the growth of conurbations.
5. **Specialization** occurs in certain **tertiary industries**, especially for the export of capital, specialized personnel, and services to less advanced regions. This stage is typified by the emergence of the city with huge office blocks, because these tertiary industries are even more spatially concentrated than secondary activities.
6. A further stage may be added to the usual model, when **quaternary activities** are developed and the region specializes in the production and refinement of ideas and processes for export.

The stages of economic growth

A related development-stage model has been proposed by Rostow. From an examination of data for fifteen countries over a long period, Rostow suggested that all nations could be placed along a continuum of development which is marked by five stages: traditional society, preconditions for take-off, the take-off to self-sustained growth, the drive to maturity, and the age of high mass-consumption (Fig. 11.6). The critical part of the model is the identification of a short period during which growth within a country becomes more or less automatic. This is the **take-off stage** which he thought marks the watershed in the life of a modern society. At this point he expected the following to occur: the rate of productive investment rises from about 5 per cent of national income to over 10 per cent; one or more major manufacturing sectors emerge to act as a leading sector(s) in the economy; political and social institutions are transformed to allow this growth to become a natural state of affairs. This theory has greatly influenced students of economic development, but is now viewed more critically.

Fig. 11.4 *Employment in the U.S.A., 1870–1950*

year	agriculture	mining	forestry	fishing	manufacturing	services	total active population
	percentage of total active population						
1870	51·47	1·49	0·25	0·22	21·14	25·41	12 505 923
1890	40·62	1·96	0·54	0·26	24·30	32·31	22 735 661
1910	32·46	2·53	0·45	0·18	27·92	36·45	38 167 336
1930	21·45	2·02	0·36	0·15	28·89	47·13	48 829 920
1950	11·57	1·54	0·36	0·13	23·92	62·48	60 200 847

Source: extracted from Perloff, H.S., *et al., Regions, Resources, and Economic Growth* (Bison/ University of Nebraska Press, 1960), Appendix A1–7

Examples

Figs. 11.4 and 11.5 demonstrate the link between the sector model and the process of urbanization which tends to accompany economic growth. Fig. 11.4 shows the percentages of the total population employed in various activities in the U.S.A. The total workforce has noticeably increased in the eighty-year period. During this time the relative importance of the primary activities (agriculture, mining, forestry, and fishing) has declined, whereas that of manufacturing increased at first but later fell, while tertiary employment increased steadily.

Again for the United States, Fig. 11.5 illustrates the increasing urbanization of its population over time. It also indicates, however, how large differences in the extent of urbanization can exist between major regions. Note the Mid-Atlantic states where the degree of urbanization has always been considerably above the national average, compared with the South East states where the opposite is true. The high levels of urbanization are associated particularly with the emergence of a dominant tertiary sector.

Friedmann's attempt to identify stages in the economic growth of Venezuela (Chapter 12) provides useful supplementary evidence for all three models (Fig. 11.6). Venezuela and most other countries have not yet reached the fifth stage of economic

Fig. 11.5 *Urbanization in U.S.A.*

	urban percentage of total population		
	1870	1910	1950
U.S.A.	25·2	45·7	59·0
New England	44·4	73·3	74·3
Mid Atlantic	44·1	70·2	74·0
Great Lakes	21·6	52·7	65·7
South East	9·5	19·4	42·5
Plains	18·9	33·2	49·9
South West	6·9	22·5	55·5
Mountain	13·9	40·7	51·8
Far West	31·2	56·0	62·7

Source: Perloff, H.S., *op. cit.*, p.19

Fig. 11.6 *Stages of economic growth in Venezuela*

stage	leading economic sectors	corresponding Rostow stage	approximate dates	total population (millions)	per cent of population		per cent of active population by sector of employment			
					rural	urban	primary	secondary	tertiary	quaternary
1a	hunting, fishing, subsistence farming (Indian)	–	pre–1500	?	100	–	100	–	–	–
1b	mining, (gold, silver, copper, pearls)	traditional society	1500–1600	?	?	?	?	?	?	?
1c	commercial agriculture (sugar, tobacco, hides, cacao, coffee)		1600–1920/5	2·8	85	15	75	10	13	2
2	oil	preconditions for take-off	1920–25 1945–50	5·0	60	40	45	18	31	6
3	consumer goods (import substitution) industries; creation of a heavy industrial base (steel, petrochemicals, electric power); automobile manufacture and assembly	take-off	1945–50 1965–70	10·0	40	60	30	20	40	10
4	manufacturing industries for export (producer goods; consumer durables)	drive to maturity	1965–70 1990–2000	20·0	30	70	25	25	35	15
5	quaternary services	mass consumption	1990–2000 2050?	50·0	5	95	10	20	45	25

traditional society: pre-Newtonian science, technology and attitudes; limit to attainable level of output per head; potential of resources not realized.

preconditions for take-off: increased international trade; external influences considerable; modern methods exist alongside traditional society; new nationalism emerges.

take-off: the watershed in the life of modern societies; old traditions/resistances finally overcome; growth basic to society. Investment/savings 5–10 per cent of national income at least.

drive to maturity: 10–20 per cent national income steadily invested; industries fade as well as others growing; long intervals (60 years) of sustained growth.

mass consumption: resources allocated to social welfare + security; cheap mass automobile = decisive element.

Source: Friedmann, J., *Regional Development Policy: A Case Study of Venezuela* (M.I.T. Press, 1966), p. 128.

growth. The U.S.A. is one country that can be said to have reached that stage when the tertiary and quaternary sectors are dominant and urbanization is almost total.

Problems and applicability

The major problem with the sector theory is that it is only a partial theory of national or regional economic development. Change is induced from within rather than from outside the nation or region, so the impact of the demand of other nations or regions is neglected. An **export-based theory** of development, which emphasizes the role of external demand, complements the sector theory. In it development occurs as the region responds to external demand and investment, which leads to the growth of export industries. These, in turn, create an internal demand for goods and services which are then provided within the region. Employees in these new jobs also demand goods and services and so the effect of the original export-based industry multiplies. This important **multiplier effect** (Chapter 12) is ignored in the sector theory.

The sector and development-stage theories underplay the interrelationships between regions that occur during development. These seem to be important since the regions usually appear to be at different stages. The following chapter examines these spatial interrelationships in detail.

The sector theory may be criticized for its simplicity. Some jobs are very difficult to classify. The sectors are very crude aggregates, and mask enormous differences within sectors, even in elasticity of demand and productivity. The complexities of industrial change, the different resource bases of regions, and the interaction with and learning from more advanced regions also suggest that there will be many types of development sequences. The development-stage model is just one of many possible sequences.

Rostow's model is open to similar criticism. As with most stage models, it is easier to recognize them retrospectively than to estimate the present situation and predict the future. Even retrospectively, many researchers have failed to observe the key take-off periods in various countries. So although the concept has been readily adopted in the literature on economic growth, there is little empirical evidence for it. Rostow's model has also been criticized for putting too much emphasis on capital formation and too little on, among other things, the degree to which capital can be used productively.

The sector and development-stage theories have been useful as a framework for the collection of data on employment structures and productivity, both of which are used as indications of development. Two implications of the theories have also had policy ramifications. First, the theories suggest that the activities of private organizations and governments can determine the rate at which the economy of a region will evolve from one stage to another, for example in the supply of infrastructure such as transport and power facilities. Many governments' regional development policies consist largely of the provision of infrastructure. Yet this is a necessary, but not a sufficient, condition for economic development. It is also an investment in place, or region, rather than people, who could be helped to move into areas with perhaps more growth potential. Secondly, the theories imply that there is a relationship between economic growth and the presence of **growth industries** within a region. Such industries have experienced a greater than national average increase in employment, real income per capita, or production value, for example electronics and chemicals in Great Britain during the 1960s. The derived policy advocates the presence of growth industries in backward areas. However, not all fast-growing industries have the great multiplier effects which are usually needed to obtain self-sustained growth within a backward region. For example the oil-refining at Milford Haven, South Wales, has had a limited impact on local employment.

Governmental promotion of development has become increasingly common in the twentieth century, with the initiation of five-year national plans and of regional policies. The sector model has become very important since debate has arisen as to whether investment should be evenly spread in all sectors (**balanced growth**) or concentrated in one set of activities (**unbalanced growth**) in order to propel the nation into the take-off stage. The U.S.S.R. chose until recently to invest primarily in heavy industry, largely ignoring agriculture, consumer goods, and transport. Other countries have concentrated first on cheap consumer goods for export, only later investing in more sophisticated goods and heavy industry. The best solution depends much on the resource base and political system of the nation.

Conclusion

The sector and development-stage models are useful frameworks for study and the collection of data. It must be remembered, however, that they are only partial models, and that they do not neatly fit all regions in describing their past or predicting their future development. Along with the demographic transition model, they suffer the same problems of most evolutionary models that are applied to regions. External contact may be very different for two regions which are at the same stage at different times. Regions may have different political, social, and economic structures, and different distributions of natural and human resources. Any of these could lead to varying sequences of development. More attention should be paid to the underlying dynamics of the models, for example demand elasticity and productivity, than to the stages.

Bibliography

Brookfield, H., *Interdependent Development* (Methuen, 1975)
Clark, C., *The Conditions of Economic Progress* (Macmillan, 1940)
Hauser, P.M., and Schnore, L.F. (eds.), *The Study of Urbanization* (Wiley, 1966)
Hoover, E.M., *An Introduction to Regional Economics* (Knopf, 1971)
Perloff, H.S., *et al., Regions, Resources, and Economic Growth* (Bison/University of Nebraska Press, 1960)
Rostow, W.W., *The Stages of Economic Growth* (Cambridge University Press, 1960)

Essay questions

1. What factors have stimulated growth of large cities in the underdeveloped countries? (Cambridge, 1975)
2. Consider with examples the relation between industrial development and rapid urban growth. (Oxford and Cambridge, 1974)
3. 'The concept of stages of economic growth as outlined by Rostow must be regarded as a failure.' Discuss this statement with regard to other models of economic growth with which you are familiar. (Manchester University)
4. Outline the main characteristics of the regional 'development stages' and 'export base' models. Which model provides the more satisfactory framework for the analysis of regional economic growth and why? (Cambridge University)

Chapter 12

Economic development in space

Introduction and link

The preceding chapter examined some models of economic development. However, the changing spatial relationships during development were only implied. In this chapter the spatial element is emphasized. It examines the role of space in development through the introduction of a number of concepts. It demonstrates the emerging interdependence of regions within a country via the **core-periphery model** or **theory of polarized growth**, as it is sometimes known. In contrast to the evolutionary models of the previous chapters, the dynamics, particularly the spatial dynamics, of development are more carefully identified. This contrasts markedly with most traditional approaches to development which emphasized the differences between countries at one time, mainly with regard to their utilization of natural resources, but paid little attention to dynamics or to the changing spatial relationships between regions within a country.

The main authors of the work discussed are Gunnar Myrdal, a Swedish economist, Albert Hirschman, an American economist, and John Friedmann, an American regional planner. Numerous geographers have applied and developed these authors' original contributions.

Main aim

The main aim of the concepts and the model is to demonstrate how and why regional imbalances in development occur and how eventually the regions of a nation are spatially integrated over time. In short, it examines the development process in its spatial dimension.

Basic principles and Friedmann's model

Economic development is a very complex concept. Development demands the emergence of new institutions, new forms of production, and, from a geographical viewpoint, changes in the internal structure and interrelationships of regions. It is facilitated by the mobility (geographical as well as inter-firm) of factors of production like labour, capital, resources, and land (owing to changes in tenure), and by a willingness of the population to accept change. Development is something more than **economic growth** which simply involves the expansion within a region of, for example, production and consumption.

Classical theory states that any **regional imbalance** in real wages or job opportunities will be resolved by the migration of firms to the poorer areas where they can benefit initially from lower wage bills. As a result of the migration of firms, less competition for labour in the richer areas and more in the poorer areas leads to an equalizing of wage rates. Empirical observations discredit this theory since, without government encouragement, firms often fail to migrate, and **selective migration** of young, better-qualified labour from poorer to richer areas reduces the stimulus to firms to migrate.

More recent theories recognize that a regional imbalance is more likely. The adage, 'to him that has, shall be given' seems to apply. They also identify the major role of innovation adoption (Chapter 9) in development. Innovations may be institutional, technical, or cultural. Some major innovations, such as the extended application of science to problems of economic production, combine elements of all three. The locations of innovation generation and initial adoption, then, become of major geographical significance, particularly if the same locations keep recurring over time.

The **process of cumulative causation** (Fig. 12.1) in part suggests that the adoption of innovations is most likely in areas of rapid economic expansion which possess the appropriate resources and entrepreneurial attitudes and where change is socially acceptable. Thus successfully growing areas attract even more economic activity directly or indirectly by means of the enhancement of further invention and innovation possibilities. Growing areas thus maintain their initial advantage. The process is circular and cumulative. It is particularly applicable to the growth of large metropolitan cities which in their later stages become the centres of quaternary activities with their institutions specifically geared to creativity and change.

Fig. 12.1 *The circular and cumulative causation process, including multiplier effects*

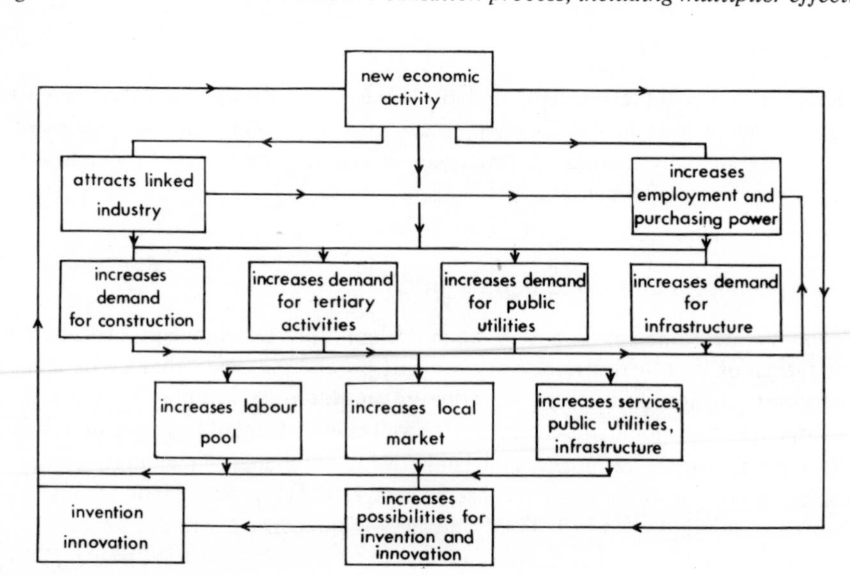

Fig. 12.2 *Vicious circles or downward spirals typical of the periphery*

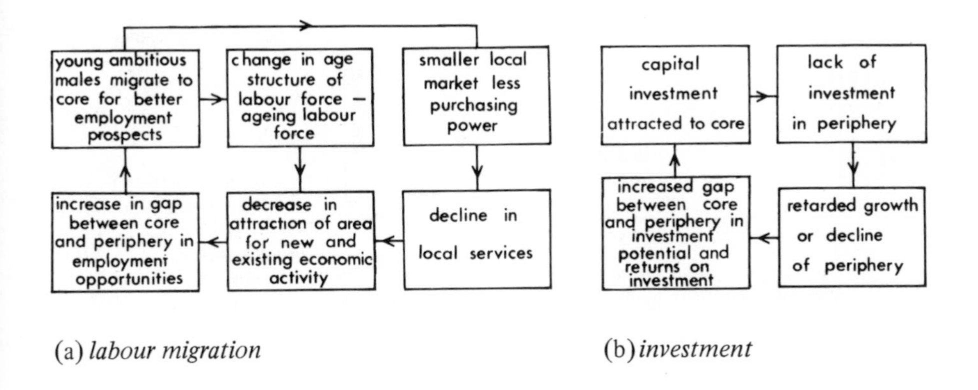

(a) *labour migration* (b) *investment*

The process of circular and cumulative causation also involves the **multiplier effect** (Chapter 11) (Fig. 12.1). A new or expanding economic activity in an area creates extra employment and raises the total purchasing power of the population. The extra population and greater purchasing power increase the demand for houses, schools, consumer goods, and services, thus creating even more employment. The new industry itself demands local goods and services. It may also attract linked industries which use its products or supply it with materials. These lead to further increases in employment and expansion in services, public utilities, and construction. The larger labour pool, expanded local market, and improved infrastructure and services attract even more economic activities which need this increase in city scale or threshold level (Chapter 1) to make production profitable. They benefit from the **agglomeration economies** (Chapter 3) that the larger city allows. Thus the process is cumulative and growth becomes self-sustaining.

This process of growth in a given area or city must be fuelled. Migrants, potential entrepreneurs, and capital are attracted from less advanced surrounding areas. Raw materials for the industries also flow in. This process of spatial concentration of resources into a **core** or **centre** is called **backwash** (Myrdal) or **polarization** (Hirschman). At the same time as it permits **virtuous circles** or upward spirals in the core, it sets off **vicious circles** or downward spirals in the **periphery**, or less advanced areas. Two examples are shown (Figs. 12.2a and 12.2b).

How then do the peripheral areas develop? Growth is supposed to **spread** (Myrdal) or **trickle down** (Hirschman) from the core. The expansion of the core increases demand for food and resources from the periphery. The core may also provide the necessary machinery, fertilizers, or new hybrid crops to permit the increases in agricultural productivity to meet the demand. Other innovations like consumer goods may diffuse from the core (Chapter 9) as real incomes increase. Decentralization of branch plants from the core is further stimulus to growth. This occurs as demand in the periphery expands and perhaps as land costs and congestion increase in the core. Government encouragement of such decentralization and its investment in infrastructure, education, and health are further forms of spread

Fig. 12.3 *Changing imbalance between core and periphery*

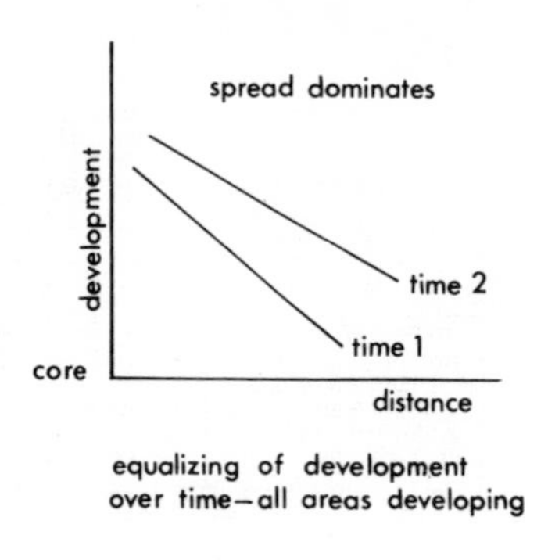

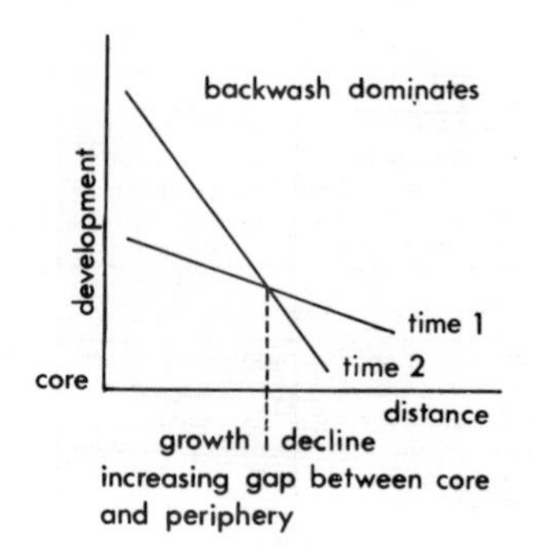

effects. Whether the gap between core and periphery widens depends on the rates of spread and backwash, as Moseley's diagrams neatly demonstrate (Fig. 12.3).

All these concepts are assembled together in Friedmann's **development model** which is outlined diagrammatically (Fig. 12.4). Stage 1 shows a relatively stable stage. In contrast, stage 2 is very unstable as it results from a disruption, often externally induced, of the spatial equilibrium maintained by a pre-industrial order.

In the early phase of industrialization the scarcity of investment means that it is impossible to exploit all opportunities simultaneously. Development occurs in one or two regions which have specific advantages over the rest. They may possess a better natural resource endowment, lie in a densely populated area and so have a large market, or be favourably located with good access to foreign markets. The initial advantage is maintained by means of the cumulative causation process as the benefits of agglomeration economies are reaped; growth will continue in the core, despite perhaps the dissipation of the original location advantages. At this stage backwash effects are stronger than spread effects, and the core grows at the expense of the periphery. In many ways a dual economy exists.

The simple core-periphery structure is gradually transformed into a multi-nuclear structure (Fig. 12.4, stage 3), as favourable parts of the periphery are developed. These may have a large regional market (isolated from the core), important natural resources, or special amenities and climate, which might bolster political demands for their development. Spread effects are now much more active nationally, but backwash effects exceed spread effects within regions, as growth within regions is spatially concentrated.

In stage 4 (Fig. 12.4) the intermetropolitan peripheries are absorbed into the metropolitan economies. Here local and national backwash and spread effects seem to be generally in balance. It is to some extent an ideal stage, but Friedmann suggests that others, not yet identifiable, might follow.

From this development model four types of areas can be designated: the core, upward transitional areas benefiting from proximity to the core, downward transitional areas distant from the core in the periphery, and resource frontiers in the periphery. Both upward transitional areas and resource frontiers may become secondary cores.

Fig. 12.4 *Friedmann's development model*

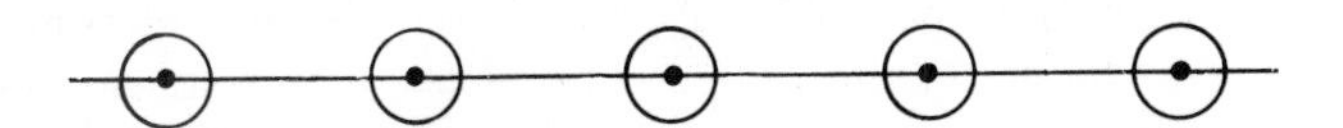

Stage 1. Relatively independent local centres; no hierarchy. Typical pre-industrial structure; each city lies at the centre of a small regional enclave.

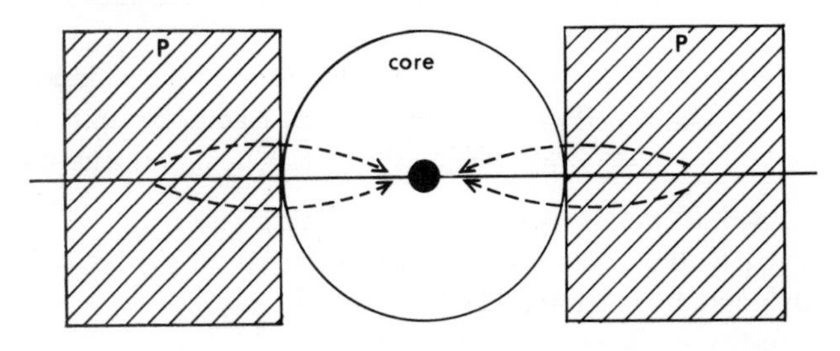

Stage 2. A single strong core. Typical of period of incipient industrialization; a periphery emerges; potential entrepreneurs and labour move to the core, national economy is virtually reduced to a single metropolitan region.

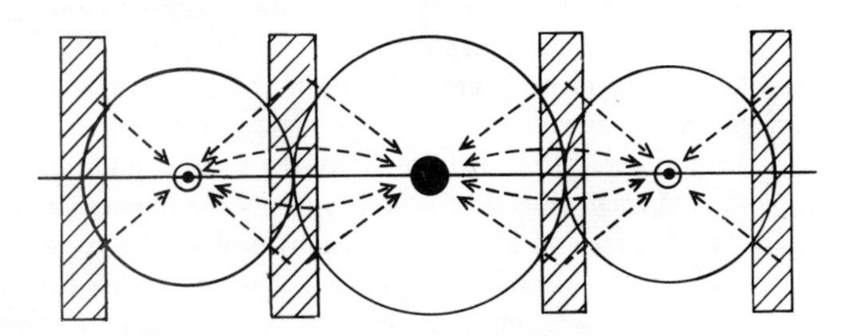

Stage 3. A single national core, strong peripheral sub-cores. During the period of industrial maturity, secondary cores form, thereby reducing the periphery on a national scale to smaller intermetropolitan peripheries.

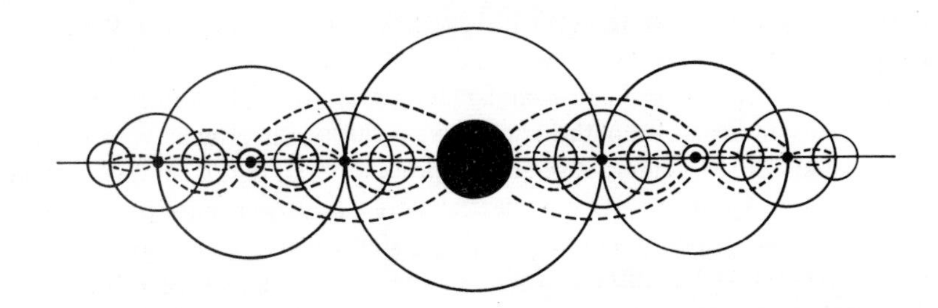

Stage 4. A functional interdependent system of cities. Organized complexity characterized by national integration, efficiency in location, maximum growth potential.

1. **The core region** is the focus of the national market, large-scale, nation-serving industries and the seedbed of new industry and innovations.
2. **The location of upward transitional areas**, relative to core regions and natural endowments, suggests the possibility of greatly intensified use of resources. They are characterized by net immigration and by increasing investment and agricultural productivity.
3. **The poverty of downward transitional areas** is due to their unfavourable locations relative to the rest of the nation; poor, deteriorating, resource bases; and traditional ways that do not allow for or promote change. They are typified by low productivity per man and unit of land, low life-expectancy, and a high rate of selective out-migration.
4. **Resource frontiers** are areas where new resources are discovered and exploited. Along with core regions, they perform a critical role in generating impulses of economic development and transmitting them elsewhere in the nation.

From the model it can be seen that cities play a key role in development. Growth is centred in them, and innovations beginning in the larger cities diffuse down the urban hierarchy (Chapter 9).

Author's example: Venezuela

In Friedmann's *Regional Development Policy, A Case Study of Venezuela* many of the major aspects of his development model were observed. Although in this work he did not attempt to identify precisely the four stages in the model, many similarities to the model are apparent.

His main study period was 1936–61, at the start of which cities in Venezuela were few, scattered, and small (Fig. 12.5). In 1936 only the population of Caracas had exceeded 100 000. Maracaibo (75 000), a distant provincial city, was the only other city of any size. In the Andean region, San Cristobal alone (of the many small trade centres) had achieved any size. Similarly in the east only Cumana and Ciudad Bolívar had attained more than local importance. Venezuela at this time, then, consisted of a number of town-centred regional economies, having little trade with one another and governed from the centre with difficulty. Port hinterlands were predominantly orientated north–south, and east–west movement was restricted. This period in Venezuela's history was similar to stage 1 in the development model.

As oil was extracted, the Caracas area emerged as the single national core (stage 2), and migration flows from the periphery, a backwash effect, were becoming significant (Fig. 12.6). A cumulative growth process began in the core. Government expenditure, the location of commercial and industrial enterprises, foreign immigration, and the expansion of the banking system created a pattern of economic and social linkages that continued to make the core attractive to investors. The national market for consumer goods was concentrated in this core. Meanwhile the outlying provinces shared, to only a limited degree, in national progress.

As oil development intensified, peripheral sub-cores, such as Maracaibo, Barquisimeto, and Valencia, were established. Migration from the periphery to such

Fig. 12.5 *Distribution of urban population in Venezuela, 1936*

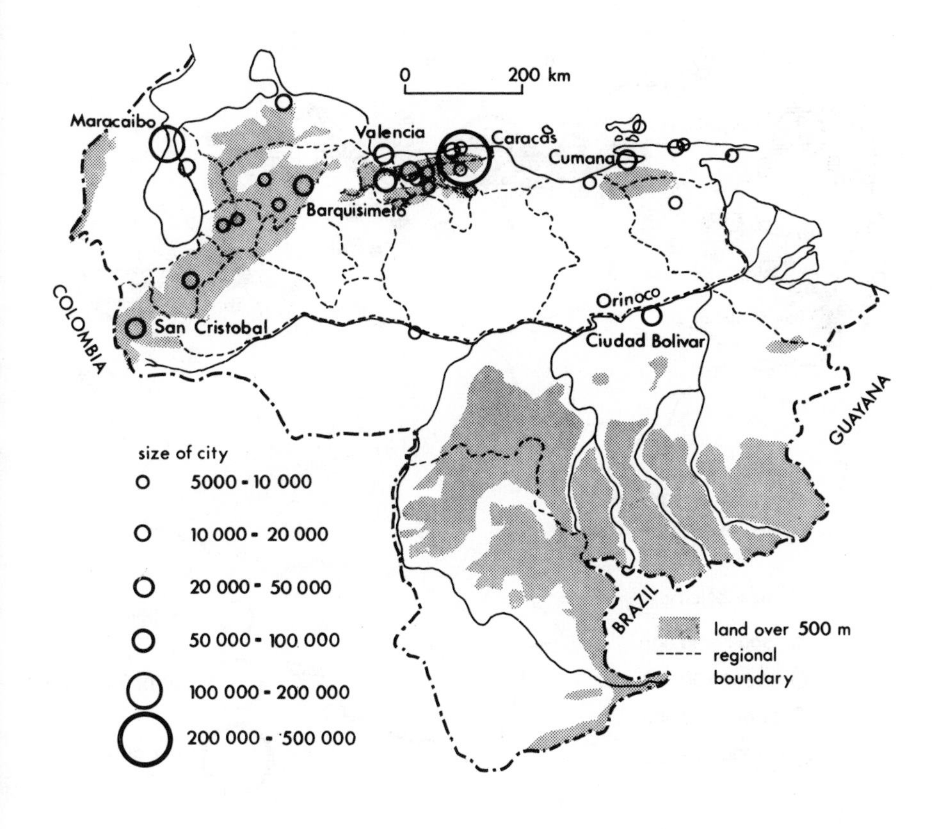

Fig. 12.6 *Internal migration: Venezuela, 1936–50 (in thousands)*

region	out-migration	in-migration	net internal migration
Western Oil States	57	95	38
Mountain States	119	1·7	–102
West Central States	76	14	–62
East Central States	112	274	161
Llanos	45	43	–2
Eastern Oil States	29	79	50
East Coastal States	69	2	–67
Guayana	25	8	–17

Source: Friedman, J., *Regional Development Policy: A Case Study of Venezuela* (M.I.T. Press, 1966), p. 141

Fig. 12.7 *Distribution of urban population in Venezuela, 1961*

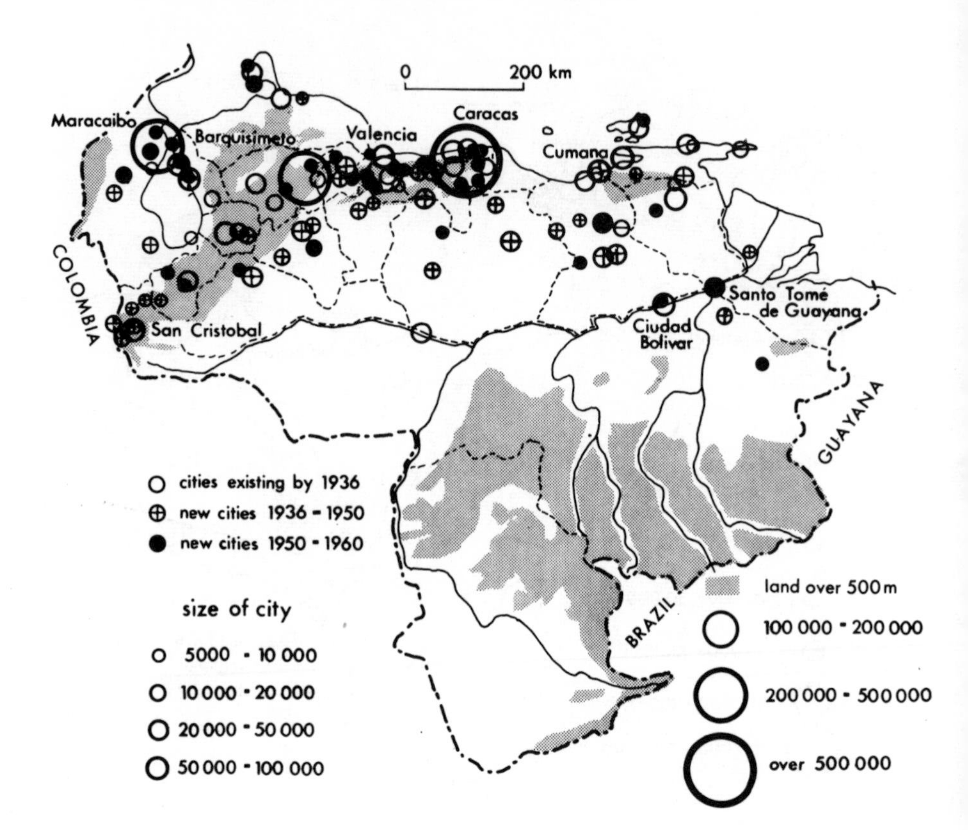

secondary cores was observed (stage 3). At the same time spread effects from Caracas were noted in the adjacent Valencia Basin into which industrial expansion, not possible in the physically constrained site of Caracas, had spilled over. In 1958 the government began to develop the new city of Santo Tomé de Guayana, and this began a policy for regional development which has since been maintained. This was mainly a government response to the actual or threatened relative decline of the periphery.

Certainly a more complex, interdependent system of cities had emerged in the twenty-five year period (Fig. 12.7). This interdependency had been partly a result of substantial road building in an east–west direction. Many concepts used by Friedmann could therefore be observed in the Venezuelan example. Caracas and its immediate environs emerged as the national core and grew by cumulative causation and agglomeration economies. Downward transitional areas such as the western mountain states were seen in marked contrast to upward transitional areas (for example Valencia Basin) and resource frontiers (for example the iron ore development in Guayana). Strong peripheral sub-cores such as Maracaibo emerged. Many of the remaining areas were part of the periphery and suffered from vicious circles.

Problems and applicability

Since the author's example has been examined at some length, other examples are not illustrated. It is not difficult, however, to think of countries which, at least superficially, fit Friedmann's model. The Sao-Paulo/Rio de Janeiro area is the obvious core of Brazil. The Cairo/north Nile valley area is the core of Egypt. Even in planned spatial economies the core-periphery structure can be discerned, with, for example, the Moscow region being the core of the U.S.S.R.

In Great Britain the South East/West Midlands area, the centre of the national market, may be viewed as the core. The old industrial areas like the North East, North West, and South Wales threatened to become downward transitional areas, but, partly with government assistance, have maintained their status as important secondary cores in the periphery. Parts of the rural periphery, such as mid Wales and highland Scotland, are more like downward transitional areas, while part of the North East coast, near the North Sea oil, especially round Aberdeen, is showing signs of being a resource frontier.

In the U.S.A., too, the main core of the manufacturing belt and the secondary core of California are rather obvious. Again government assistance and contracts have partly helped to revive old-established mining and industrial areas like Appalachia and New England. The rural parts of the South and South East were very much downward transitional areas, while the South Texas complex with its petrochemical and chemical industries was once a resource frontier, now with the space program more a secondary core. Florida certainly has been an upward transitional area with its special climate and amenities. These comparative advantages have led to a boom in fruit growing, tourism, and the retirement and real estate industries for people from the core.

However, the spatial development of both the U.S.A. and Great Britain is more like that of stage 3, where the simple core-periphery model has given way to a multi-nuclear structure. The problems lie more in the intermetropolitan peripheries than in the periphery as a whole. This is certainly the case at the scale of the European Economic Community, where the Golden Triangle (including north-east France, the Ruhr, and Benelux) has been regarded as the core.

Although it is easy to point to areas within countries and classify them according to Friedmann's model, it is more difficult to substantiate these classifications since there has been little data collected on a regional or sub-regional basis. So the multiplier effects and the processes of backwash, spread, and cumulative causation are difficult to observe directly, although there is often plenty of indirect evidence for all except perhaps spread. Unfortunately, the indirect effect is often misleading. For example, it might be thought that London's Heathrow airport has had an extensive multiplier effect on the area west of London. Yet much of the economic activity has been attracted there for other reasons. In some ways the airport even repels activities, for example because of noise. So although these processes are often discussed in the literature they are difficult to observe directly.

These theoretical ideas have been adopted by many governments in establishing **growth centre policies**. They have become aware of regional imbalance, and for political, social, and (arguably) economic reasons, have sought to reduce it. These policies have involved investment in selected towns in the periphery which will, it is hoped, attract growth industries, so setting the cumulative causation processes into operation. Incentives are offered to attract industries to the periphery, sometimes particularly to these centres, while industrial expansion is often discouraged in the core. By concentrating investment in these mini-cores, it is hoped that via spread effects, the surrounding area will benefit. Spread effects, then, are crucial to the success of the policies. Thus the core-periphery ideas have been applied at a regional or even sub-regional scale. A good example of such policies is the French regional planning objective of creating *métropoles d'équilibres* to act as counter-magnets to Paris. Lyon, St. Etienne, and Grenoble are such urban areas in the Rhône-Alpes region.

There have been a number of problems encountered in applying growth centre policies. In some cases, as in the U.S.A. (1960s), investment has been ill-advised because it has been spread too thinly in too many centres and been on a worst-first, greatest-need basis, rather than on a greatest-potential basis. The result has been that these centres continually absorb investment without achieving the aim of self-sustained growth by means of the cumulative causation process. It seems that towns have to be of a certain threshold size before this will occur. Thus larger and better-off towns have been expanded, often at some distance from the area of greatest need. This makes spread effects even more crucial for the success of the policies.

However, first industry must be attracted. In many cases it has been difficult to attract the right kind of industry, namely propulsive growth industries which have extensive multiplier effects. In reality wholesale relocation is unusual. More often branch plants are opened, but these have ties outside the area and are often the first to close in a depression. Even when firms have relocated, the multiplier effects have often been found to be much less than expected, because the firms have retained their links outside the area rather than buy locally. However, in many cases the growth centres have indeed grown.

What is more questionable is whether they have successfully spread this growth to the surrounding areas. Some spread effects occur in the commuter-field of a town, but even then it has been shown, at least for the expanded towns of East Anglia, that people spend more money on shopping in more distant, larger centres like Norwich and Cambridge than in the local villages. Growth is thus **trickling up** to larger towns on the edge of the area rather than trickling down, or spreading to, smaller ones within it, as hoped. It is difficult, however, to assess the success of the application of the growth centre idea, partly because of the short time scale and partly because fluctuating government policies on the location and type of assistance have created so much uncertainty.

Two major themes appear from this application. First, by attempting spatial redistribution of real income, it is possible that the overall growth of the country is hindered. The restrictions on expansion in the metropolitan cores may mean that new growth industries are never established. The country is then robbed of its 'seedbed of new industry and innovations'. Policies of redistribution or minimizing regional imbalances may, therefore, be more appropriate to developed, rather than developing nations. Indeed, it may be argued that regional imbalance is a necessary concomitant of the process leading to take-off. Secondly, it is apparent that these policies invariably mean investment in place rather than people. Infrastructure is provided in and industries attracted to the poorer areas, rather than investment being made in training the people and assisting them to move to areas of greater potential. It may be that for the success of such policies some local movement of people will be required in the future.

Conclusion

Friedmann's model is a useful non-quantitative description and explanation of spatial development within countries. As with much geographic thought, it not only reflects changes in reality, it mirrors changes in the ways researchers view reality. As well as reflecting development, its spatial structures also reflect changes in scientific thought, from the simple core-periphery form to the more complex multi-nuclear structure. Cities are important parts of both structures. As has been seen from the discussion of processes and policies, cities play a key role in development. Research into these processes operating within and around cities has been further stimulated by recent government interest in regional development policies. The geographer has thus become more involved in doing research for governments, and giving advice to governments and to larger groups like the European Economic Community on allocation of its regional fund.

However, government involvement in spatial development makes it even more complex to model. Given that few, if any, countries have reached Friedmann's fourth stage, looking into the future it seems less likely that his possible fifth stage will reflect the operation of market forces than that it will resemble a spatial outcome which has been planned. With this increasing emphasis on what *should* happen, it is not surprising that many geographers in all branches of the subject are doing research which has direct application to policy. Although the aims of this research are rather more applied, it is still appropriate to use, among others, a scientific approach.

This chapter is a fitting conclusion to the book because it incorporates many of the ideas and principles that have been established, via various scientific approaches, earlier in the book. With its emphasis on policy-making, it also brings the discussion back from the abstractions of earlier sections to the real world, which is the focus of all geographical endeavour.

Bibliography

Blunden, J., Brook, C., Edge, G., and Hay, A., (eds.), *Regional Analysis and Development* (Harper & Row, 1973)

Friedmann, J., and Alonso, W., (eds.), *Regional Development and Planning: A Reader* (includes article by Hirschman), (M.I.T. Press, 1974)

Friedmann, J., *Regional Development Policy: A Case Study of Venezuela* (M.I.T. Press, 1966)

Hansen, N.M., *Growth Centres in Regional Economic Development* (Collier-Macmillan, 1972)

Manners, G., Keeble, D.E., Rodgers, B., and Warren, K., *Regional Development in Britain* (Wiley, 1972)
Moseley, M.J., *Growth Centres in Spatial Planning* (Pergamon, 1974)
Myrdal, G.M., *Rich Lands and Poor* (Harper & Row, 1957)

Essay questions

1. Outline the problems of regional development and planning in any one country you have studied. (Cambridge, 1975)
2. 'Over very long periods the pattern of regional disparity within a country may change significantly.' Discuss this statement, using geographical examples. (Oxford and Cambridge, 1975)
3. What factors may cause regional differences in prosperity within a country? (Oxford and Cambridge, 1974)
4. How far do you agree that the map of economic prosperity in Britain is best viewed in terms of a basic centre-periphery, rather than north-south, pattern? (Cambridge University)

General questions

1. What do you understand by the term 'friction of distance'? How does its effect on geographical patterns vary according to the topics under consideration? (Oxford and Cambridge, 1974)
2. Give examples to show how geographical techniques can reveal the effect of *one* of the following:
   (a) distance,
   (b) accessibility,
   (c) agglomeration. (Oxford and Cambridge, 1975)
3. Holiday-makers rarely occupy a stretch of beach so that their spatial distribution, viewed from overhead helicopter, could be described as even or regular. Draw and annotate some beach sketch maps in order to illustrate some of the likely reasons for this. (Oxford and Cambridge, 1974)

Index